The Story of Monsanto

Faith, Hope and $5,000

THE TRIALS AND TRIUMPHS
OF THE FIRST 75 YEARS

by Dan J. Forrestal

Simon and Schuster
New York

Designed by Irving Perkins
Manufactured in the United States of America
1   2   3   4   5   6   7   8   9   10

Library of Congress Cataloging in Publication Data
Forrestal, Dan J.
Faith, hope, and $5,000.
Includes index.
1.   Monsanto Company—History.   I.   Title.
HD9651.9.M6F67   338.7'66'00973   77-7339
ISBN 0-671-22784-X

Foreword

An underwhelming and unreported event of November 29, 1901, was the birth of Monsanto Chemical Works in St. Louis, Missouri. A man named John F. Queeny started it all, with $1500 of his own money and $3500 in borrowed funds.

In contrast, Monsanto Company on its 75th birthday in November, 1976, was a major presence on the world business scene, as evidenced by these end-of-the-year statistics:

> More than $4¼ billion in annual sales
> More than $360 million in annual net income
> Almost 60,000 employes
> Almost 100,000 shareowners
> And 150 plants and 135 offices in 43 countries of the world
> Plus 108 subsidiaries and affiliates outside the United States

This book bridges the 75-year gap.

Late in 1974, Charles H. Sommer, who was then chairman, recommended that the oncoming diamond anniversary should encompass but transcend nostalgia. He suggested, "The Monsanto story merits telling. Perhaps somewhere in it will emerge the reasons for the company's spirit over the years." President John W. Hanley, later to become chairman as well as president, endorsed Sommer's recommendation and wondered, "Are there any lessons from the past impacting the future?"

The historical narrative that follows is the product of the Sommer-Hanley assignment. It makes no pretense of being complete. To the contrary, it contains—quite arbitrarily—only those portions of the history which the author believes to be significant and/or interesting. Happily, an Appendix contains a parade of appropriate biographical sketches and a chronological list of products over the years, and thus helps compensate for incompleteness in the body of the book.

Inclusions and exclusions were relegated to the journalistic judgment of an observer whose roots were deep in journalism prior to his 1947 entry into Monsanto, and whose Monsanto career included longtime residency in the director of public relations chair prior to his request for early retirement in 1974 to engage in counseling.

Other authors, no doubt, would have done it differently. No two would have gone the same route. This observer freely admits he may have tarried over certain people and events at the expense of unmentioned people and events. Those things he found least fascinating received short shrift or no shrift. As a result, it is inescapable that some people and events important to the 75-year scene have been slighted.

Monsanto's top management left up to him the uncomfortable and imprecise task of including and excluding events, a burden whose consequences he was not only willing but eager to bear.

To the degree this narrative succeeds in meeting the expectations of the reader, credit must be allocated to the many people who cooperated beyond need or duty. Information came from far-flung outposts—from A. Sidney Hill, retired Far East star salesman now re-reveling in the stimulating sights and sounds of Hong Kong; from Mrs. Thomas P. Berington, daughter of and last family link to Monsanto's founder, living in the calm quiet of Worcestershire, England.

The author's constant colleague and intrepid fact-checker in the endeavor has been Michael A. Blatz of Monsanto, whose diligence traces back to Dr. Kent Forster of Penn State, the man who first sparked Mr. Blatz's interest in history, and to Dr. Alfred B. Sears of the University of Oklahoma, who guided Mr. Blatz's graduate studies.

Constant support was also furnished by Karen L. Robertson and James K. Webb, the author's assistants, who kept brandishing dictionaries, atlases, thesauri and other primitive reference weapons to support their endless but constructive insubordination.

Monsanto not only permitted but encouraged the author to sprinkle his manuscript with pro and con material. The author had unrestricted access to information. He was even advised not to get too hung up on "who gets credit for what?" No box score for personal accomplishments was involved. The chips fall where they fall.

There are quite a few irreverent and controversial items in the book, which some Monsanto people probably wish had been overlooked. Yet, with credibility as the goal, the author needed free rein.

The journalistic method employed has each chapter attempting to stand on its own feet, without regard to the contents of other chapters. This advantage necessitated a negative trade-off involving some seemingly inadvertent or careless (but, in fact, quite deliberate) repetition here and there.

There may be those who will say objectivity and credibility are difficult to achieve when an alumnus undertakes the writing of a history of his alma mater, for employes and shareowners and for general public sale. Some critics may even choose to see the author as sort of a helpless Trilby, performing under the hypnosis of a corporate Svengali. So much for the liability, to the extent it exists.

On the asset side of the ledger, the author most definitely knew what questions to ask. He had had a close-up, inside, eyewitness view of a large number of the company's adventures and, in fact, had been an active participant in many. Having hung on to this corporate roller coaster for more than 27 years, he had at least an opportunity to try to transmit some of the assorted flavors behind the scenes and to try to make some of the company's principals a bit three-dimensional rather than the stuffy stereotypes so often and awkwardly held in awe in company puff pieces.

Monsanto is neither the largest nor smallest, oldest nor newest American business venture. There is no evidence that the founder intended his company to be symbolic of the American mode of private enterprise. Early-day motives were less noble, more pragmatic—such as survival. Yet as things worked out, there was—and is—a lot of American symbolism in the Monsanto story. This wide-angle view of the first 75 years, therefore, provides some insight into what it took to create and nourish a science-based company in the competitive scene of twentieth-century America.

(In a limited number of instances, the author was able to update some material into 1977. Yet, by and large, this is a 75-year history of Monsanto, covering the period between the company's incorporation November 29, 1901, and December 31, 1976.)

—D. J. F.

Contents

CHAPTER I

How It All Began

IT had been one of the longest days of 1976 for the man from Monsanto headquarters.

He had awakened early on a cold December morning at the Dorchester Hotel in London and had arrived at Heathrow Airport at 9:30 A.M., allowing a 90-minute cushion for the scheduled 11 A.M. departure of Pan Am flight 101 for New York.

But there had been a double problem: a delay caused by nasty weather, which brought the incoming Pan Am 747 late into London, and a delay-on-top-of-a-delay caused by "the need for a slight mechanical adjustment."

He had been due to arrive at Kennedy Airport, New York, at 1:35 P.M., but, alas, it was almost 5 P.M. when he disembarked from flight 101. Could he get over to the domestic side of the sprawling airport complex in time to make his 5:55 connection with TWA flight 703 and thus get home to St. Louis on time, at 8:27 P.M.?

It took some scrambling, but he did it.

He went through immigration in a hurry; his baggage tumbled onto the carousel without delay; the trip through customs went smoothly and rapidly. Instead of waiting for a shuttle bus to take him from the international side to the domestic side of the busy airport, he grabbed a taxi for the short trip to the TWA terminal building. Things even went fast as he checked through Checkpoint Charlie's baggage-inspection machinery—and he made his connection, granted with not too much time to spare.

As he settled into his TWA seat, musing on the events of the long day, he found himself wondering, Did Orville and Wilbur Wright have the foggiest idea all this would be happening 73 years after Kitty Hawk?

Fatigued but pensive, he also reminisced on the buoyant business nature of his trip. He had paid his first visit to Seal Sands, a flourishing industrial community on the northeast coast of England, where Monsanto was installing $250 millions' worth of sophisticated hardware to further its stake in petrochemicals. And the weary traveler also found

11

himself wondering, Did a man named John Francis Queeny have the foggiest idea all this would be happening 75 years after he founded an insignificant little company called Monsanto Chemical Works?

The answers to the Wright and Queeny questions are the same: Probably not. Yet, allowing that the Wrights were inventors and dreamers, one will never really know what they envisioned. But John F. Queeny was no inventor. He wasn't a scientist. He wasn't even what is known as a technical man. "In the early days, he settled for mere survival," John F. Queeny's only son, Edgar, was to comment in the mid-sixties. "My father used to say, 'If we can make it 'til tomorrow, we'll be all right.'"

It seems safe, therefore, to conclude that the founder of Monsanto did not envision Seal Sands, did not envision a vast petrochemicals complex 4000 miles from home, and most certainly did not envision his company laying $250 million on the line anywhere in the world.

It seems equally safe to say that if he could return for "one more day" he would be thunderstruck by such end-of-1976 Monsanto statistics as: 150 plants and 135 offices in 43 countries; 60,000 employes; 100,000 shareowners; and $4 billion in assets.

An analysis of John F. Queeny's activities and motivation starting with 1901, when he founded Monsanto, would be insufficient. After all, in 1901 he was forty-two years of age and had already accumulated a substantial share of adventures—some joyous, some disastrous.

He was born in Chicago on August 17, 1859, the eldest of five children. His parents, John and Sarah (Flaherty) Queeny, had both been the children of immigrants from Ireland's County Galway.

Six years of public schooling was the sum total of his formal education.

In 1871 his father was receiving a rather comfortable income in rental payments from several modest buildings he owned, as well as what he was able to earn as a carpenter-contractor. Tragedy hit hard that fateful year of 1871—the year of the Great Chicago Fire. The effect on the Queeny family was shattering. The Queeny buildings were wiped out and, of course, the flow of income from them ceased.

The twelve-year-old boy, John Francis, quite plainly couldn't afford the non-income-producing luxury of continuing his education. So he walked the streets of the fire-ravaged city in search of a job. It took him several months to find employment, as an office boy in the drug firm of Tolman and King—at $2.50 a week.

In a short time he advanced to the responsibilities of delivery boy. (Years later, his employer recalled: "He wore out more wagon wheels than any boy I ever had.")

During the seventies, eighties and early nineties, John F. Queeny doggedly and persistently fought his way up, serving in the sales department of Tolman and King before accepting a position as buyer for the drug firm of I. L. Lyons of New Orleans. In 1894 he went to New York as sales manager for Merck & Company.

In retrospect, it can be said that 1896 and 1897 involved substantial milestones, all ultimately bearing on the development of what is known today as Monsanto Company.

Milestone No. 1: In 1896, in Hoboken, N.J., John F. Queeny married Miss Olga Mendez Monsanto.

It was a storybook romance, a union of rather different cultures. Queeny brought to it a combination of vision and vigor, an indomitable spirit, and a very large measure of self-reliance engendered by the exacting requirements of the already-competitive business system of the New World. Olga Monsanto brought the gentleness, grace and charm of the Old World.

Her Spanish father, Maurice Monsanto, was the son of Don Emmanuel Mendez de Monsanto, an aristocrat who had been knighted by both Queen Isabella II of Spain and King Frederick VII of Denmark. Her German mother, Emma Cleaves, was a daughter of a private secretary to King George IV of Hanover.

The three Monsantos—father, mother and daughter—had abandoned Europe and had taken up residence on sugar plantations on the island of Vieques near Puerto Rico, and on St. Thomas in the Virgin Islands, before moving to New York in 1878.

There seems to have been unanimity among early watchers of Monsanto Chemical Works that Olga Monsanto Queeny gave her husband's company more than her name.

She provided a sensitive balance for her ambitious and hard-driving husband. She is often credited with contributing to her husband, and later to her son, Edgar, a crucial "leavening influence." Years after she died, a principal executive of the company who knew the family well declared, "I think the influence of that wonderful woman on that rugged Irishman was one of the basic keystones of the company's success."

Milestone No. 2: In 1897, John F. Queeny brought his bride to St. Louis, where he accepted the position of purchasing agent for Meyer Brothers Drug Company, which was then one of the largest wholesale drug houses in the nation. The words "to St. Louis" are the point of this milestone.

Milestone No. 3: On September 29, 1897, a son was born. His parents named him Edgar Monsanto Queeny.

To latter-day Monsanto-watchers who wonder, Was this industrial enterprise mostly plan, mostly fortuitous accident, or a mix of both?, there are three speculative and teasing responses.

1) John F. Queeny would probably have "founded something." Or, at least, this was the judgment of his son, Edgar, almost 65 years later. "He had a relentless stirring within him," was the son's observation. But, obviously, without the maiden name of the young lady he married,

John F. Queeny would not have called his St. Louis-born company Monsanto. And he would not have had the same sensitive, compassionate guidance and support from a partner whose beneficial influence seems to have been encouraging, ennobling and enduring.

2) If John F. Queeny had not come to St. Louis to work for Meyer Brothers, and ultimately to engage in a bit of early-day, riverfront "moonlighting" in order to set up his own chemical shop, would he have had the environment to start a chemical company somewhere else? He had learned about the synthetic sweetening agent, saccharin, at Meyer Brothers—and saccharin was the first product manufactured by Monsanto Chemical Works.

3) To be sure, no one knew in 1897 that an infant christened Edgar Monsanto Queeny would grow into a man of heroic stature and become dominantly responsible for taking the company from a "lost ball in the high weeds of chemistry" to a major multinational presence in the world of science and commerce.

It is easy now, with the perspective of hindsight, to see the three legendary figures who "made" Monsanto: John F. Queeny, Olga Monsanto Queeny and Edgar Monsanto Queeny.

THE year 1899 brought the scourge and ravages of fire back into the life of John F. Queeny, as though his earlier experiences with fire in Chicago had not been sufficient.

In that year of 1899 Queeny lost $6000 in his first extracurricular experiment, when his East St. Louis Sulfur Refinery burned down on its first day of operation—uninsured. It was later determined that a spark had exploded the finely ground sulfur dust in the one-building factory. Something of John F.'s fiber was revealed on the day of that fire. Because Mrs. Queeny was giving a party in the evening, her husband said nothing to her of the calamity when he returned home, waiting instead until the following morning to break the news.

John F. Queeny was forty-two years old and the city of St. Louis was one hundred and thirty-seven years old when Monsanto Chemical Works came into being, without fanfare and almost without notice, in 1901.

Known even then as the Gateway to the West, St. Louis boasted of being the fourth-largest city in the nation in population—575,238—and manufactured output—almost $400 million a year from its 7000 factories. (Ironically, the 1977 population of the city of St. Louis is a bit below 575,238.)

The St. Louis *Republic*, the morning newspaper, predecessor of the *Globe-Democrat*, called its hometown the fastest-growing and "most prosperous city in the Union." Principal avenues of commerce were chewing tobacco, streetcars, dry goods, footwear, hardware, fuses, drugs, paints, oils, gloves, millinery, farm implements, general apparel, clay products, paper, trunks, groceries, glassware, furniture, hides, candies, stoves, lumber, flour—and chemicals (Mallinckrodt Chemical Works had started its operations in North St. Louis in 1867).

Yet, alas, the charm of this fur-trading post on the mighty Mississippi, with picturesque steamboats going north and south, had by 1901 given way to what today's observers would call urban blight. The waterfront was drab and dirty. Less than one half of the 900 miles of streets of this "most prosperous city" were paved. The rest were mud paths dotted with punctuation marks called sinkholes. Taxes were low. Municipal services were minimal.

When 1900's Mayor Henry Ziegenhein was chided by the press for insufficient illumination of the city's thoroughfares, he rebutted with a still-referred-to classic: "Vell, we got a moon yet, ain't it?"

The city's most unfortunate trademark was the smoke-filled air, which hovered like a constant umbrella—somewhere between a medium and dark gray. When a visiting tenor in 1901 canceled his performance with a local opera company because smoke had "choked my lungs," he added this commentary: "I have seen only one place beat St. Louis— Peetsburgh."

On a happier note, the citizenry's spirits were lifted by the prospect of brighter days when the United States Congress, in March of 1901, approved a proposal for a St. Louis World's Fair in 1903 (subsequently postponed until 1904) to commemorate the 100th anniversary of the Louisiana Purchase. To get ready for an influx of visitors from all over the world, St. Louis began to roll up its sleeves for a massive job of civic clean-up.

In such an environment, practically no one noticed—and indeed there was no mention in the press—when on November 29, 1901, John F. Queeny filed papers of incorporation in the Missouri state capitol at Jefferson City for Monsanto Chemical Works.

Why did he name the company after his wife? is an oft-asked question. It is suggested it may have been imprudent for him to have called it Queeny Chemical Works, in light of the fact he edged into his new venture on a moonlighting basis while still holding on to his job as purchasing agent for Meyer Brothers Drug Company.

This is not to say he kept any secrets from his employer. He had the full encouragement of Carl F. G. Meyer, president. (Today, Carl F. G. Meyer III, grandson of John F. Queeny's boss, comments with amusement, "My grandfather would be as surprised as John F. Queeny if both could see today the size of the Monsanto empire, spawned as a part-time adventure for the making of saccharin.")

This man named Queeny, who had the impulse to do his own act on his own time while working for Meyer Brothers, was tall, fine-boned and outwardly rather distinguished. He had dark hair and a sandy-red mustache. He was determined and ambitious. He was regarded as a good companion at poker and billiards. And he had a charming wife, Olga, a four-year-old son, Edgar, and a two-year-old daughter, Olguita.

He was in his fifth year as purchasing agent for Meyer Brothers.

By 1901, Queeny had saved another $1500—an accomplishment in itself considering the worth of a dollar in that era—and was ready for another try at starting up his own company. One might add "again!— only two years after the fire at the sulfur company!"

At Meyer Brothers he had learned much about saccharin, a supersweet chemical which was derived from coal tar and was discovered quite by accident at Johns Hopkins University in 1879. The infant U.S. organic chemical industry had shown little interest in the product and, in fact, it was being manufactured only in Germany in 1901.

For several years Meyer Brothers had been importing the synthetic sweetener and selling it to a growing list of customers.

Queeny felt confident that an enterprising American could make some money by producing this wonder product in the U.S. and selling it to manufacturers of soft drinks, candy and tobacco and to other big sugar-users.

The arithmetic was impressive. One pound of saccharin would do precisely the same sweetening job as five hundred pounds of sugar. Sugar was selling for $.06 a pound; saccharin was selling for $4.50 a pound.

Saccharin, therefore, provided equal sweetening for less than one cent a pound, which means it was more than six times cheaper than sugar. Queeny regarded this as a substantial advantage—one that would enable him to become a pioneer in the sense that he'd be the first and only U.S. manufacturer, plus he'd be able to turn a tidy profit in the doing.

But . . .

His $1500 was not enough capital upon which to build a chemical company. He calculated he'd need at least $5000. He turned to the banks. They said no. They wanted tried-and-true collateral. And the chemical industry in 1901 was something less than Fort Knox in the eyes of the local bankers. Queeny's plans left them unimpressed.

From out of the blue there appeared a man for whom Queeny had recently done a small favor: Jacob Baur, president of Liquid Carbonic Acid Manufacturing Company, Chicago, a company specializing in making ingredients for soft drinks.

Fifty years later, Jacob's brother Oscar recalled the circumstances clearly: "Shortly before Monsanto was formed," he said, "Liquid Carbonic had been making a large amount of Epsom salts, and Queeny was able to sell a substantial amount of our product through Meyer Brothers, where he was the buyer. . . . Queeny was a man of high character. All his transactions with us were satisfactory. . . . He was anxious to sell us stock in his proposed new company, but we considered this too risky. We preferred to make a short-term loan, which was promptly repaid when it became due. The loan was made by Liquid Carbonic, not by my brother, Jacob."

The amount of the loan was $3500. Liquid Carbonic also agreed to purchase a five-year supply of saccharin, contracting for not less than 6000 pounds a year.

And so, with $5000 capital and one very reliable and reassuring customer, Queeny was ready to start his new company.

He would work earnestly through most of the day—7 A.M. to 3 P.M.—at Meyer Brothers and would devote the rest of the time to his new industrial offspring. But who would make the saccharin and keep the new enterprise humming? Who would help him crank up Monsanto Chemical Works?

EARLY in 1901, Queeny had actually tried to persuade his employer, Meyer Brothers, to manufacture saccharin instead of importing it from Germany. But his employer perceived little in the way of a profitable future from the product. His employer said no.

So Queeny set out to do some investigating on his own. By summertime he had arranged for the Sandoz Company of Basel, Switzerland, to supply this nonchemist with the nine-syllable, tongue-twisting, crucial intermediate necessary for the saccharin process—ortho-toluenesulfonamid.

Sandoz had also agreed to export to St. Louis an expert proficient in the manufacturing of saccharin—a Ph.D. chemist, no less, from Zurich, named Louis Veillon.

Chemist Veillon, who thus had the distinction of being the first employe hired by Monsanto Chemical Works, arrived in St. Louis on December 31, 1901, only a month plus two days after the incorporation papers had been filed. When Founder Queeny met Veillon at Union Station, here's what greeted his eyes: an elegant young dandy of twenty-six, with a pointed beard and continental clothes topped by a fur-lined greatcoat.

(Many years later, Edgar Queeny wondered: "I wonder what they said. On occasion, my father used to grunt. But he had a hearty handclasp.")

Louis Veillon was the youngest son of a Swiss army officer, and a graduate of the Federal Polytechnic Institute at Zurich. Little did he realize on that New Year's Eve the central role he'd be playing as Monsanto's first "technical man"—at $100 a month. He'd be involved in the hard, dirty job of building and running a chemical plant on a shoestring, coaxing along rickety machines, and hiring unskilled workers who had never heard of chemistry, much less saccharin.

At 10 A.M. the next day, the dawn of a new year, the two men set out in Queeny's buggy to inspect three plant locations that had been advertised for rent.

Considering Queeny's unhappy experience with fire in Chicago in 1871 and in East St. Louis in 1899, one wonders what went through his mind when he and his Swiss employe took a "plant tour" of an unused section of the Diamond Match Company near the riverfront on dingy, dirty South Second Street. The structure they inspected was flimsy—and tens of thousands of matches were stacked along the walls of an immediately adjacent building.

But that's the site they picked! Veillon's analysis had a strong influence. He pointed out that the warehouse had a ceiling high enough for the three platforms he would need to erect for establishing the saccharin process.

(Today, in 1977, the John F. Queeny plant is still located on South Second Street, where it all started in the dawning days of the new century. Until 1957, Monsanto also had its general headquarters at this same location.)

Queeny was not one to rush his new Swiss employe into any precipitous action. He gave the good doctor 31 days to hire three laborers and to purchase apparatus, to hook it all together, and to put the saccharin process "on stream."

And Veillon almost made the deadline, missing it by only a few days.

Scrounging for hardware was Veillon's most difficult task, keeping in mind that the expense budget under which he operated was both meager and ill-defined. The solution: secondhand equipment, stem to stern.

Queeny had already bought a sputtery old steam engine ($200) and an ancient boiler ($500). Veillon found a pump, scales, kettle, pipes, filters and four big wooden tanks, all pre-owned, as today's euphemism says it. A used centrifuge, alas, was not available. A brand new one had to be purchased ($1000!).

Even before all equipment was in place in the plant Queeny was pestering Dr. Veillon for one little trial batch. He even offered to pick up the check for luncheon at the nationally famous Southern Hotel— at about where the Busch Memorial Stadium complex now stands— when the first sample was produced. Yet, when the batch was ready, both were disappointed. It didn't taste sweet at all.

But Queeny followed through with the luncheon plans anyway. As things developed, they took a small sample of the product with them and, while eating, they offered the waiter a taste. "My, that's sweet," was the waiter's comment.

As the story goes, the two pioneers, suddenly realizing that their taste buds had been deadened by the saccharin dust and fumes in the plant where the first batch had been manufactured, leaped up and jigged a victory dance around the table.

On February 5 there occurred what Veillon later referred to as "the inauguration of the works, with engine under steam." Fittingly, February 5, 1902, was the Queenys' sixth wedding anniversary. John F. and Olga Queeny were undoubtedly a bit proud, though unaware of the empire to follow, when they went down to the plant in the evening and climbed to the top platform, where Veillon handed Mrs. Queeny "a bunch of roses I had fastened to one of the oxidation tubs up there."

When the first satisfactory batch of saccharin, almost ready to sell, was produced in small quantity on February 14, John F. Queeny couldn't restrain his enthusiasm. He handed out the corporation's first bonuses: two dollars each to the three laborers who had helped coax the hardware into assembly—plus a box of Havana cigars to Veillon, who had made it all happen under circumstances that were primitive and discouraging, but exhilarating.

(Before leaving this inaugural event behind, a flash-forward to a mid-1965 appraisal by Edgar Queeny: "My father did it all somewhat as a challenge, somewhat on an impulse, *but largely because he was sure it could be done*. Market research? If he had taken time to accumulate the kind of data which is commonplace today, he probably would never have started the company. If all the information he needed on saccharin could have been fed into a computer in 1901, the computer would have blown a fuse.")

An old sheet in careful penmanship shows commercial-quantity manufacturing of saccharin actually started on March 6, 1902. Sales in March were $998.14; in April, $1930.17; in May, $1843.47; in June, $3937.93; in July, $2707.31; and in August, $1512.88—making total sales for the first six months $12,929.90. Even though profits were still several years down the road, these sales numbers were encouraging, all by themselves.

From 1902 to 1904, the "owners, directors and officers" met ten times for purposes of policy, operations and for keeping a close watch on the fragile financial condition of the infant company. During this time Queeny was both president and treasurer; Veillon was the corporate secretary. A lawyer, John W. Rossiter, served as vice president.

In 1904 and 1905, President Queeny moved toward diversification and added two additional products, caffeine and vanillin—products that he had also become familiar with at Meyer Brothers, where, it should be noted, he continued to serve as a purchasing agent, through all mornings and early afternoons.

Such a growing chemical company quite plainly needed another technical man. Where to turn? Switzerland, naturally. From what institution of higher learning? The Federal Polytechnic Institute at Zurich, naturally. What kind of a person? A chemist, naturally, and in this case one who was working toward his Ph.D. degree when he was summoned from afar.

Gaston DuBois thus became the second Swiss scientist to come across the water and to cast his lot with an upstart American industrialist in

St. Louis. After DuBois had accepted the assignment, he received a piece of correspondence from Queeny asking him to study processes for making caffeine and vanillin. However, all evidence suggests that what really lured DuBois to St. Louis was not chemistry but, instead, a desire to see the World's Fair.

He arrived April 20, 1904. Many years later DuBois was to tell how disappointed he was that his job at Monsanto was so totally time-consuming, and that he saw so little of the Louisiana Purchase Exposition in Forest Park. Indeed, he visited the fair only once, for a few hours on the Fourth of July of 1904.

Veillon, by this time glorified by the twin titles of Corporate Secretary and Plant Manager, welcomed his Swiss compatriot warmly. The two became constant working companions and fast friends. They had been fellow students in Zurich only a short time back. Now they were both pursuing their careers in a new land of adventure, 4500 miles from home.

DuBois later recalled that even though it was springtime when he arrived in the United States, much of the nation from New York to St. Louis was white with snow. But St. Louis offered a dull contrast. His destination was "dirty, muddy, smoky and very ugly." Prior to his arrival a room in South St. Louis had been rented for him "in a building reached through a dark passage. There was one window that opened onto a brick wall three feet away. Luckily, the room had a gas light, which I burned constantly when I was there. The room had been selected because it was within walking distance of Monsanto. My starting salary was only $75 per month, which didn't allow for carfare."

His first task upon arriving at the chemical works was to unpack a heavy case he had shepherded all the way from Switzerland—a case containing books, a platinum crucible, an hydrometer and a thermometer.

The thermometers previously in use at Monsanto were found, upon checking, to be quite inaccurate. DuBois further recalled: "We used to go to the School of Pharmacy to borrow thermometers. In those days we borrowed almost everything—wrenches, chain hoists and so forth—but we got along pretty well."

It became evident in 1904 that Queeny had scored a coup in terms of the talent, skills, ingenuity and willingness of his two Swiss chemists. Thus, when it also became evident that there should be a chemical engineer on the payroll along with the two chemists, it was unsurprising that Queeny should seek out a man who had been a classmate of Veillon and DuBois in Zurich.

Dr. Jules Bebie had not only attended the Polytechnic Institute but had also studied at the University of Zurich, where he received his Ph.D. degree in chemical engineering. He arrived in St. Louis early in 1905, completing the "technical triumvirate from the Swiss Alps" destined to help Founder Queeny plot a course of rapid, though often precarious, expansion.

Not only was the expansion precarious; even the early days of "saccharin only" were touch and go.

Shortly after Monsanto Chemical Works began shipping rather substantial—and somewhat profitable—amounts of saccharin to Liquid Carbonic and other companies, the powerful German cartel known as the Dye Trust began to take notice of this new little company in St. Louis—a company daring to compete with the Germans' "proprietary" product.

The six companies in the Dye Trust had already learned how to deal with American upstarts. Their method was simple. It was effective. And it was ferocious. They would simply cut the price of a given product below the cost of manufacture until their U.S. competitors—struggling along with infinitely smaller product lines—were bankrupt. And then, having vanquished the competition, they'd raise their prices as high as the traffic would bear.

Between 1866 and 1880, to discourage a stubborn company named Dow, they drove the price of bromine from $6.00 a pound to $.28 a pound. They were particularly eager to discourage new companies from getting into what they regarded as their special province—organic chemicals.

There is some evidence suggesting Queeny may conceivably have thought, at least for a while, that his little enterprise would be too puny for the Germans to notice. However, the facts are that the Germans lost no time in spotting this tiny newcomer in American industry. The methodical monopolists abroad quite obviously believed in killing off competitors before they grew big enough to be really bothersome.

Swiftly and without mercy, the Dye Trust dropped the price of saccharin—from $4.50 a pound to $4.00 to $2.00 to $1.00.

Queeny sold his horse and buggy and borrowed on his life insurance. His workdays were endless—mornings and afternoons until 3 P.M. at Meyer Brothers; late afternoons, evenings and Sundays at Monsanto. Largely as the result of German price reductions, Monsanto showed a loss of $1512.04 for the year 1902 and $70.63 for 1903. The Germans even went so far as to try to intimidate Sandoz into cutting off its supply of the nine-syllable intermediate. They were playing for keeps.

The U.S. Government and the U.S. sugar industry likewise made things difficult for this fledgling St. Louis company. The U.S. Department of Agriculture's Bureau of Chemistry wasn't too sure about an edible product made of coal tar, and it established a "poison squad" and chose saccharin as a target. In Queeny's earlier years in the drug business he had become a staunch advocate of purity and an arch-foe of adulteration. He had in fact been a one-man minority on a national Committee on Trade Practices, and had helped lead a winning fight for endorsement of a national pure food and drug law by the National Wholesale Druggists' Association.

An ad hoc task force appointed by President Theodore Roosevelt subsequently gave saccharin a clean bill of health. A popular writer on the subjects of food and health, Alfred W. McCann, nonetheless stuck to his guns and wrote: "Saccharin is as false and scarlet as the glow of health transferred from the rouge pot to the cheek of a bawd." No offense to this early burst of investigative journalism, but such a scarlet start-up of Monsanto was not exactly what Queeny had had in mind.

Saccharin was even attacked on the grounds that it had no food value and thus added no calories—three score years before Diet Pepsi, Tab and Sugar-Free Seven-Up. Yet, by persistence, Queeny was able to achieve recognition for the product's demonstrable advantages. It was a boon for diabetics. And it provided an easily packaged, compact, economical way to accomplish a lot of sweetening for a growing list of customers.

Queeny and his lieutenants also saw the hand of sugar interests behind the smear campaign aimed at discrediting his product. The enmity was not only natural, it was expected.

So Queeny had antagonists on three fronts: the Germans, the U.S. Government and the sugar industry, all looking askance at the struggling little company on South Second Street near the St. Louis riverfront.

Things got worse before they got better.

In 1904 Monsanto lost $2058.05. At one time its working capital was down to $204. But the following year Monsanto turned its first profit: $10,600.

In 1905 Queeny said adieu to his friends at Meyer Brothers and became the St. Louis representative of Powers-Weightman-Rosengarten Co., a Philadelphia drug house. Even though things were looking up at Monsanto, he still felt he needed the security and income from part-time employment at an established drug firm. For that matter, it was not until 1908 that he felt he could cut loose from other employment and settle in as the full-time president·of Monsanto Chemical Works.

Saccharin remained the dominant product, but the introduction of caffeine and vanillin helped fortify the company's financial position— especially caffeine, which was credited by DuBois with "keeping us solvent for ten years."

John F. was, above all things, resolute. No detail escaped his eyes. Whenever he had a few spare hours away from the plant site, he'd be persuading new investors to advance fresh capital, beseeching a bank for a line of credit, fending off his own creditors, scouring the land for new customers, and trying to build up Monsanto's reputation for quality and integrity.

And whereas Monsanto later would add products largely on the basis of logical chemical relationships, during those early years products were added whenever Queeny—out of his knowledge of the drug business and his study of supply and demand and costs and competition and know-how—saw a chance to make a few more dollars in earnings.

Among these additional products were: phenacetin, for controlling fever, in 1906; chloral hydrate, a sedative, in 1908; phenolphthalein, a laxative ingredient, in 1909; glycerophosphates, for tonics, in 1912; and coumarin, an additive to enhance flavorings, in 1914.

Queeny's restlessness was most frequently evident in his incessant urge to travel—to get out there and locate new customers for his growing line of chemicals. From his train window he'd observe factory signs along the way and would jot down the names in a little notebook. He would later approach these prospects by letter with the phrase "perhaps in your business you use chemicals."

Policy meetings with his three Swiss colleagues would take place two or three evenings a week at the Queeny home. At the start of each meeting Queeny would draw from his pocket a handful of paper slips made from incoming envelopes salvaged by an office staff regimented into keeping a supply of "scratch pads" from all possible sources, and particularly from the unused insides of envelopes.

Each slip of paper Queeny brought out for his policy meetings noted some company problem or opportunity. If the subject was adequately covered, a decision made and accountability established, Queeny would tear up the slip. If not, back into his pocket the scrap of paper would go, to be pulled out again—and, if necessary, again and again—at subsequent meetings. Queeny's rule was absolute. His decisions were final. But he listened eagerly to the comments of his associates, particularly since they knew chemistry and he didn't. More often than not, he heeded their comments and counsel, and he thereby provided a sense of involvement and teamwork—qualities which were to become indelible characteristics of the company and which would be intensely nurtured by his son, Edgar, in future years.

He was stubbornly dedicated to "writing things down." Early in his career, as his son explained years later, John F. had learned the pitfalls of loose, undisciplined, totally oral communications. He was sufficiently sensitive to the problem to realize the written word was the clearest way to spell out accountability. He had many things on his mind and didn't want to risk forgetfulness in this exciting period of busy day upon busy day. Veillon summed it up when he said, "John F. Queeny taught us how to work."

The work brought triumphs as well as heartaches during the precarious first ten years at Monsanto. Sometimes when cash flow was a problem, Queeny would pay his principal associates partly in money, to meet their immediate needs, and partly in stock. The associates may not have realized it at the time, but this opportunity to acquire stock in lieu of cash led to their eventual enrichment and sharing in the material fruits of the long, hard hours of labor in the early days.

In the years prior to World War I the pros and cons of saccharin continued to reverberate across the land.

Reference was made earlier to President Theodore Roosevelt's task force coming out on the side of Monsanto's synthetic sweetener. Here's a glimpse into the fray of that day:

While John F. Queeny was still championing his cause and still bucking the U.S. sugar interests, with help from absolutely no one anywhere, he learned that Teddy Roosevelt was a constant and enthusiastic user of the sweetening agent made in downtown South St. Louis.

So Queeny, an ardent believer in putting things in writing, sent a letter to Roosevelt, setting forth data in support of saccharin's safety, and inquiring, gingerly and discreetly, into Roosevelt's personal sweetening proclivities.

In a letter dated July 7, 1911, the former U.S. President's reply included the following statement:

"I always completely disagreed about saccharin both as to the label and as to its being deleterious. . . . I have used it myself for many years as a substitute for sugar in tea and coffee without feeling the slightest bad effects. I am continuing to use it now. Faithfully yours, T. Roosevelt."

This encouraging endorsement from Teddy Roosevelt was regarded by Queeny as a small triumph in itself. In a period when seldom was heard an encouraging word, this testimonial from on high was a major boost to his marginal morale.

It was an exciting era in the American industrial revolution, and Monsanto Chemical Works became a part of the excitement, providing products for a growing list of manufacturing industries—including the drug and food industries and, all of a sudden, others beyond them.

In 1908 Henry Ford introduced his famous Model T. The following year Robert Peary discovered the North Pole. Meanwhile, Monsanto was on the move, nurturing its "nest egg" products, as Queeny called them, and promulgating its messages about its products in ever-widening ripples.

Even Lady Luck smiled when fire again raged at Queeny's left elbow —in an adjacent building at the Diamond Match Company, in 1910. Damage to Monsanto property and stocks was minimal, and things looked so promising that Queeny decided to purchase the burned-out property of his stricken neighbor and to use this ground for expansion of his company.

In 1913, Monsanto demonstrated its clout and bravery by opening a New York office, at Pearl and Platt Streets. In 1915 nitrochlorobenzene was added to the product line, to be followed shortly by phenol. Phenol, a product on which Queeny took a chance, thus became the first enduring and basic chemical building block in the Monsanto catalogue— and it remains a basic building block today.

CHAPTER II

World War I and Its Aftermath

Respectable earnings of $81,000 in 1913 and $150,000 in 1914 leapfrogged to $561,000 in 1915 and to $905,000 in 1916 for Monsanto. The company's sales passed the million-dollar mark for the first time in 1915.

War had broken out in Europe in 1914. The ambitions of Germany's Kaiser Wilhelm von Hohenzollern were no military secret.

The last thing John F. Queeny needed during the tense period was a letter, dated August 11, 1915, from a man named Coney Sturgis, director of the Sturgis School Preparatory Department in Ithaca, New York. The letter concerned Queeny's one and only son, Edgar, who was then seventeen years of age.

Choicest morsels of the letter concerned the "current grades of Edgar Monsanto Queeny," to wit:

> Chemistry—working well, absent twice.
> French 2—poor.
> Pl. Geom.—93%.
> English B—65%, slow, not doing his best.

Plus . . .

> The boy has got it in him, if we could only wake him up.
> He does not do things in a finished kind of way.
> The next point is his Spanish. He is supposed to have two hours a week, on Tuesdays and Fridays. But on both occasions since your visit here he came in and said he had not prepared his lessons. Also, he was supposed to come and make an appointment for physics but he didn't come in. We were unable to get him on the telephone to remind him of it. Later he said he had forgotten all about it.
> I told Edgar he should take his exercise between four and six in the open air. Yesterday at five o'clock I saw him sitting on a railing outside the Ithaca Hotel. I should judge he was there about a half an hour. This is, of course, no way for a boy to take his exercise.
> He oversleeps once or twice a week. At the present rate, he

hasn't the slightest chance of getting into college this fall, unless he
has a sudden conversion—and I am going to try to bring that about.
Yours very sincerely,
Coney Sturgis

Let it be said without delay, in the fall young Edgar did get into
college—Cornell. And the record shows he ultimately woke up. But
1915 at Sturgis was not his finest academic hour.

Elsewhere on the home front all was quiet and orderly in the
Queeny household. The family now lived in a large and rambling house
on tree-lined Hawthorne Boulevard in South St. Louis. Mrs. Queeny
was always ready to add a welcoming touch when people from Monsanto came in, for business meetings in the evenings or for social
occasions. The only other offspring, a daughter, Olguita, was now sixteen years old and was attending school nearby. She was an earnest
student. She was particularly delighted when Messrs. Veillon, DuBois
and Bebie came in for dinner on Sundays. She called them her three
Swiss uncles.

But that Edgar . . . Worrying his father that way . . . A father who
had enough worries anyway at the chemical works.

EVEN though today's popular adjective "multinational" was not in
vogue in the dawning years of the twentieth century, the plain fact was
that Monsanto was born and bred of multinational origins and influences. A founder with Irish forebears married a lady with Spanish forebears and set up operations in French-founded St. Louis with the aid of
three Swiss chemists in order to compete head-on with the Germans in
the world saccharin market.

All along Monsanto had relied on feedstocks from Europe, principally
from Germany. Less importantly, Monsanto had begun exporting some
finished products to Europe. Yet the company's dependence on Europe
—and the then-young American chemical industry's dependence on
Europe—was probably never sufficiently appreciated during those earlier, prewar days, when peaceful, snail-paced yet orderly traffic on the
North Atlantic was a matter-of-fact sort of thing. In later years Edgar
Queeny recalled his father saying, at a meeting in Washington, D.C.,
"Prior to World War I, Germany was a mecca of chemical education
and chemical technology and was a fountainhead of raw materials,
intermediates and finished products, bolstered by hard-earned 'lead
time' and by national support of a government which understood the
importance of this emerging industry."

Monsanto—a small and struggling company in those early days?
Yes. Domestic, South St. Louis-ish and parochial? No. John F. Queeny's
sights knew no boundaries.

Yet Queeny was above all things an American—and proud of it. And he was convinced that the still-adolescent American chemical industry could provide his country with better services, better health, better food —and greater national strength. But he worried about the industry's environment for growth, considering that so many chemical products from Europe were flooding into the country at low prices, often because they were manufactured at lower labor rates.

There was no U.S. tariff in those days. And Queeny felt there was little understanding about the relationship of a strong chemical industry to a strong America.

There are no known records dealing with Queeny's reaction in 1914, when Archduke Francis Ferdinand of Austria was assassinated in Sarajevo by a Serbian terrorist named Gevrilo Princip—an event which historians and journalists later called the spark which ignited World War I. Yet, with the 20-20 vision of hindsight, this can be said: The shot that killed the archduke should have been heard loud and clear by Queeny, if for no other reason than that it signaled the start of a vast new assortment of problems and a vast new assortment of opportunities for American industry—and for Monsanto.

Despite, or because of, the efforts of President Woodrow Wilson in the interest of peace, there had been sufficient uneasiness to suggest to all Americans—including Queeny—that the day might not be far off when the usual, taken-for-granted to-and-fro commerce with Europe would be curtailed.

Prior to America's entry into the war, a British blockade had brought a sudden halt to shipments to the U.S., including chemical shipments. Had chemical shipments been vital to the German economy? Consider this: After the British blockade was established, a German submarine, the *Deutschland*, was dispatched with the specific assignment of eluding the British net—in order to deliver driblets of drugs and dyestuffs to America. And the *Deutschland* got through!

The situation of being isolated from Europe was difficult for many U.S. citizens to comprehend. After all, most Americans had relatives "over there." Access to European markets for U.S. products and access to European materials for the U.S. seemed as logically ho-hum as the sun and the moon. It had never been any other way. Those who tried to sell the need for American self-sufficiency during an era of apparent sufficiency (and reliance on imports) had a hard package to peddle. The horn of plenty had been too reliable too long.

Even the consequence of the British blockade was viewed by many as only a passing inconvenience in world trade. The interruption of normal trans-Atlantic commerce seemed temporary in light of its traditional presence.

The telling blow came in 1917, when the U.S. entered "the war to end all wars" on the side of the Triple Entente—when it sent its soldiers, sailors and marines to fight in the fields, trenches, skies and waters of Europe "to save the world for democracy." In short order, America began to realize that a whole new way of living—and dying—had become commonplace.

Of the 4,743,826 Americans who served their country and of the 315,000 U.S. casualties suffered between April 6, 1917, and November 11, 1918, when the Armistice was declared, Monsanto sent its share into service, many of whom would never return to what one soldier called "that sweet land of saccharin on the banks of the Mississippi River."

As in all wars, the devastation was incalculable, the adjustments beyond belief. Monsanto of 1917–1918 was only a minuscule, teen-aged cog in the industrial machinery of the nation. Yet Monsanto was destined to be shaken harshly into sudden maturity by the force of war-related events.

The company whose birth was dependent on a polysyllabic intermediate from Switzerland now found all of Europe, the "storage depot," closed down.

World War I forced the American industrial community to take a fresh look at its traditional "make or buy" decisions. The new imperative was to "make"—from the ground up, at home. Self-sufficiency became the cry of the land. *The New York Times,* in a forceful editorial, called upon the U.S. chemical industry to stand on its own feet (an earlier cry akin, it now seems, to today's clamor for less dependence on Mideast petroleum).

Edgar Queeny, looking back years later on the crunch that bore in on his father, remarked, "It was the first time Monsanto had to look all the way upstream in order to look downstream. Hard work and ingenuity were the only answers. There was no choice other than to improvise, to invent, and to find new ways of doing all the old things. The old dependence on Europe was, almost overnight, a thing of the past."

In sum: A company that had been beleaguered by incessant start-up woes, yet had been an industrial Horatio Alger in reaching its adolescent stage, was now confronted with an entirely new mix of imponderables. John F. Queeny, motivated by the double demands of profitability and patriotism, had just the right assessment of the predicament: a crisis. As it so happened, a slogan he had earlier borrowed for his company from his wife's family crest, *"in bello quies,"* was equally appropriate. Its meaning: "steadfast in strife" or, more literally, "calm in war."

The demands on Monsanto were overpowering. Old customers increased their orders. New customers sprang up like jacks-in-the-boxes. The Federal Government became a prime customer for the first time.

Concern on South Second Street centered on the availability of raw materials and intermediates for "making our own building blocks" and on rearranging processes so that available supplies from domestic sources could be employed. This called for new chemistry and new chemical engineering. In many cases, Monsanto knew all about the raw materials that were needed as the components of various intermediates it had been purchasing. Yet there was a difference, Monsanto learned, between a chemical formula and a chemical process.

What Monsanto did not know were things like the precise mixtures, temperatures, pressures, catalysts, techniques and equipment for "stirring" raw materials into intermediates. And the gap had to be filled, one way or the other—and fast.

When Monsanto researchers went to technical libraries to dig deeper, it became clear that the Germans had: 1) anticipated the war, and 2) anticipated that American researchers would be storming the libraries in a scramble which a latter-day journalist would call "a hectic game of catch-up football."

What did the Monsanto "detectives" find in the libraries? They found that pages of descriptions of German processes had been torn out of the books.

Something more subtle was also discovered. In those books where the pages had not been torn out, the Germans had quite frequently—and perhaps intentionally—been vague and misleading.

Yet, by and large, the battle of establishing new technology was won. How? "By working hard and even by making mistakes" was the explanation offered by Jules Bebie, the No. 3 Swiss import on John F. Queeny's team.

Phenol, which is, among other things, an effective antiseptic—and is also known as carbolic acid—was strongly in demand by the Surgeon General's office during the war period. It was used to maintain cleanliness in hospitals, camps and battlefield locations. A coal-tar product, it was a "best seller" for Monsanto from 1916 onward, and was destined to become a key product in the decades to follow, particularly in plastic resins.

The year 1917 brought with it another significant development— Monsanto's addition of acetylsalicylic acid, or aspirin, to its product catalogue. To be sure, no one at the time realized Monsanto would become the world's largest manufacturer of this early "wonder drug"— a distinction which still holds true today. Happily (for Monsanto) a U.S. patent protecting the Bayer Company of Germany expired in 1917. John F. Queeny leaped at this opportunity.

Phthalic anhydride, an intermediate, joined the list of the company's products in 1918. Here again was an item destined to be a longtime star on the stage of chemistry, particularly in plastics and plasticizers. However, Monsanto began making it because imports were cut off and because it was needed for phenolphthalein, an ingredient for laxatives.

In 1918, faced with the need for a deeper and broader market line and for expanded facilities to better accommodate the requirements of a war-fed American economy, Monsanto made a very large decision— the decision to be a more-than-one-factory company. The reach for a second production unit didn't require a very long arm. The reach was simply directly across the mighty Mississippi to the Commercial Acid Company, just south of East St. Louis, Illinois, and a mile due east, as the crow flies across the water, from South Second Street in St. Louis.

Commercial Acid's principal products were sulfuric acid, zinc chloride, chlorosulfonic acid and salt cake, an impure form of sodium sulfate—new strengths to mix in with or add to Monsanto's requirements. Prior to this purchase, Monsanto's ranks stood at 288 employes. Commercial Acid added another 310.

To supervise operations "across the river," Monsanto hired Dr. Lloyd F. Nickell, an assistant professor of chemistry at Washington University in St. Louis—a man destined to advance to important positions for the company in the U.S. and in England. In turn, "Doc" Nickell, as he was called, brought with him a student, F. B. "Bert" Langreck, who was later to become a legendary "No. 1 chemical engineer" within the company's technical community.

"Profiteer" was an ugly word that raised its head during the World War I turmoil, referring to any businessman who took advantage of an unusual circumstance and put money into his own pocket without regard to the national interest or the long-term consequences of his behavior.

A quote from Gaston DuBois sums up the Monsanto philosophy: "John F. Queeny could have sold saccharin in England during the war for $45 to $50 a pound. But he insisted on restricting its sale at 25 to 30 cents a pound to U.S. customers who had contracts." Queeny took care of his "regulars," as he called them, feeling that if he were loyal to them they'd repay that loyalty with continuing and increasing purchases.

Yet, understandably, the war did give Monsanto muscle, plus an unforgettable lesson that, again to quote DuBois, "the impossible is accomplishable." The year of the Armistice, 1918, showed Monsanto with sales of $9,450,000.

Financial growth was not the only reward for exemplary performance on the home front. From the U.S. War Department came a Certificate of Merit for the people of Monsanto, along with this citation:

"For their unceasing efforts, particularly in experiments in the manufacture of chemicals and drugs which had never before been made in this country, which were . . . of exceptional importance to the Government."

The crunch had not all been in vain.

It is insufficient to examine the Monsanto of the World War I period only in terms of products and growth. It was a digital company then, as now, of course. Survival is a digital exercise for all businesses.

But Monsanto was not (and is not) only digital. It was standard operating procedure to treat people as people, individuals as individuals. An observer in 1915 had commented on "the thing that separates and embellishes Monsanto—its respect for employes and its willingness to permit individuals to be individualistic, within the confines of teamwork and common goals, of course." Special care had been taken to welcome the Commercial Acid employes in 1918—so they'd not feel swallowed up by the headquarters operation of the company in "the big city across the river."

To better indicate the kind of·organization Monsanto was during the war years, two small biographical inserts will help give the flavor of what it was like to work there in the company's second decade.

Victor E. Williams, eighty-two, lives an active and comfortable life in Garden City, New York. He retired as Monsanto's regional vice president in New York in 1962. He still gets together with some of his old cronies from the chemical industry. No alumnus alive can look back as far into Monsanto experience as Vic Williams. The story spins out best in his own words, as follows:

> When I was twenty years old, early in November, 1915, I wanted to be a ballplayer and my father wanted me to be an electrical engineer. Yet my path in life was actually determined by my mother's aunt, who, somehow, had met John F. Queeny and who had written a letter to Mr. Queeny in my behalf, explaining I was seeking employment. Mr. Queeny's response had been to the effect, "We're only a small company and I don't think we have anything for the young man, but ask him to come down for an interview and perhaps I can arrange for him to get a job at Meyer Brothers."
>
> On the fateful day of my appointment, I got off the Broadway streetcar at Lafayette Avenue and began to walk two blocks east to Monsanto. I didn't have to walk very far to encounter a most disagreeable aroma coming from the chemical plant. It was mostly from tea waste used in the early process of manufacturing caffeine. Well, I got halfway down and decided, "This is not for me." So I turned around and went back to Broadway, figuring the best thing to do under the circumstances was to catch a streetcar and head back home.
>
> While waiting for a northbound trolley, all of a sudden I said to myself, "What will I tell my mother?" This horrible thought prompted me to head back east on Lafayette and to enter a door of Monsanto with a request to see Mr. Queeny. Actually, I was hoping he'd not have a job at his smelly plant but would, instead, refer me to someone at Meyer Brothers, as his letter to my mother's aunt had indicated.
>
> His was the only private office in the place. When I was ushered in to meet him, the first thing he did was give me a piece of paper and ask me to write my name. This I did—in flowing penmanship—unaware as I was, at the time, that he put great emphasis on legibility of writing and that he, indeed, was quite justifiably proud of his own penmanship.
>
> Then he wrote down a series of multiplication tables on another sheet of paper and asked me to work them out. Little did he know that math had been my specialty in high school. I had enjoyed all forms of math, including calculus, and had even done some tutor-

ing in the subject. Consequently, it was no strain at all to knock off the Queeny numbers with dispatch. And it was quite obvious that he was favorably impressed. Was I impressed? I was so captivated by the man that I forgot about the smells.

So he offered me a job as office boy. "How does thirty-five dollars a month suit you?" he inquired. "Fine," I replied. He explained the hours were 8 A.M. sharp until 6 P.M., with three and a half holidays a year—Christmas, Decoration Day, Fourth of July and half of Thanksgiving. Then he asked, "Do you know the name of the company?" I said, "Monsanto Chemical Works." More in seriousness than in jest he added, "That last word in our name explains what everybody does around here. Everybody works!"

I showed up promptly at 8 o'clock the following morning—and that was the start of my 47-year adventure with Monsanto.

In November of 1915 there were 20 office and lab employes and 75 hourly employes. I was promptly instructed to save every paper clip. Also, we carefully kept all incoming envelopes so that we could slit them and use the inside portions for our own notations, interoffice memos and even our expense accounts.

Three $5 increases took me up to $50 a month prior to the time I decided to enlist in the Army in 1917. I'll never forget the day I told Mr. Queeny I'd rather enlist than be drafted. "Very good, Victor," was his instant reaction. "We'll continue paying you for a full year while you're in service and will have a job waiting for you when you come back."

While I was serving with the artillery in France, paychecks came monthly from Monsanto—by boat, of course, and quite delayed. After twelve paychecks had arrived, I figured there'd be no more. But I very well recall the day a thirteenth check arrived. Quite promptly I wrote Mr. Queeny from the battlefield and suggested that perhaps an error had been made. He wrote back, also quite promptly, assuring me there had been no mistake and that the thirteenth check had been quite deliberately dispatched. As things turned out, I was paid for each and every month I was absent for war service. There was, of course, no government requirement for Monsanto to do this, just as there was no government requirement to guarantee military personnel that jobs would be waiting at war's end.

While in Europe I had wondered what kind of a job I'd have upon my return. I had been an office boy and had also been a clerk in the order and billing department before the war.

Upon my return to South Second Street in 1919, the smells smelled sweeter and Monsanto looked like a corner of heaven. And a warm welcome was awaiting. Mr. Queeny suggested I take off a few weeks to become acclimated to civilian life—with pay. I took only a week, and then I returned for a brief assignment in the export department.

Quite often in those days Mr. Queeny would ask me to come into his office. He'd say, "Someone in our organization has made such-and-such a mistake. I'm sure, Victor, if you had done this you would have learned by it and avoided ever making such a mistake again."

Founder John F. Queeny as he looked in 1924.

Olga Monsanto Queeny, the founder's wife, for whom the company was named. The photograph was made in 1923.

Mr. and Mrs. John F. Queeny with their children, Edgar, six and Olguita, four, in the back yard of their South St. Louis home in 1903.

as follows:

machinery $5851.54
Process 2000.00
Stock on hand 4629.93
Cash " " 120.28
Accts. receivable 1289.50

Total — — $13891.25

Capital Stock $5000.00
Accts. payable 1836.28
Accts. payable
to M.B.D. Co 2917.63
John F. Queeny 617.58

Total 10371.49

Expenses paid since
commencing $5007.20
Manufacturing com-
menced March 6, 1902
Sales March 998.14
" April 1930.17
" May 1843.47
" June 3937.93
" July 2707.31
" August 1512.88

Total sales to date, 12929.90

A report of the first six months of business of Monsanto Chemical Works.

"If we don't sell you, we both lose money"

ACETPHENETIDIN
(Phenacetin)

VANILLIN

IRON BY HYDROGEN

MONSANTO CHEMICAL WORKS
SAINT LOUIS

One of the company's first advertisements, circa 1910.

The founder's original chair and rolltop desk.

The company's first transportation vehicle. The photo was made in the early 1900s.

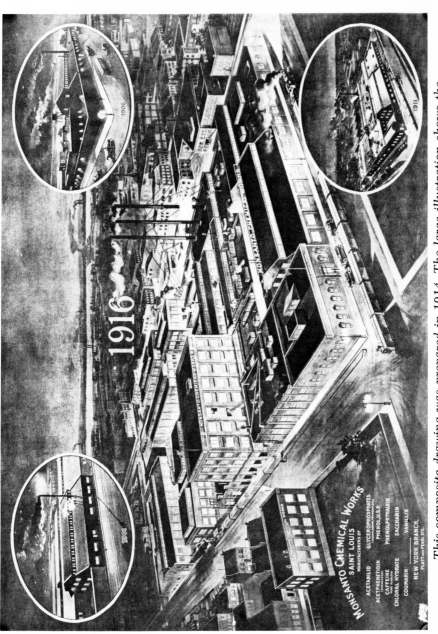

This composite drawing was prepared in 1914. The large illustration shows the way the company was expected to look in 1916. In fact not all the expansion was realized. The small insets depict the facilities as they were in 1901, 1906 and 1911.

Edgar M. Queeny as a lieutenant (j.g.) in the U.S. Navy during World War I.

Naturally, he was referring to some oversight or shortcoming on my part. He knew it and I knew it. But he usually worded his reprimands in that manner.

In 1925, Monsanto was greatly strengthened by the arrival of John W. Livingston, a chemist who had been with Allied. This was the man who subsequently brought in Dr. Lucas P. Kyrides from the University of Michigan, a man who in turn was responsible for summoning some great technical people into the company.

Mr. Queeny was fair but firm. No chemist, he would become upset when someone told him something couldn't be manufactured on the basis of Monsanto's know-how and equipment. He'd often reply, "Goddammit, they can do it in Germany and there's no reason why we can't do it here."

In those days we referred to all our products by number in our internal phone calls, memos and discussions. Saccharin was, of course, No. 1. Vanillin was No. 2 (even though it came on stream late and was, in precise fact, No. 3). Caffeine was called No. 3. And so forth.

When did I meet Edgar Queeny for the first time?

In 1920, after Edgar had returned from service in the Navy, his father asked him to sit with me and to inquire into the nature of my duties. Edgar spent an hour and a half listening to the various details of my job in the flavors and condiments department. During the whole time I rambled on, he just sat there and didn't say a word. And when I ran out of things to say, he didn't utter a sound. He simply got up and left.

In 1928 there was a big reception at the Queeny home in South St. Louis, honoring Olguita Queeny and her new husband, Tom Berington of London, following their wedding abroad. Everybody was in tails. During the height of the party I found myself sitting on the steps with Edgar Queeny. He lost little time in commenting, "This is boresome; let's get out of this place." So we got into his roadster and headed for a speakeasy—at 60 miles an hour.

In 1920, long before Monsanto went public, Walter R. Phemister, the treasurer, told me he was trying to scrape up $1000 in cash to help in the purchase of a house. A share of Monsanto stock was then worth $62.50, but Phemister told me, "I'll let you have seventeen shares at sixty dollars each."

Scraping up $1020 wasn't easy. My father advanced me $200, but I still needed another $820. So I went to a bank. Keep in mind that in those days the chemical industry wasn't regarded by bankers as a mature industry. It took a lot of persuading—but I got the loan.

Later, when I advised Mr. Queeny that I had negotiated the loan, he commented, "I am proud of you for having such faith in the company during this shaky period." And when he learned my loan payments were to be $25 a month, he advanced my salary by that amount—which means my first purchase of Monsanto stock, almost 57 years ago, cost me only the interest rate on the loan.

The early twenties were really rough. For a while it looked like Monsanto simply wouldn't make it. To assure continuing employment for his people, Mr. Queeny even went so far as to try to sell Monsanto to DuPont. But DuPont said, "No, the price is too high." Subsequently, Mr. Queeny was able to negotiate a loan from National City Bank of New York. He called the loan a lifesaver.

It should be added that when business finally did improve, a few years later, DuPont contacted Mr. Queeny to indicate that this prestigious company would now be willing to consider acquiring Monsanto. Mr. Queeny's brusque response was "Monsanto is not for sale at any price."

After Edgar became president in 1928, his father went to England, not only to provide management strength for his British affiliate, but also to give Edgar a free rein in his new responsibilities. One day in 1930, when Edgar Queeny was visiting me in the New York office, a cable came in for him from his father in England. My secretary brought the cable into my office and handed it to Edgar. It carried the news from John F. Queeny that he had just arranged for Tom Berington, Edgar's rather recent brother-in-law, to go onto the British company's board. Edgar was most upset by the news, not because he didn't admire and respect Tom Berington, but because he was sensitive to the potential abuses of corporate nepotism and also sensitive to the need for delicate handling—perhaps even extrasensitive because he himself was the founder's son who "made it." His comment in my office that day: "From now on any executive or supervisor who is ever affiliated with Monsanto will earn his job and not be hired because he's a member of anyone's family." Shortly thereafter, he introduced a specific anti-nepotism policy to the Monsanto board—and the policy was promptly promulgated. [Author's note: this policy has been continued ever since.]

Edgar Queeny began delegating authority to a much greater degree than his father had ever done. John F. Queeny used to sit at his desk, smoking Havana cigars, inspecting all incoming letters and invoices when they arrived and inspecting all outgoing letters and invoices before they left the premises. But Edgar didn't hover over such details.

Edgar believed very deeply in the importance of letting people handle their own responsibilities. Sometimes when he'd come into New York I'd tell him about a few problems and I'd outline what I proposed to do—just to make sure I had his approval. He'd always say, "Vic, you know more about that than I do. Go ahead." Quite often I'd remind him, "Okay, but don't forget I make mistakes." And he'd come back with "Who doesn't?" He didn't believe in the short leash.

Jules H. Kernen, eighty, perennial personnel manager at the "main plant" on South Second Street, lives in the area known as "down by the Gravois"—which means in deep South St. Louis near Gravois Boulevard in the part of town once known as "little Germany." Kernen retired in 1961. He still looks a little like Jimmy Durante, as his friends have said all along, affectionately. And he still has a thick and colorful accent, tracing to his upbringing in the French region of Switzerland. Kernen keeps constantly active and sees his many old Monsanto friends frequently. Like Vic Williams, he came aboard Monsanto in 1915, only two weeks after Williams' arrival. His memories of early Monsanto are best captured in his own language (unfortunately without the colorful accent), as follows:

I was not imported by Monsanto like my distinguished Swiss predecessors, Messrs. Veillon, DuBois and Bebie. Actually, I had never met these three Swiss compatriots prior to joining the company. But you can be sure we had some great times together once I joined their ranks.

Before I came to Monsanto late in November of 1915, I was engaged as a French teacher and French tutor in St. Louis. It was an interesting assignment, but it didn't keep me sufficiently busy. I was working only a few hours a day. I was bored.

So, on my own, I knocked on Monsanto's door—and was hired by John F. Queeny to come in as timekeeper at the adjacent plant—the one and only plant Monsanto had in 1915.

Shortly after I arrived, Gaston DuBois told me of the tribulations of the company's early days. He told me, for example, how in 1906 John F. Queeny had issued an official edict that henceforth payday would be each Monday instead of each Friday. The reason was that on a given Friday John F. Queeny didn't have enough money to meet his payroll. He surmised that a check would be forthcoming from Coca-Cola, for caffeine, on Monday. He guessed right. The check did come in, and he was able to pay his people. Life moved on. But it was all touch-and-go.

I remember the early days quite vividly. The hours were long—Mondays through Saturdays. And I always used to come in on Sundays too. I used to take the Tower Grove streetcar to and from work. It went as far as the City Hospital at 14th Street and Lafayette. So it was necessary to walk the rest of the way. Quite often when I was going home on the trolley people would ask, "Why do you smell that way?" and sometimes they'd be more complimentary by asking, "Why do you smell so sweet?" I'd simply tell them I worked at Monsanto in a blend of many aromas, mainly saccharin and coumarin.

When I started at Monsanto, John F. Queeny was the only person there who had an automobile. DuBois bought one in 1917. Bebie bought one in 1918. I couldn't afford one until 1930.

John F. Queeny was fifty-six years old when I came to work in 1915. He was powerful, vigorous and determined. Whenever he lost his Irish temper he gave the impression of being Jehovah blowing fire from the heavens. On the few occasions when he'd take off in the evenings, one could often find him and Mrs. Queeny at the Ritz Theatre on Grand Boulevard and Hartford Street in South St. Louis, not far from their Hawthorne Boulevard home.

Louis Veillon was a human dynamo. He was often high-strung and impatient—and sometimes quite unreasonable. But he was a real square shooter.

DuBois was a suave man of distinction. People at the plant called him "Gum Shoe" because of his ability to appear suddenly and quietly from nowhere. He would turn up unexpectedly at any part of the plant.

Bebie had a dry wit and was modest and unspectacular. He was probably the most humane of the three early Swiss.

I recall so well the year 1916, when Queeny and Veillon were prime movers in the organization of the St. Louis Safety Council. Two years later we at Monsanto hired our first full-time safety engineer.

And I'll never forget March 14, 1918, when a pipe fitter persuaded about three-fourths of our plant work force of 500 to leave their jobs. It was Monsanto's first strike. And it lasted six days. We were able to keep the plant operating at full capacity, with salaried employes lending assistance. We brought all working employes down to the plant in trucks, with police protection, because we were afraid things would get rough. Actually on one occasion stones were thrown at Mr. Queeny's automobile. Its windows were broken, but he wasn't injured.

When the strike ended, all employes were welcomed back—except the persuasive pipe fitter. We increased wage rates by three to nine cents an hour, depending on work classification. No demand had been made for union recognition.

The plant personnel department was a busy place during the war years. In 1917 we established our first medical dispensary and began the practice of pre-employment physical exams.

During the war years of 1917 and 1918, about 125 women were hired to take over jobs formerly handled by men—as chemical operators, drill press operators, storeroom attendants and helpers in the various mechanical departments.

By and large, the women did a pretty good job. But they had a marked resistance to night and Sunday work. Absenteeism was high and emotional problems were prevalent. The intermingling of the sexes also brought many complaints from wives of male employes. And, of course, extra expenses were incurred in providing special clothing and separate restroom and locker facilities.

Prior to 1920 the bulletin board was the principal general communications medium enabling plant employes to see printed material relating to Monsanto policies and activities. In 1920 we had a contest to find a name for a new publication to be distributed to all employes in the company. And I am happy to report two hourly paid women employes of Plant A—both of whom suggested *Current Events* for the name—were the winners of the contest. This publication remained until 1939, when it was transformed into the highly effective *Monsanto Magazine*, which picked up the job of carrying Monsanto information externally as well as internally.

Other dates I remember? Workmen's Compensation became a law in Missouri in 1927. In 1929 group insurance was made available for our employes. The year 1932 brought vacation with pay. And in 1940 we started our first pension plan.

The first labor contract for the plant was written in 1940. The previous year three plant employes, John Gratz, Wilbert Gusky and August Schneider, had become actively interested in organizing within the AFL. And in October, 1940, the NLRB supervised an election to determine if more than 50 percent of the employes wanted union recognition. The result: 50.8 percent voted for a union and 49.2 voted negatively. Thus, we had a union. I'll never forget the night of the election. I was invited to Bevo Mill, a popular restaurant in South St. Louis, with Vice President John Livingston and a few other people. We had asked one of the election referees to phone us at the restaurant as soon as the results were in. Needless to say, we were a bit disappointed. We had counted on employe loyalty to swing the thing the other way.

Later, many who voted for the union told us the only reason the union had made headway was because the wage increase plan under the so-called merit system had not been administered fairly. That was an important lesson. We learned it the hard way.

Looking back on the whole experience of working at Monsanto, I simply can't describe all the enjoyment I had and all the friends I made from 1915, when I started, until 1961, when I retired. I still chuckle when I remember that retirement dinner in the Gold Room of the Jefferson Hotel, with everyone in the room—hundreds of people, including Edgar Queeny—each wearing a mask with my funny face on it. Imagine that! A roomful of Jules Kernens.

The *St. Louis Globe-Democrat* once reported that during my career I hired 10,000 people. That's probably not far from being true. And I recall so many of them, and I remember how earnestly most of them worked for Monsanto. And don't forget this: I started as chief timekeeper and wound up personnel director of the plant. But regardless of titles, I was the personnel fellow at the same plant for 46 years. And that's why I always say I never really got a promotion. I never wanted anything else but that which I was lucky enough to receive. Monsanto was a way of life. I'll never forget it. The only period I wish I could forget was that terrible depression era after World War I. That was a nightmare.

It was almost as difficult to brace for peace as it had been to brace for war.

Monsanto, like the rest of America, was unready for many of the reverberations of peace.

John F. Queeny had taken a step toward readiness in 1919, when, on January 20, he asked Gaston DuBois to become Monsanto's second president—while staying on himself in the continuing and increasingly demanding roles of chief executive officer and chairman of the board. DuBois had not sought this accolade nor the fresh pressures which were part and parcel of it. His duties remained essentially the same, though under new stress. He later explained to a colleague: "I was a technical man at heart and didn't really want to be president." But he took the job.

DuBois had traveled extensively with Queeny and had been an eyewitness to his superior's adroit salesmanship. Additionally, having been in on Monsanto's arrangements of bondage to lending institutions, he knew the day would come when Monsanto would have to reckon with paying back the loans.

The inevitability that such a day would dawn was not exclusively the worry of that "fox terrier of research," President Gaston DuBois. John Francis Queeny, an old poker player from the days of whisky and cigars at the Southern Hotel, also was fully cognizant of what it meant to toss an IOU-type scrap of paper into the pot. He knew "settling up" was part of the game.

Monsanto's World War I growth had been fueled not only by sales and earnings increases, an acquisition (Commercial Acid), new products and new technology. It had also been fueled by fresh capital, which was needed to finance the progress. By 1920, Monsanto's postwar hangover involved a $3,200,000 debt—$1,200,000 to banks in direct loans, and $2,000,000 in corporate bonds purchased by institutions. Monsanto was defying the law of gravity by going upward at precisely the same time it was going downward.

This tug-of-war-era economics was, the records suggest, only partially anticipated by Queeny and his headquarters staff. Some war-inflicted aftermaths came as total shocks.

The best vantage point from which to examine this set of predicaments is 1920—shortly after the closeout of the war. Queeny was chairman and boss; DuBois was president and No. 2. Queeny was sixty; DuBois was only thirty-nine.

Later on, in 1960, John F.'s son, Edgar, was to philosophize that chief executive officers should step aside at sixty years of age and provide access for younger men to take over the burdens of corporate leadership. In 1920 Edgar's father, unquestionably fatigued by the strains of World War I, was faced with the enervating burdens of war's aftereffects.

Debt, scourge that it can be, was not his only problem. Other worrisome influences abounded to keep him from making debt a constant concern.

The whole supply-and-demand mechanism of the postwar years was seriously out of kilter, not just for Monsanto, but for the entire American industrial complex.

Much of the industrial apparatus mounted for war was promptly outmoded by peace. Most products that were all of a sudden urgently needed were in insufficient supply. More seriously, there was virtually unlimited supply of most products *not* urgently needed. Industrial inventories—accumulated when production had reached peaks—became "What'll we do with it all?" stockpiles—storage nightmares in themselves, distress merchandise awaiting shoppers.

Monsanto was not simply stuck with excess inventories. It found itself with a production capacity far exceeding postwar needs.

In short order—surprisingly short order—it found the Germans back in business on some products, cutting prices. It found its costs up and its revenues down. Sales fell from $9,450,000 in 1918 to $8,432,698 in 1920.

When Edgar Queeny was asked in the early fifties to recount the Monsanto problem he best remembered, his answer was "The hard times of the early twenties."

But John F. Queeny was as adventurous as ever, hard times notwithstanding. He and Louis Veillon took a trip to England to scout there for idle war plants which might be available at bargain rates. During the course of the visit they met a man named Norman Graesser, who was president of a chemical company founded by his father, Robert Graesser, in 1867. The upshot of this meeting was Monsanto's 1920 purchase of one-half interest in R. Graesser, Limited.

Why? For one reason, the Graesser company was Great Britain's leading producer of phenol. For another, the same John F. Queeny who was adventurous enough to step across the Mississippi to acquire Commercial Acid was also adventurous enough to step across the Atlantic for a foothold in Europe. (Eight years later Monsanto was to acquire the remaining 50-percent interest of the British company and thus embark in earnest on its multinational pursuit.)

A classic irony of 1920 was this: While Monsanto was investing in a phenol-based company in North Wales, the U.S. was swimming in a postwar phenol surplus of 35 million pounds. Yet Monsanto later turned the latter situation to its advantage, serving as contractor for selling off the government's surplus at a commission.

The year 1921 was the real villain. That's when the postwar depression set in. By springtime the 1100-man working force at the plant on South Second Street—called Plant A—had been cut down to 25 people, and the Commercial Acid facility across the river—called Plant B—was virtually shut down for a three-month period. Struggling to hang on to its chemists, Monsanto gave some of them jobs as watchmen. In desperation, John F. Queeny sold a large portion of his stock and thus relinquished the majority control which had been so important to him.

Sales, which had been $8,432,698 in 1920, fell to $3,727,000 in 1921. Even more distressing, profits became losses.

Perhaps the most embarrassing episode of all came in 1923, when the big creditor, National City Bank of New York, sent in a "watchdog" named Beverly Harris and insisted he be given the title of president while overseeing the running of Monsanto. For the rest of his life, Harris—an easily provoked, stubborn but otherwise likable chap who had most certainly not solicited the six-month sit-in assignment—liked to tell the story about his tenure as "the most expensive flyswatter in the Midwest." He explained that John F. Queeny had taken the position, "If the bank insists we economize to get back on our feet, there are obviously no funds available to install a window screen in President Harris's office."

This particular visitation by a New York banker was not only an uncomfortable experience but was also, on the more positive side, a trigger for many latter-day references—in the forties and fifties—to the risks of heavy corporate debt. Indeed, it was not uncommon in later years for Edgar Queeny to share with his colleagues the story of the creditor from New York who imposed a sit-in in 1923, and not uncommon for Queeny to caution his associates on the importance of keeping a conservative debt-to-equity ratio.

The discomforts of 1923 went beyond enforced hospitality for an unwelcome visitor. Gaston DuBois, bumped down to vice president, described the war-expanded company as "fumbling and uncoordinated as an overgrown boy at his first dancing class." He admitted, "We were inefficient; the entire structure had to be rebuilt."

Technological advancement was retarded—but didn't come to a halt. In 1925 Monsanto chemists and engineers established an important breakthrough in making sulfuric acid with a vanadium catalyst instead of using the then-usual and expensive platinum. (From the twenties on, a substantial amount of Monsanto profits has come not only from sulfuric acid sales but also from fees obtained for designing vanadium-catalyst plants for other companies around the world. As of 1977, more than half the world's sulfuric acid manufacturing facilities use the Monsanto method.)

But most steps on the mid-twenties road to recovery were slow. In 1926, with sales back over $5,000,000, Monsanto was once again in a somewhat healthy financial condition, aided by a more stable national economy and by almost doubled ranks of customers. And in 1927 John F. Queeny permitted underwriters to sell a block of his stock to the public, in order to clear up some personal as well as business debts. In the process, he opened the way for Monsanto's capital expansion and future growth by making it a public company with its stock listed for the first time on the Chicago Stock Exchange and New York Curb Exchange.

In the following year, 1928, having learned he was incurably ill with cancer of the tongue, he turned over the presidency of the company to his thirty-year-old son, Edgar—and then left promptly, at the age of sixty-nine, for England to acquire the remaining 50 percent of Graesser and to stay there for more than two years, running that company and nursing it through a wide variety of crunches.

By then the career of this indefatigable Irishman was beginning to wind down. He returned to St. Louis in 1931. In his final months he was weak, helpless and barely able to speak. When he did talk, he inquired about Edgar—and about day-to-day progress at Monsanto.

John F. Queeny died on March 19, 1933, shortly before Germany bolted from the League of Nations to plan an invasion into the Rhineland and set the stage for World War II.

CHAPTER III

The Mysterious East

CHINA, the world's most populous country—more than 900 million people occupying 3½ million square miles—is separated from Monsanto headquarters by 8000 miles and by a way of life even more distant than that.

The most recent Monsanto-related bridging of these two worlds occurred in October of 1976, when Monsanto's chairman and president, John W. Hanley, visited Peking as a member of the delegation of the National Council for U.S.–China Trade.

Hanley very well knew he was visiting more than a somewhat-inscrutable Communist country in the Far East. He knew that in setting foot on Chinese soil he was entering a wide and wondrous land where over several decades during an earlier period the name Monsanto had become a legend and almost a household word.

Far from the protocol and formality of the 1976 visitation, Monsanto's earlier experiences in China had been as fiction-like and melodramatic as a Humphrey Bogart movie, filled with suspense, intrigue and high adventure.

The story began in 1923 and ended in the late forties.

In 1923, both John F. and Edgar M. Queeny had met at the Blackstone Hotel in Chicago with a British-born sales agent from Shanghai, Herbert M. Hodges.

In Shanghai earlier that year Hodges had been visited by a Russian named M. Teplitsky, whose specific errand was summed up in one question: "Where can I purchase some saccharin?"

Hodges had told his White Russian visitor he'd look into the matter and report back. Subsequently, Hodges had thumbed through a copy of the New York–published *Oil, Paint and Drug Reporter* to locate the world's principal manufacturers of saccharin, and had dispatched inquiries to all of them, soliciting information on price and availability.

The response Hodges had liked best was the one from Monsanto. And the outcome was that meeting in Chicago.

The result of the Chicago meeting was this: Hodges took on the

41

Monsanto account on an exclusive basis forthwith—and remained the company's "man in the Orient" until 1936.

Upon his return to Shanghai, in 1923, Hodges not only opened up a line of business with the inquisitive M. Teplitsky, but he also embarked upon a campaign to sell many hundreds of tons of Monsanto saccharin in all parts of China.

Hodges knew that throughout that vast country—and particularly in the hinterlands—transporting sugar was a prodigious and unending task. Heavy sacks were carried on the backs of mules and human beings. This struck Hodges as being primitive and inefficient. After all, he reasoned, saccharin is lightweight and it's 500 times sweeter than sugar. Further, he said to himself, saccharin can be easily packaged in one-pound tins to protect the product and to make it easy to sell, to handle, to store and to use.

With his eye on opening up all of China as a market for saccharin, he contacted Monsanto anew, following his return to Shanghai. Neither he nor Monsanto realized then that they were inaugurating a new era of broad international relationships based on St. Louis shipments of a single product—the very product upon which the company had been founded.

Up until the early twenties, a large part of the commerce with China had been handled throughout the land by middlemen known as "compradores." Hodges saw their period of influence declining; further, he saw a larger market opening up if he could supply the 5000 medicine shops which could sell saccharin directly to the Chinese populace.

Monsanto's initial tin can for one pound of saccharin, designed expressly for the Far East market, had a key-type can opener on the bottom. This seemed like a good idea until Hodges discovered that some crafty Chinese were engaging in the following trickery:

They'd lift the key and tear it off.

They'd drill a tiny hole at some point where the key had been attached.

They'd empty half the saccharin.

They'd add some neutral powder, like borax.

They'd carefully resolder the key.

They'd sell the loose saccharin on the black market.

It was plain to Hodges that such skulduggery could not be tolerated— to the extent that he and Monsanto could do anything about it. They did effect some control by eliminating the key and turning instead to a can that required puncturing with a sharp opener.

Yet the Chinese weren't easily discouraged. Some shady operators found ways of breaking into the new one-pound cans by ingenious techniques that would have defied Charlie Chan.

Example: An elderly woman in a Chinese waterfront loft developed a special bit of craftsmanship. She became expert with a fine drill, using it to pierce a tiny hole through a portion of an obscure letter painted near the bottom edge of the can. Adroitly, slowly and patiently, she would remove a quantity of saccharin, replace it with some filler, seal up the hole and then make the pilfered saccharin available on the black market. Even with a magnifying glass it was difficult to locate the precise point of the woman's skillful handiwork.

To prove to St. Louis that its "improved" saccharin cans weren't 100 percent tamperproof, Hodges would send back to Monsanto choice samples of Oriental ingenuity. When St. Louis was finally convinced, Hodges received a cable saying "the impossible has occurred."

There were even Chinese attempts to make copies of the can itself.

Monsanto tried a variety of devices to assure that the end-users would receive unadulterated saccharin, including a fabric enclosure to shroud the sweetener and to make difficult the dishonest job of shaking the fine grains through a small hole in the can.

It was important, also, that the cans be hermetically sealed to keep the sweet powder dry. Yet this protection ultimately became the tool of those adept in the art of rascality. Here was Hodges' analysis: "On the one hand, the fact that our can was hermetically sealed and could even stand immersion in water gave it an advantage over competitive brands. Yet it facilitated smuggling, which was prevalent in the waters between Hong Kong and Chinese ports. Nets containing the tins could be thrown overboard for convenient recovery later, or towed underwater when entering a harbor to avoid customs duties."

Considering that the Chinese consumers of saccharin couldn't read the English language, Hodges suggested the saccharin cans should have some simple symbol—one that could be recognized instantly. Monsanto responded by putting an artist's sketch of a large pine tree on every can, so that all a customer would have to do was point to a pine tree to receive Monsanto saccharin. (It was a primitive example of what today's sophisticates search for: instant corporate identity.)

And so it went. "Something new and different all the time," Bert Hodges used to say.

During the late twenties and early thirties he began to broaden his Monsanto product line and to sell such items as vanillin, coumarin and aspirin in the Far East. These Monsanto products were accepted in almost direct proportion to the skill with which they had been crated for shipment from St. Louis. Hodges composed his own "sales literature" in Shanghai, detailing the kinds of wood and even the kinds and number of nails used in the shipping containers. Not only the Monsanto products but also their packagings proved popular.

It should be stated that Hodges, intrepid as he was as Monsanto's super salesman in the Far East, didn't do his work alone. For many years he was aided by an assistant named A. Sidney Hill. When Hodges moved to St. Louis in 1936, Hill took over—and had his own set of Chinese puzzles to solve. In addition to his other duties, he was faced with a continuation of the old cat-and-mouse exercise, that of tracking down and trying to prevent adulteration of saccharin. Tricky tampering kept him on his toes.

Hill also faced some puzzling problems under the heading of "accounts receivable."

Among his favorite stories is this:

An importer in Harbin, a principal city in Northern Manchuria, owed $6000 for Monsanto saccharin. Pleading inability to pay, he offered as "good faith" 350 barrels of Korean herring.

Rather than let the debt lie dormant, Hill went to Harbin. Horse-drawn sleighs filled the streets. Upon encountering his debtor, he was led to a cold-storage house, which was simply a roof over a large hole in the ground that was partially filled with blocks of ice from the Sungari River—and with herring.

As Hill recalls the incident, the owner of the storage facilities, a Mr. Prekatchikoff, complicated the deal by insisting on the payment of storage charges for herring that had been, Hill learned, in inventory for two years.

Hill's options were few. He decided the best thing to do was to go to a local bazaar and find fish dealers who'd bid on the aging fish. The dealers' first bid was the equivalent of nine dollars a barrel. When Hill protested, they looked more closely into the storage hole and took another sniff—and offered eight dollars.

Fearing that additional negotiations would alter the bid to seven dollars, Hill took the money—amounting to something less than $3000 —and, after paying Mr. Prekatchikoff his storage fee, he got out of town, resolving that thereafter he'd be more cautious in extending credit to saccharin importers in Harbin.

On balance, both Hodges and Hill were able to get most of their shipments of saccharin legitimately into the hands of Far East consumers despite smugglers, adulterators and other villains. But it was a hard fight against what Hodges once called "the active minority."

During World War II, Sidney Hill and his wife and three children, ages eight, six and four at the war's outset, were interned near Shanghai by the Japanese. For two years and five months, the five Hills lived in a room 13 feet by 14 feet. Hill had a daily routine: finding coal for heat and for boiling water, removing garbage, and "general coolie work"— and locating that rarest of wartime commodities, soap. Happily, he had been able to include among his internment belongings one tin of Monsanto saccharin. "Bartering the saccharin, bit by bit, kept us in soap for the duration," Hill recalls.

After the war Hill lost no time in reopening his Shanghai office. But things were not to remain settled for long. Shortly before the Communist takeover in 1949, Hill and his family got out.

After visiting the States, he and his family returned to the Orient, but this time to Hong Kong, where Monsanto subsequently installed its own sales employes, with Hill's assistance, and established a full-fledged office to market all product lines in the Far East.

When star salesman Hill retired in 1966, he was not only the honored guest but also the principal speaker at a Monsanto-sponsored dinner in St. Louis. He recalled the excitement of the old days when Monsanto saccharin was a favorite product throughout pre-Communist China and the neighboring area, peaking as high as 200,000 one-pound cans a year. And he remembered how "that one can of saccharin helped pull the Hill family through the long period of internment by the Japanese."

When he was asked, "Weren't all those experiences rather taxing?" he replied, "I think it was good for us all. It strengthened our character."

CHAPTER IV

Edgar Monsanto Queeny

THE company's 1977 product catalogue includes man-made fibers, herbicides, plastics, rubber chemicals, phosphates and detergents, petrochemical raw materials and intermediates, packaging systems, and so forth.

Such 1977 chemical heavyweights in the Monsanto product line were nowhere in sight on that May day in 1928 when Edgar Monsanto Queeny succeeded his father as president, yet were firmly established on that September day in 1962 when Edgar Queeny physically moved himself, his furniture and his files away from the company, which had never seen the dawn of a Queenyless day since 1901.

Actually Edgar Queeny had stepped down as board chairman in 1960, remaining in his less-active days as Finance Committee chairman and in other roles for two years until his sixty-fifth birthday, upon which occasion a colleague dropped into his office for a visit. Here's the visitor's report:

"They had called him 'Old Stone Face.' Only his friends and close associates knew he wasn't as cold as he looked. They knew he was inwardly warm and sometimes downright sentimental. Yet there he sat on his final day in D Building [executive headquarters] at Creve Coeur. When he looked up, upon my entrance, do you know what? Edgar Queeny was crying."

The distance between 1928 and 1962, in perspective, is rather short in terms of a company transforming from provincial obscurity in the midwestern U.S. to a position of worldwide stature. And this period, measuring less than half the life expectancy for the average American, was dominantly, dramatically and singuarly influenced by the leadership of a single person—Edgar Monsanto Queeny.

On the day of his departure in 1962, Edgar Queeny could have said, "Sales are well over $1 billion. We have almost 45,000 employes and 80,000 shareowners. And we are represented by manufacturing, office, laboratory or sales personnel and agents in 40 nations of the world."

Similarly, when he assumed the responsibilities as president in 1928,

he could have said, "Sales are $5½ million. Earnings are almost
$700,000. We have 1000 employees and 55 shareowners. And we've got
three plants in the U.S., plus a small company in Great Britain, plus
sales offices in New York, Chicago, San Francisco and London."

His father had accomplished the necessary first steps for Monsanto.
Staking out the claim had taken a heavy hammer. "He had the joy of
bringing something into being," was Edgar's analysis of his father's
efforts. John F. Queeny had tenaciously and doggedly given the company
vitality, and even some degree of financial stability.

The son, therefore, didn't have to start from scratch, to borrow
wrenches, to plead with bankers as a beleaguered, moonlighting entrepreneur while holding down a regular job as a purchasing agent at a
drug company.

The ultimate evolvement of Monsanto, characterized by "passing
along" to succeeding waves of management, was in fact set in motion
in the transfer of presidential responsibilities from father to son. One
had left the other a heritage upon which to build—an evolvement continuing ever since in the form of new links in a lengthening chain.

The son, Edgar, added not only breath. He added breadth. He provided momentum and, in doing so, he brought Monsanto along from
what Gaston DuBois described as an awkward "overgrown boy" to a position of international accomplishment.

And he did it inch by inch.

But the principal words are: He did it.

Significantly, no known business observer, scholar, analyst, journalist,
historian or any other kind of Monsanto-watcher has ever come to a
conclusion other than "Edgar Queeny built the company."

It is clear and irrevocable and indisputable that Edgar Queeny personally guided his father's company to heights so lofty that, as one insider put it, "Monsanto undoubtedly exceeded even the most fanciful
Irish dreams John F. ever had."

There is some evidence that the father wasn't 100 percent sure the
son would buckle down to the task with sufficient seriousness, application and resolve. On one occasion, John F. confided to a family friend:
"Edgar wants to change everything; he's going to ruin Monsanto."

The two had much in common and much apart.

People who knew both have contributed the following adjectives:

For the father: stubborn, determined, single-minded, aggressive, hard-
headed, Irish, tireless, energetic, constant, considerate and warm.

For the son: stubborn, intelligent, creative, visionary, suave, aloof,
sophisticated, independent, cool, aristocratic, sensitive, headstrong, brilliant, decisive and intuitive.

The father was partial to cigars; the son chain-smoked cigarettes.
They both enjoyed their share, or more, of bourbon (father) and Scotch
and martinis (son) during nonwork interludes.

What precisely did Edgar Queeny do between 1928 and 1962?

How, precisely, did he pull it off?

Which, precisely, were the techniques he employed?

Such simplistic questions, often asked, do not find neat and tidy answers. Edgar Queeny was not a standard package of easy-to-define (much less easy-to-anticipate) skills and techniques lending themselves to easy, latter-day analysis for inquisitive MBA students wondering "What was his special secret?"

If a single word has to be found from the laundry list of adjectives—as a pacifier for those who insist that every man has to be encapsulated in a single word—the word is "intuitive."

Above all, he was intuitive.

His longtime secretary once commented, partly in jest but partly in seriousness, "he can see around the next corner."

Infrequently, in those wistful moments when his wistfulness became audible, he'd admit to seat-of-the-pants judgment unguided by formalities, and also admit to an impatience with "ribbon-clerk thinking," which demanded prosaic, orthodox plodding through the usual and traditional tedium of normal business practice.

Sensing as he did, as far back as the thirties, that the American chemical industry would grow dramatically to the degree that it was creative, daring and entrepreneurial, he found his niche in being creative, daring and entrepreneurial.

Risks were worth taking when potential rewards so firmly outweighed the penalties for occasional mistakes, in Queeny's view.

During the Terrible Thirties, when most of industry was pulling in its horns, his bold, decisive style quite directly led to acquiring companies; to venturing into a wide variety of equities in strange lands; to fostering the kind of research that required back-breaking budgets; to experimenting with untested ideas; to pioneering in the use of new business equipment and systems; and to persuading his colleagues to join in reaching, reaching, reaching.

Plus, he was not only a Queeny; he was not only Edgar M. Queeny; he was (and this is not an inconsequential point) Edgar Monsanto Queeny, something of a walking symbol and synonym for the corporation itself.

Aided by a touch of quiet remoteness, he inadvertently but assuredly generated a wisp of mystique and charisma in the halls of leadership.

There are those—including some who worked closely with him for many years—who say that Edgar Queeny was unquestionably the right man in the right place during his time, but that he may have been less right later, in a more institutionalized, more depersonalized and highly computerized era of American industry.

Yet those same observers also add such pragmatic comments as: "He could glance at a balance sheet and zero in on the crux," and "He'd often amaze his own financial people by the solutions he'd envision and propose," and "He was so challenging it was hard to keep up."

It's a moot point whether he ever realized that when people used to walk by his office and see him sitting there, pensive and alone, they often wondered, "What's he thinking up now?"

He was always the boss.

Monsanto flowered under his care.

An early synopsis of Edgar:

He was born September 29, 1897. The only other child, his sister, Olguita, arrived in 1899.

His early years were largely unrecorded, perhaps because there was little requiring unusual attention. He attended a public grammar school in South St. Louis—but so did practically everyone else in his neighborhood peer group.

If an early uniqueness could have been found it might very well have been this: He didn't do very well at a prep school at Pawling, New York, and had to be sent to a more expensive tutoring academy, Sturgis School Preparatory Department, Ithaca, New York, for individual attention. But he gained admission to Cornell University in 1915 and majored in chemistry. He later commented, "It was all my father's plan and, after all, he was paying the bills."

Perhaps the first clue of Edgar Queeny's creativity was visible during college, when he dabbled in journalism on the Cornell *Widow*, the school's magazine. Although he had the title of business manager, he found opportunities to try his hand at writing and editing. Even with this experience, there is no evidence that anyone predicted this young man would someday be recognized as a gifted writer (and a miserable speaker).

Queeny's collegiate career was cut short by the advent of World War I. He completed his sophomore year and then hastened to join the U.S. Navy as a seaman in 1917. Promptly transferred to the Naval Officers Training School at Newport, Rhode Island, he was commissioned an ensign. After a brief stint at a naval base at Plymouth, England, in 1918, he received orders to report to Mare Island, California, for sea duty on a destroyer—duty that never materialized.

Mare Island was more than a stopover in his brief Navy career. It was the place where Queeny met Ethel Schneider, daughter of a Washington, D.C., architect, who was visiting her uncle, Captain Edward Beach, then the commandant of the Mare Island Navy Yard. In June, 1919, Queeny was discharged from the Navy, with the rank of lieutenant junior grade. He married Miss Schneider in Washington five months later. In 1921 a son was born in St. Louis but died very shortly after birth.

There were, obviously, two roads for young Queeny to consider in the postwar period: A) returning to Cornell and B) moving into Monsanto to help his father during a troublesome period of readjustment. Both father and son agreed on the latter, particularly since Cornell offered to send along a diploma conferring a "war degree."

A ready-made job for the son of the founder? Yes. An easy road smoothed by family favoritism? No. There are frequent comments to the effect John F. seemed stricter and to demand more of his son than he did of his other employes. "The son always rises" was an unfunny joke to John F.

Charles L. Fetzner, an alumnus who currently lives in California and who started with Monsanto as a fifteen-year-old office boy in 1919, recently recalled his first meeting with Edgar Queeny:

"Edgar came over to my desk with a fancy drafting set he had picked up somewhere. Someone had told him I had studied drafting at McKinley High School. He was determined to figure out how the thing worked. It develops he was trying to make a design—an oval. Subsequently, he did find out how to do it and he created a symbol that was used in Monsanto advertising and labels, starting in 1920, an oval design featuring the words, 'Chemicals of Quality.'"

Edgar Queeny's first assignment involved advertising and sales promotion, and in 1920 he served more or less as publisher and editor-in-chief of the publication *Current Events,* a house organ for distribution to all the company's employes.

Young Queeny's early career included positions in export sales and in general sales, and by 1923 Edgar Queeny had calling cards printed with the title Vice President and Sales Manager.

His associates promptly learned Edgar was a decisive sort of fellow, often impatient with those who would procrastinate and delay and shuffle their feet and enable competitors to move out in front.

Perhaps because he liked decisiveness, Edgar Queeny promptly became fond of John W. Livingston, vice president in charge of manufacturing. Livingston is quoted as having said, in the mid-twenties, "You could get an idea in the morning, discuss it at noon, and get it going in the afternoon." Livingston disdained red tape and delay. He also commented, "In the organic chemical industry, the fellow who moves fastest gets the profits. The man who is second gets a much lesser prize, and the third and fourth fellows get left out in the cold."

Edgar liked this type of thinking.

In 1928, when Edgar became president, here was the lineup: John F., now off to England to acquire the remaining 50 percent of Graesser-Monsanto and to stay abroad and actually manage the British company, was chairman of the parent company's board of directors. The founder's second and third Swiss lieutenants, Gaston DuBois and Jules Bebie, were still very much involved, as vice president and assistant vice president, respectively. Both were heavily engaged in the company's growing technical effort. But Louis Veillon, the founder's first employe, who had arrived from Switzerland on New Year's Eve of 1901, had retired in 1926, still exhausted, he said, from the long hours and seven-days-a-week schedules imposed by World War I, and by the physical and mental strain of the recession of the early twenties.

From the outset of Edgar Queeny's presidency it was apparent he would operate in a style quite different from that of his father. The first and most immediately recognizable difference was that Edgar not only preached delegation of authority, but he practiced it.

Prior to 1928, much of the internal and external communicating had been spontaneous and unplanned—in meetings and by telephone. The establishment of the company house organ, *Current Events,* had been a new step forward. But it did little to help the day-to-day communications requirements of a growing company.

The new president was aware that internal communications shortcomings existed. Quite often employes "across the river" in Illinois had expressed a wish to be "tuned in" more often. On the East Coast, the New York office was complaining, "St. Louis forgets we are here."

As suggested by the earlier establishment of a publication for employes, Edgar's initial concerns were of an in-house nature. He understood the relationships of information to morale and of morale to productivity. He also appreciated the human requirement of the workers to be kept informed so that they would feel like an integral part of the whole.

But he was also sensitive to the relationship between external communications and corporate reputation. He knew that outsiders, unaware of Monsanto's totality, would be inclined to judge the company by small and commonplace omissions or commissions. He knew that a single salesman could make long-lasting friends or enemies. And he knew that a little thing like telephone manners could turn on or turn off a caller.

The extent and sensitivity of his concern are illustrated by the following memorandum, dispatched in 1929:

GENERAL BULLETIN

To: Key Personnel, Plants and Offices   DATE: 9–13–29

Upon my return to the office after an extended absence, I have come across several instances where incoming mail has not been promptly acknowledged.

Letters have been received regarding a subject with which the party in our organization who is most familiar is not available, and the letters have been held over unanswered pending that party's return.

While no doubt the receiving party really anticipated only a few days' delay, other developments considerably stretched the time before the letters in question received consideration and were answered.

This is not *Monsanto courtesy* and is very apt to leave with the sender an impression of slack business methods in our company.

We cannot afford such an impression on the part of anyone having business relations with us. Therefore, *acknowledge receipt of all letters promptly,* stating what action has been or will be taken. *Let the sender know the letter has been received and that Monsanto is on the job.*

Edgar M. Queeny

Plainly, this directive merits consideration by American industry in 1977. The friendly scolding in it is as appropriate today as it was almost 50 years ago.

In 1927 Edgar Queeny had undertaken a quiet campaign in concert with his father to make Monsanto a public company, with listings on the Chicago Stock Exchange and New York Curb. But this was only an interim step in Edgar's view. He had the so-called "big board" in sight. And on October 10, 1929, he took the big jump and put Monsanto where, in his words, "we belong"—on the New York Stock Exchange.

In 1929 and through the early thirties the United States suffered an unprecedented period of harsh and trying predicaments, including the Great Depression. Industrial production plummeted; unemployment was prevalent; banks failed; the nation's morale was depressed.

It was precisely then that Edgar Queeny decided to implement his expansion plans for Monsanto: to move into Australia; to try out a new kind of annual report to shareholders; to reincorporate under the laws of the State of Delaware; to move into New England; to put new emphasis on research; to establish a new industry-wide record in freedom from lost-time accidents; to acquire a phosphorus-based company in the South; and—importantly—to bolster corporate profitability.

Later in the thirties Monsanto continued on its Depression-born path of expansion by acquiring a prestigious Ohio-based research laboratory and an Eastern company specializing in a then-new field of chemistry called plastics.

The thrust didn't slow down. Edgar Queeny permitted no slowdown. Consequently, the growth into new fields continued into the forties, fifties and sixties. Some of the growth was by acquisition, but most was internally conceived, internally nourished and internally accomplished.

Many people who knew Edgar Queeny well, looking back, say the same thing: He liked new things.

Actually, he liked new things in an almost boyish way.

Example: When a Monsanto product trade-named Resloom, a melamine-based resin that made natural fibers stain resistant, was introduced into drapery material, Edgar Queeny enjoyed giving impromptu demonstrations. On one occasion he showered a bottle of Coca-Cola onto draperies in order to prove with delight: "No stain!"

Example: When Monsanto developed sturdy plastics for refrigerator parts, no one more enjoyed jumping up and down on the new components than Edgar Queeny. A friend who witnessed such an exhibition said, "He looked like a fiendish child."

Yet it all went infinitely deeper. Although he did like new things, he felt diversification would foster the most rewarding environment for employes, shareowners and customers.

To many he was an enigma. To many he was "hard to read." But what seemed to some to be aloofness was simply a lifelong case of shyness. He was much more of an introvert than an extrovert. He disliked the public limelight and often fled from it, despite his recognition that any corporate leadership role carried with it the responsibilities and opportunities of providing a company with a "voice."

Public recognition was welcomed, when merited, provided the recognition was for Monsanto and not for its principal officer.

Through most of his active years, Edgar Queeny carried his tall, thin body with the untiring stride of an Indian. Of medium-dark complexion, he was what the ladies used to call "dark and handsome." Yet more often they would say, "remote and quiet and cool and dark and handsome."

Perhaps his most enduring characteristic was the quantity and quality of silence. His ability to outwait any colleague or visitor in conversation was a trait he never abandoned. It was particularly unsettling to those who expected the normal give-and-take, who weren't accustomed to silence as a mode of response.

Anecdotes abound on how people reacted. The most frequent concern was "I wonder what he was thinking while I was doing all that jabbering."

It wasn't uncommon for people to hasten to the office of someone else and unburden a series of post-conference apprehensions, frequently leading off with "Edgar looked bored." Others would say such things as "It takes two to make a discussion; it was disconcerting to observe him yawn during my presentation."

One visitor remarked, "Edgar's look of boredom was contagious. I found myself becoming bored by my own remarks."

From time to time Edgar would further communicate his attitude, or impatience, or contemplation, or boredom, or whatever, not by saying something (which was rare) but by the simple expedient of getting up and walking out of the room. People unaccustomed to this were inclined to regard it as a bit impolite.

Some self-assured people, undaunted by Queeny's silence, would report that they'd begin speaking at a normal pace and then, noticing a continuation of Edgar Queeny's nonresponse, would increase the tempo of their talking if for no other reason than to get the experience behind them.

If such treatment in the "icehouse" was not enough to unnerve the conversationalist, Edgar Queeny had an extra bit of behavior, which approached habit proportions. He would put his gangling legs up on his desk and stretch out almost horizontally to further accent an attitude charitably described as "most casual."

When Edgar did speak, the guest in his office would often wish he could return to the earlier minutes of total silence. The sudden emergence of speech would often be simply a condensed conclusion or a mumbled yes or no or, even worse, "some of the roughest questions any man could ever ask." His penchant for getting to the central point of an issue, once he decided to open his mouth, was a quality recognized, admired and sometimes feared by his associates.

A distinguished journalist, a senior editor of *Fortune* Magazine from New York, who was assigned to investigate the emergence of Monsanto as a substantial influence on the horizon of international business, decided not to be unnerved and outsilenced by Edgar Queeny. Advised beforehand what he was getting into, he resolved not to be intimidated by the nonresponse of his industrialist host.

The journalist confided to a few friends, "When I visit Queeny I intend to use his own tactics. I will not rush into conversation or try to bridge periods of silence by my own cover-overs and by clumsy efforts to make things conversationally comfortable."

Here is the journalist's report of the outcome:

> Edgar had been gracious enough to invite me out to his home, Jarville, on Mason Road in St. Louis County, for a 9 P.M. interview. I had met him before, briefly, and looked forward to a session where we'd be alone. After stating the reason for my visit in a concise manner, I sat there, waiting for a reply. Nothing happened. The "game" was on.
>
> In retrospect, I am convinced Edgar Queeny knew what was up as soon as he discerned I didn't fill the gaps of silence by further questions or comment.
>
> Time passed. I found myself lighting several cigarettes and tightening a shoelace.
>
> Actually, I had not asked a direct question at the outset. Maybe I should have. I simply made a few statements, outlining the nature of my assignment. The silence was neither approval nor disapproval, I suspect.
>
> I must admit Edgar appeared to be thoughtful. Perhaps, I said to myself, he regarded my mission and my opening observations as somewhat profound. Perhaps he was cogitating.
>
> More time passed. Neither of us uttered a sound. We were quiet as mice. On one occasion when I crossed my legs, my chair moved a bit—and this seemed like quite a bustle under the circumstances.
>
> Edgar then picked up a newspaper and glanced at the front-page headlines. It must have been a dull news day because the paper didn't retain his attention for very long. And most assuredly it did not attract any comment.
>
> After what seemed like an eternity, I finally came to the conclusion that Edgar Queeny was outwaiting and outwitting me and that he'd emerge the victor for the pure and simple reason he was more accustomed to conversational silence than I was.

So I jettisoned my plan and broke the silence by a direct question. Queeny smiled when I spoke, sensing—I am sure—that I had had the temerity to try his own strategy within his own household.

It was a bold and silly experiment which brought me to defeat. Once the "game" had been exposed and once I had a direct question hanging in the air, awaiting response, Edgar Queeny spoke up and told me what was on his mind—in short, substantive and thoughtful sentences.

When it was finally time for me to leave, he even invited me to visit him downtown for a second interview if my requirements had not been fully met. I wound up getting the information I wanted, but I didn't beat Edgar Queeny at his own game.

It would be a mistake to think Edgar Queeny always played the element of silence like a trump card in conversational bouts with others. Evidence suggests he resorted to such gamesmanship only when such strategy was appropriate.

Not being garrulous was, more deeply, a basic part of his chemistry and personality. When business or social functions demanded, he was gracious and sometimes even charming, but never chatty. In company meetings he spoke up only when he had something to say.

Yet, when he picked up a pen or pencil, Edgar Queeny became a sensitive and articulate writer, as willing and eager to participate in this form of expression as he was reluctant to indulge in excessive talking.

In 1931, after examining annual reports from many U.S. corporations, Queeny decided shareowners deserved not only more information but, also, information prepared and edited in a way to make it more understandable and palatable. In Monsanto's 1931 Annual Report, he wrote: "I am departing from past practice and have elaborated this Annual Report into a 'year book' . . . with charts and illustrations . . . and with information of a general nature which should be of interest to anyone participating in the ownership of our company." Prior to 1931, the Monsanto Annual Report had been an inoffensive six by nine inches. He took it up to "magazine size." In the later thirties, he experimented with unique embellishments, such as inserts of clear plastic sheeting and use of coumarin-scented ink.

The 1933 Annual Report marked the quiet, unheralded change from Monsanto Chemical Works to Monsanto Chemical Company. It also brought Edgar Queeny in fuller expression:

"This account of stewardship covers a most colorful twelve months into which were crowded the depths of despair of March and the great new confidence of December—the hesitancy and hoarding of February and the rush to spend in July—a condition first of no orders and then back orders."

Anticipating government intervention which would tend to limit corporate freedoms in the New Deal era of Franklin Delano Roosevelt, Queeny continued:

"At this time, when it is being urged upon the American psychology to accept the doctrine that the profit increment should be minimized in the American economy, and that proficiency should be penalized in order that incapacity and inefficiency might share and profit by the achievement of others, it is appropriate to introduce into this letter the words of a great humanitarian. On March 21, 1864, Abraham Lincoln said to a committee from The Workingmen's Association of New York:

" 'Property is the fruit of labor; property is desirable; it is a positive good in the world. That some should be rich shows that others may become rich, hence just encouragement to industry and enterprise. Let him not who is houseless pull down the house of another, but let him labor diligently and build one for himself, thus by example assuring that his own house, when built, shall be safe from violence.' "

In the ensuing years, Edgar Queeny was to become an ardent foe of those New Deal policies which seemed to penalize the American business system. He was also to become an ardent foe of high national debt. But he wasn't anti-New Deal across the board, as evidenced by this additional paragraph in the 1933 Annual Report:

"The spirit of the New Deal has brought about a national sympathy for fair and liberal dealing with labor, and a growing realization and acceptance by industrial management of the rights of labor and of the importance to national welfare of its adequate remuneration. We are and always have been in harmony with this spirit."

Edgar Queeny went on to explain: "The forty-hour week had been adopted in our plants early in 1932. In July of 1933, the five-day, forty-hour week was initiated among the office and salaried force. . . . In view of our policies, no adjustments in our rates or hours were required under NRA [National Recovery Administration] operation. Believing that workers should share with shareowners in our substantial earnings this year, a bonus of one week's pay was voted by the Board of Directors for each employe who had been with us for one year and lesser amounts to new employes. This was paid at the same time we increased our dividend to shareowners."

Not one to parade his personal emotions, Edgar Queeny had a restrained last paragraph in his 1933 Annual Report letter to shareowners, as follows:

"It is my sad duty to record the death on March 19, 1933, of my father and your former chairman of the Board of Directors, John Francis Queeny, whose foresight led him to found Monsanto Chemical Works in 1901 and to pioneer in the American manufacture of organic chemicals. His courage and tenacity and integrity continue to be an inspiration to the exceptional co-workers he had gathered about him."

It is interesting to compare that sparse tribute from Edgar Queeny with the language of a journalist who understood the nature and impact of the founder's contributions. The journalist went a bit further than the founder's son and provided an historical perspective when he wrote:

"He [John F. Queeny] drew together thousands of separate lives, nourished and directed their talents, teamed their energies, held them together by his courage, and welded them in time into a richly productive organization, an enduring whole greater than the sum of its parts, including himself. To say he contributed nothing to science is to say George Washington contributed nothing to American independence because he never invented or built a gun or in the Revolution never fired one."

In a special message to employes, customers and shareowners, following his father's death, Edgar Queeny came full face with what he regarded as his responsibility to state his philosophy of business. He wrote:

"The affairs of every corporation are so inseparably bound up in the interests of employes, shareowners and customers that unless proper regard and consideration are given to each, the management is doomed to failure. These three factors constitute a fundamental business triangle, the sides of which misfit unless kept in proper relation to each other. That is the job of management."

As government taxation and constraints increased during the mid-thirties, and as government debt soared in an era of unprecedented social and economic experiments, Queeny observed in a 1935 letter to employes: "It is lamentable that the great body of citizens, whose votes are being bought with mortgages on the nation's future, do not realize that they are but receiving tomorrow's pay today, and that in the inevitable reckoning everyone will be called upon for tribute."

Searching for better ways to conduct business, Edgar Queeny brought onto the Monsanto board in 1935 a strong outside—or nonemploye—director. This was Walter W. Smith, a St. Louis businessman and civic leader with 35 years of experience in banking. Queeny reasoned that Smith would bring a valuable extra dimension to the board's deliberations.

Edgar Queeny was preparing an agenda for a board meeting in 1938 when he was informed that his mother, Olga Monsanto Queeny, for whom the company had been named, had died while visiting her daughter, Olguita, in England. Again, the most articulate tribute did not come from Edgar Queeny. It came from a research director, Lynn A. Watt, who wrote in *Current Events:* "Mrs. Queeny's life was so closely interwoven with the lives of her husband and family that some future commentator or historian is in danger of giving credit to those around her when, rightfully, the rewards should be shared."

Sensing the need for professional handling of communicating the company's viewpoints to inside and outside audiences, Edgar Queeny established a corporate department with specific communications responsibilities in 1939. Even though the term "public relations" was somewhat in use on the national business scene, Queeny decided to forego this nomenclature for a year and instead called the new unit the Department of Advertising and Monsanto Practice. Many business observers have wondered, at the time and since, why he chose this unusual name. It was so uncommon. The words "Monsanto Practice" were particularly unusual.

Here's why:

Assignment No. 1 for the new department (beyond advertising) was the task of updating and distributing, internally, the company's Manual of Business Practice—a document which later became known as the Organization and Procedures Manual and then, later, the Management Guide.

Edgar Queeny related the word "practice" to the word "policy." He reasoned that a company needs four fundamentals in the formation and maintenance of a reputation: 1) practices, or policies, 2) performance, 3) behavior, and 4) communication to and from audiences, or constituencies, whose understanding and support are crucial.

In establishing a charter for Monsanto Practice, Edgar Queeny specified that Monsanto should expect only *merited* understanding and support. And his knowledge that "everything starts with having the right rules and regulations" is illustrated by the unusual name he selected—Practice—for what later became known as the Industrial and Public Relations Department.

In 1977, scholars speaking and writing on the subject of corporate reputation occasionally are tempted to "discover" the need for the same basic four ingredients Edgar Queeny set forth as guideposts for the staff of Monsanto Practice 38 years ago.

In establishing this communications-related department, Edgar Queeny was cautious not to imply that the group would be responsible only for the carpentry of communications and media techniques. He knew that no faulty policy or product could be "saved" by communications techniques. He knew that actions speak louder than words. Queeny wrote the following for the company's manual in 1939, when a formal public relations policy was spelled out:

"It seeks to identify Monsanto with that which in an individual would be good morals and good manners. So-called good public and employe relations will be determined by the way we treat our employes, by the way we treat our shareowners, by the way in which all our business and community contacts are handled. In other words, whether we accomplish our purposes, or fail in their accomplishment, will depend on the way we do things, and the way in which our corporate character is interpreted and identified." Up to 1977, no one has said it better, nor meant it more earnestly.

Queeny's interest in corporate communications also extended into the field of advertising. "Serving Industry Which Serves Mankind" was adopted as a company slogan in 1939. Most of Monsanto's early advertisements were confined to so-called trade publications, read primarily by people in the many and varied industries the company served.

In the late thirties and early forties Edgar Queeny provided both the encouragement and the budget for experiments in advertising which transcended the old-fashioned direct approach "to customer audiences only." He decided that a public company—even a public company with no merchandise offered directly to the public—should make at least a modest endeavor to become better known by the public. He reasoned that shareowners might gain by having their company better known, and that recruitment of new employes might be facilitated if Monsanto could become a somewhat familiar name, beyond those industrial customers who knew Monsanto because they purchased its products, and beyond those suppliers who knew Monsanto because they sold products and services to it.

The company's first major national institutional ad appeared in *Fortune* Magazine's issue for October, 1939, a full-page debut headlined "I Owe So Much to the Man I've Never Met." The illustration featured a photo of an attractive woman looking directly at the reader. The text material explained how consumers using end-products improved by chemistry were, quite obviously, unaware of "the man" in the laboratory whose discoveries were serving the public interest in a hidden, unappreciated sort of way.

"We're not a consumer goods company; we have nothing to sell directly to the man on the street," a few of Queeny's executive associates commented, particularly when they learned national advertising carried a fat fee, adding materially to the "cost of doing business."

Queeny simply requested his Advertising Department to explain: 1) He had authorized the expenditure, and 2) *Fortune* Magazine was read by many businessmen who should know more about "who we are and what we make."

A year later, in 1940, the company dropped its oval symbol and its longtime slogan, "Chemicals of Quality," and introduced a corporate trademark which was to be prominent in advertising and on labels, signs and tank cars for more than 30 years—the big, bold "block M."

JUST as World War I shook the timbers of Monsanto, so did World War II. In both cases the effect was severe, challenging and long-lasting. Yet there was one principal difference: The America that had little appreciated the chemical industry during World War I was more alert 20 years later to turn to chemical plants and laboratories for the accelerated requirements of a wartime economy.

To some degree, Edgar suffered the same shock waves as were felt by his father. Just as foreign imports were cut off in the earlier era, a broad range of foreign raw materials and intermediates was also to some extent denied before and during World War II. Yet, by Pearl Harbor Day the chemical industry had become at least somewhat self-sufficient, compared to its "orphan status"—to use the founder's words —two decades earlier.

Queeny observed: "The same federal government which had harassed industry in the thirties with experimental 'remedies,' inquisitional commissions and exhausting taxation found, upon war's advent, the industrial arm of the nation was its most important ally."

The government needed synthetic rubber for tires; it needed pharmaceuticals and detergents; it needed plastics and apparel; and before the hostilities were to end, it would need chemists, physicists and engineers to make the first atom bomb. Monsanto was among the leading science companies in the nation which contributed to these and other urgent calls to duty.

Edgar Queeny's deep feelings of patriotism and pride in America had a new outlet. Yet when V-E Day and V-J Day had passed, and when a newspaper reporter asked him to sum up all that Monsanto had contributed, Queeny found only four words: "We did our part."

The forties brought more than war-forced production. The decade also brought a novel-sized book and "two new outsiders" onto the Monsanto scene.

The book, *The Spirit of Enterprise,* was published in 1934 by Charles Scribner & Sons. The author: Edgar M. Queeny. In it, this industrialist who felt somewhat bruised by the antibusiness antics of the New Deal decided to state his case for America, for the importance of the individual, for personal freedoms—and for the role of the business system in furthering the well-being of the nation.

Edgar Queeny had some convictions and he wanted a forum in which to express them without constraint. Thus, the book.

Well promoted by the publisher, it was widely bought and intensely read, particularly by those Americans hungry for chewy reading, for unvarnished viewpoints, for head-on collisions with the antibusiness establishment.

The book not only offered glimpses into economics, government and science, but also revealed glimpses of the author. He had done his research well—so well, in fact, that the homework prompted him to change and even reverse some of his earlier opinions. And he said so.

Insights into the Queeny personality and character were not confined to between-the-lines interpretations alone. He went so far as to draw the following picture of himself:

"Thus I recognized my two selves: a crusading idealist and a cold, granitic believer in the law of the jungle."

And he added: "For a time, the more I read, the more confused I became. Business did not have clean hands; but its critics and detractors were not fair or honest toward it, either."

Considering all the other pressures, one wonders how Edgar Queeny found time to do the research required for *The Spirit of Enterprise,* much less the actual writing. When he was asked about it, he commented: "I told some of my friends I'd do it—and I was stuck with the commitment. I had no other course than to do it. In a way, it was kind of a safety valve. Many of the things in it were unplanned, but a few pet convictions needed airing."

THE "two new outsiders" brought into Monsanto were as much Queeny's idea as was *The Spirit of Enterprise*. They were to have a profound and lasting effect by wielding "extraordinary and beneficial" influence on the company's affairs.

In 1945, Charles S. Cheston, a prominent investment banker at Smith Barney & Company, Philadelphia, was elected to the board to begin a period of service which would last for 14 years, until his death. In 1947, Fredrick M. Eaton, a distinguished New York attorney who was a partner in the firm of Shearman & Sterling & Wright, was elected to the board, to begin a period of service which would last for more than 27 years. With the exception of the Queenys, Gaston DuBois and Dr. Charles A. Thomas, Eaton established the longest record of service in the Monsanto board's history.

Cheston's credentials in finance had been long admired by Edgar Queeny. Several underwriting ventures for Monsanto were handled by Cheston before he came onto the company's board. In 1947 Cheston became chairman of the Finance Committee and thus was in a position to further assist the financial planning of a growing corporation.

Eaton's credentials were similarly respected by Queeny. Eaton was not only a distinguished lawyer. In Edgar's words, "He has a lot of class; he is a very special breed."

Eaton recently recalled the following:

> I remember meeting Edgar Queeny for the first time at a luncheon at the old Ambassador Hotel in New York in 1940. I had established the New York Committee to support Wendell Willkie as the Republican nominee for president. Edgar was working hard for Willkie and had undoubtedly given him a lot of his personal funds.
>
> Edgar attended the Republican convention in Philadelphia that summer but I didn't. As you know, Willkie became the Republican candidate. Yet, I must mention in passing that subsequently Edgar found himself in disagreement with some stand Willkie espoused and he got off the bandwagon.
>
> I spent a lot of time in Washington from June, 1940, until the end of 1945. During that time I got to know Charlie Cheston quite well. In late 1946, Edgar came to talk to me about going on the Monsanto board early in 1947. I accepted readily because I knew the company.
>
> In the early years, Edgar, Charlie Cheston and I used to meet the night before the board meeting and we pretty well determined what the policies were going to be at the meeting the next day. As

I recall, at one of the early meetings prior to the board session we met at Edgar's place, Jarville, on Mason Road, and discussed having an age limit—sixty-eight years of age—for outside directors, chairmen and presidents as board members.

Charles Belknap was chairman of the Executive Committee when I went onto the Monsanto board. The president of the company was William Rand. Both were superior executives.

I remember at one meeting we were discussing an appropriations request and Bill Rand said this was the first time within his memory that the cost of a plant would be greater than the annual sales volume which was forecast. Prior to that, Rand said, a dollar of construction had meant at least a dollar of sales.

Edgar was a very powerful and determined person. He always made copious inquiries to find out what the facts were. But when he made up his mind, that was his mind, and he was very determined to carry out whatever decision he had made.

Monsanto always provided extensive knowledge of the workings of its business. Edgar saw to it that we went around to the various plant sites. We covered all the major locations, including Europe. We met the plant managers and their staffs. We knew what was going on. This was easier in the earlier days, of course, when Monsanto was smaller and when there were fewer locations.

I always felt very much involved—more so than on the average board on which I served.

Throughout the years, Monsanto not only invited and encouraged but sought rough questions from outside directors. I think the record will show there was never a meeting where I didn't speak up. Questions were never resented. I always got the answers. Monsanto was part of me—and I hope I was part of Monsanto. The company was always an open book, inviting me to turn to any page.

I have always had a great deal of admiration for Monsanto and for its people. The principal executives were not only business colleagues but friends. Edgar was singular. I had a very special sense of respect and affection for him.

The contributions of both Charlie Cheston and Fred Eaton were particularly welcomed during the post-war years, when Monsanto was poised for fresh advances. Astute planning was required for entry into synthetic fibers and for expansions in all operating divisions.

In the late forties Edgar Queeny came up with another book. This time it was what he called a "fun book"—a definitive volume, part words, part photos, part drawings of ducks in flight. Its title: *Prairie Wings*.

It was, and is, a classic. The photographs, many taken at extremely high speed, were by Queeny himself; the writing likewise; the drawings were by a close friend, Richard D. Bishop. Published by J. B. Lippincott in 1947, it was imposing in size and was almost instantly recognized by outdoorsmen as the most definitive treatment of the subject ever to come onto the market. Much of the photography was accomplished at Queeny's duck-hunting preserve, Wingmead, near Stuttgart, Arkansas —the "duck capital of the world."

The normally cautious Edgar Queeny encountered an unhappy surprise in connection with *Prairie Wings.* In 1946 he had dispatched all of the original materials—negatives, prints, drawings—to the publisher in Philadelphia. Not knowing how enthusiastic the reception would be, the publisher undertook an initial press run of only 7500 copies.

Late in 1947 Queeny asked that all the materials be returned to him in St. Louis, via Railway Express, insured. The materials, packed in several crates, never reached their destination. Virtually everyone short of J. Edgar Hoover was called into action in an attempt to locate the wayward crates. Yet, alas, they never turned up.

Friends suggested to Queeny that he authorize a second edition and that it be produced by simply photographing the pages of the first edition. When Queeny saw samples of how the new pages would look, he turned thumbs down. Mediocrity was not the right cup of tea for this perfectionist.

As a result, *Prairie Wings* promptly became a valued collector's item, as it still is today.

In 1948 a friend in Monsanto's public relations department persuaded him to transfer his attention to sound motion pictures. And by 1949 Edgar Queeny had produced—for the conservation organization known as Ducks Unlimited, Inc.—an enchanting 16mm. color motion picture, which he also titled *Prairie Wings.* Thus motion pictures became his principal hobby—particularly motion pictures dealing with the outdoors, with nature, with birds, dogs and fish—and with the animals and customs of East Africa.

Queeny found in the medium of motion pictures the ultimate opportunity for creativity. He described the challenge as "a giant keyboard onto which one can play unlimited variations of sight and sound."

He did the photography, supervised the editing, wrote the scripts, recorded the sounds, and selected the music. His barn on Mason Road in St. Louis County became "the studio," outfitted with the highest quality equipment for editing, recording and projection.

His tribute to a favorite Labrador dog, Mike, was also a film made for the benefit of Ducks Unlimited. For the sound track he engaged the services of Conductor Vladimir Golschmann and the St. Louis Symphony Orchestra. Friends recall how enthusiastic and "boyish" he was the day the music track was recorded at the St. Louis Theatre (now Powell Hall). Golschmann and Queeny stood side by side, watching cues on the screen and beckoning musical phrases to sweep up and down in synchronization with the "ballet," as Queeny called it, of thousands of flying birds.

For a salmon-fishing film in Canada, the aristocratic Edgar Queeny sat on a large, cold rock in the middle of the Bonaventure River to record—with a special French underwater camera—fish in their otherwise-undisturbed natural habitat. His movie *Silver Lightning,* perhaps the most exciting salmon fishing film ever made, was purchased by Warner Brothers for a short subject in theaters. The proceeds went to Ducks Unlimited. Edgar's wife, Ethel, was an accomplished hunter and angler and would usually accompany her husband on his outdoor adventures, whether with gun, rod, or camera—or all. It was she, actually, who initially persuaded him to take up duck hunting as a hobby.

Two trips to East Africa in the early fifties—on brief leaves of absence from Monsanto—provided his peak of extracurricular enjoyment. Using a turret-mounted camera on a heavy vehicle, Queeny got off the beaten path to record the sights and sounds of the wild. He did research into the customs of remote African tribes and even "lived in" with the Latuko tribe before producing a documentary on the customs and adventures of natives who had seen few white men and no cameras in their lives.

Latuko, Wakamba, Pagan Sudan, Wanderobo—these were among the documentaries Queeny filmed on safaris sponsored by the American Museum of Natural History, an organization for which he served as a trustee and an associate in the Department of Anthropology. Of seven films he made in Africa, three were released theatrically in the U.S.

Yet even "The Big White Father" couldn't buck the American censors. *Latuko,* in particular, caused problems—principally because it showed frontal male nudity. The Hays Office refused to give it a seal, and the Legion of Decency stamped a condemned rating on it. Queeny was shocked. After all, he said, that's the way natives look. "Go to any museum and you'll find nudity in classic sculpture. Why is it immoral for me to show it on the screen?" The Legion of Decency's executive director, reluctant to establish new precedents and unmoved by the noble reputation of Producer Queeny, said no in a picturesque way. His unceremonious message to Edgar Queeny contained three words: "Tough luck, Jack." Theatrical distribution of this film was, as a result, quite limited.

Queeny's reaction: "Let's concentrate on the other African films."

A sportsman, he was not a sports fan. Pro football and basketball seldom caught his fancy. Baseball was moderately to his liking. Yet, strangely, he used a sports expression one day when a Monsanto colleague suggested that a company-sponsored film could be produced at half the cost by sacrificing some of the quality Queeny had specifically requested.

His reply: "At Monsanto, we'll do it the big league way or not at all. I refuse to have the company affiliated with anything which smacks of minor league mediocrity." And he added, "If we do cheap little things, people might think we're a cheap little company."

One of Edgar Queeny's haunting vexations in the fifties concerned a simple word: tariffs. He had never forgotten how the Germans cut the price on saccharin in Monsanto's early days in an attempt to put his father out of business. Fifty years later, in the post–World War II period of worldwide industrial expansion, Queeny became upset by the increasing volume of chemicals coming into the U.S. from Europe and the Far East—chemicals manufactured at low wage rates and sent into the U.S. at prices that made Monsanto competition difficult.

Synthetic organic chemicals, in particular, were being shipped into the U.S. without, in Queeny's view, sufficient tariff protection for the American chemical industry. He kept repeating, "Reciprocal trade agreements with other countries are simply not reciprocal; the U.S. is disadvantaged by them."

This was a trying period. In Queeny's view, a strong America needed a strong chemical industry—and a strong chemical industry needed some protection against foreign competition.

Not all U.S. industrialists agreed with the Queeny position. Indeed, some major Monsanto customers took the opposite view. They got on the "free trade" bandwagon.

"Free trade" had a motherhood ring to it. It suggested "let all nations in the world get along nicely with each other." Queeny's position, on the other hand, seemed to some to be isolationist, provincial, protectionist, selfish and shortsighted.

Whenever and wherever he could find the opportunity, Queeny would cry out "Unfair!" Monsanto Annual Reports and Annual Meetings and *Monsanto Magazine* carried his cry. He went to Washington, D.C., to testify before a Congressional committee, and he went to Little Rock, Arkansas, to make a speech in support of "not disadvantaging our own country." His speech title there was "Tariffs or Socialism."

A close friend observed at the time, "We all know how Edgar fears the podium. He'd rather walk on nails than make a speech. He surely feels firmly about his tariff stand."

During Queeny's several short leaves of absence from Monsanto, for shooting with camera or gun or both, President Charles A. Thomas and Executive Vice President R. R. Cole made the principal decisions for a growing company.

In 1952 employe ranks were nearly 20,000. Down at the headquarters offices on South Second Street, office space was getting tight. Opportunities for office expansion in the old part of town were limited. And the company knew it would be growing vigorously in the years ahead.

Question: To stay or to move headquarters elsewhere? Question: If elsewhere, where elsewhere?

To this day Charlie Thomas insists, "If I ever made a contribution it was opposing anyone who even hinted we should move our offices to New York." Most of the discussion centered on trying to find suitable ground in the St. Louis area. For a time, property east of the Arena, south of Forest Park, seemed most promising. Yet when a decision was finally made, it was one everyone rallied around, namely to purchase about 300 acres 15 miles west of South Second Street, in suburban

Creve Coeur near the intersection of Lindberg Boulevard and Olive Street Road, a mere 15 minutes from Lambert-St. Louis International Airport.

The purchase was announced in 1952, but construction of the initial office buildings in St. Louis County didn't get underway until 1955. The move occurred in 1957.

The St. Louis city fathers didn't like "deserters." Edgar Queeny knew this. And he had some reluctance about leaving the historic offices alongside the plant site selected early in 1902 by John F. Queeny and Dr. Louis Veillon of Switzerland. South Second Street had been home for Monsanto offices for more than 50 years. The adjacent plant, by now called the John F. Queeny plant, remained—and continued to modernize.

Fredrick M. Eaton recently commented, "When the decision was made to move to Creve Coeur, Edgar knew Monsanto was going to grow to a size where we couldn't possibly live on South Second Street. What a wise decision that was. If we had stayed downtown, in space comparable to today's requirements, we would have needed South Second Street, South Third Street, South Fourth Street and South Fifth Street."

Eaton continued: "It is important for a company to have its head-quarters in its own home area. I would call this one of the reasons for Monsanto's success. It is a distinct advantage to live where you grow up and to have your 'being' there. It's far better than being 'lost' in New York City. Even though they have sometimes found it inconvenient, the outside directors have gained immensely by coming to St. Louis for dinners prior to board meetings and for luncheons after board meetings. That's the way we have all gotten to know each other—directors and officers—better. For most board meetings at New York-based companies, directors arrive shortly before the meetings and leave immediately afterward."

Other observers have said over and over how convenient it is to be headquartered a few hours from the East Coast, West Coast and Gulf Coast.

The logic of leaving downtown notwithstanding, Edgar Queeny had a few poignant moments during his final day at work on South Second Street in 1957. Some optimist tried to cheer him up by saying, "You won't have to drive east into the glare of the sun in the morning and west into the glare of the sun in the evening." Edgar replied, "Yes, but I'll miss those sweet smells of saccharin and vanillin."

A more deeply emotional day was to come—three years later, on Thursday, March 27, 1960.

The Annual Meeting of shareowners in Monsanto's A Building cafeteria—transformed for the occasion into an auditorium, with about 900 persons present—had moved along on schedule. There was the customary speech by the chairman (Edgar Queeny) and the customary speech by the president (Dr. Charles A. Thomas). In addition, there was the customary formality of counting votes for the directorships. And there was the customary showing of the annual "Monsanto Newsreel," containing motion picture highlights of the previous year.

When the audience thought the program was all but over, the chairman had a surprise in the form of "additional remarks," which were later referred to as "Edgar's swan song." An abbreviated version follows:

Before we close, may I say that my chairmanship of shareowner meetings is, I expect, coming to an end with this meeting.

Several years ago, our directors, after weighing the great physical and mental demands on a president of a company such as ours, adopted a policy—that the president then in office, and all future presidents of this company, should become board chairmen no later than when they reach sixty years of age, in order that younger men would be in a position to shoulder the enervating burdens borne by the chief executive.

The passage of years now reminds our Board of Directors to implement this policy; and I know that resolutions have been prepared for the board you have just chosen to elect, to in turn elect, when it meets this afternoon, as president and chairman of the Executive Committee—Charlie Sommer; and as chairman of the Board of Directors, the man who has shouldered the responsibilities of president with such distinction since 1951—Charlie Thomas. I expect the board will adopt, also, a resolution re-electing me chairman of the Finance Committee.

Now as this is to be my last opportunity to prattle before you, may I look back a little to 1928, when my father—having discovered that he was incurably ill with cancer—turned the presidency of Monsanto over to me, at my then mature age of thirty.

It seems to me that the intervening years have never been without serious problems. It has not been nonstop development and prosperity. One set of problems was constantly being replaced by another—globally and nationally, as well as in our company. Perhaps this has always been so and will always be as long as the sun sets in the west. Perhaps this constitutes progress, although I do not always think so. However, the challenges we faced and now face do supply the yeast and carbonization of life—the carrot before as well as the whip behind, which make the human donkey go on and on and on; for if problems are not faced and solved, no wizard can rescue anything that life's parade has trod over.

If we look back to the year before I became president, Monsanto had fifty-five shareowners, almost all of them officers of the company and their families. The 1927 Annual Meeting was held around a table in my father's office. About twenty-five people were present; the meeting may have taken as much as ten minutes.

A few months later, Lindbergh set the world's imagination afire with his flight to Paris; and it seems to me that with his flight a new age came into being—a new age which has not been confined to aviation.

Fired by Lindbergh's achievement, the City of St. Louis, in 1928, passed a two-million-dollar bond issue to buy the land which my old friend, the late Albert Bond Lambert, had assembled, to create a municipal airport, which later was appropriately named Lambert Field.

A resident and taxpayer of St. Louis brought suit to restrain the city from issuing these bonds. The temper of those times may be assessed by his petition to the court to annul the issue, in which he stated: "It will afford a starting and landing place for a few wealthy, ultra-reckless persons who own planes and who are engaged in private pleasure flying. . . . The number of persons using the airport will be about equal to the total number of persons who engage in big-game hunting trips to the African wilderness and voyages of North Pole exploration."

Now almost two-and-a-half million people will fly in and out of Lambert Field this year—and presumably not all will be ultra-reckless millionaires.

But lack of vision was not restricted to this taxpayer. A few years before this lawsuit was filed, Harvard's distinguished economics professor Frank William Taussig wrote an article which appeared in the Harvard University Press containing this estimate of the then-infant American organic chemicals industry. The professor stated:

"Regarded from the strictly economic point of view, the chemical industry does not seem to be adapted to American ways. In our technical parlance, it lacks a comparative advantage. Its processes are painfully detailed and elaborate, in which highly trained and highly paid labor is applied slowly and carefully to a variety of products. Each one of these products is turned out in small amounts; a possible exception is synthetic indigo, of which there is something like mass production. In the main, it is adapted to the German industrial ways and traditions; exact applied science, patient experimenting; a technical staff and its trained technical assistants, to be had at comparatively low salaries and wages; large scale operations but not mass production. . . . As a matter of the international division of labor, the people of the United States probably would do well to turn to other things in which they work to better advantage, and get their organic chemicals from Germany."

It has been said that old Socrates got the hemlock for spreading untested ideas—but the professor was more fortunate with his untested ideas, for, had they prevailed, there is no doubt we would have lost World War II. Today, the American organic chemical industry is the world's largest and its most efficient; even all plastics and all petrochemicals are organics.

But the professor's desolating estimate of the American chemical industry's potential was, at that time, that of most bankers and others too. At the end of 1927, the stock market was roaring; everyone, it seemed, believed in a New Era—but not for the chemical industry. Monsanto's first public financing took place in that market.

My father sold 21,000 shares of his Monsanto stock to put his affairs in order. The company sold another 10,000 shares to realize extra working capital. The issue, constituting 31,000 shares out of the 110,000 shares then outstanding, was sold to the public at $33 a share—5.4 times 1927 earnings. Such was the banking, professional and, indeed, the public estimate of the American chemical industry. In contrast, chemical shares reign among the favorites in today's stock market.

A few comparisons on a consolidated basis of the 1927 Monsanto of Professor Taussig's time and now, may be of interest:

Then we had a few domestic plants and a one-half interest in a British one; today we have twenty-two domestic plants and hold direct interests in twenty-two foreign companies which operate twenty-seven plants in sixteen countries.

Employes totaled 919; at last year's end, 31,346.

Sales were $5.5 million; last year, $811 million.

After-tax earnings were almost $700,000; last year, almost $62 million.

Assets, $8.5 million; last year, $951 million—and by the end of 1960, we may well have climbed into the billion-dollar club.

I could go on—but you know the story of our industry and of our company. I am fortunate to have had a part in this fascinating business for so long a time.

As the rest of the 1960s ticked off, Edgar Queeny became less active in the affairs of the company. Granted, he exercised occasional influence as chairman of the Finance Committee. Yet he was no longer the boss who called the shots.

In 1961 he took over the chairmanship of the trustees at Barnes Hospital in St. Louis—the hospital which would ultimately inherit virtually the entire Queeny estate. And in 1962, when he became sixty-five years of age, he moved from Monsanto headquarters to an office in the Pierre Laclede Building in suburban Clayton, Missouri, for a short stay before he gave funds to erect Queeny Tower at Barnes Hospital and then moved his office to the top floor of the tower. With each relocation he moved farther away from what he used to call "his" company.

His erstwhile investigative habits were sharply rekindled in 1964, when he learned, quite by accident, that an effort was afoot to change the name of Monsanto Chemical Company. Edgar Queeny phoned a longtime Monsanto colleague and inquired, "What's going on?" He was advised that some New York experts had decided the word "chemical" was too limiting. After all, the outside experts said, Monsanto was making fibers in the United Kingdom; it was making silicon for the electronic industry at St. Peters, Missouri; it was operating service stations (under the Lion trademark) in southern states. It was no longer *just* a chemical company.

"Edgar, the New Yorkers feel the 'umbrella' is not broad enough. They suggest going to a corporate name that's not too limiting, one which will fit regardless of the way we grow in the future."

Queeny understood. Perhaps he thought back to the time in 1933 when he regarded Monsanto Chemical Works as an outdated name.

Anyway, he knew the New Yorkers were not about to tamper with the only important part of the company's name, the word "Monsanto."

He was told, "Edgar, some people favor switching to Monsanto Incorporated; others like Monsanto Corporation; and still others like Monsanto Company." He had no preference. "I'll buy whatever Charlie Sommer and Charlie Thomas and their associates decide on," he said. And their decision was "Monsanto Company."

In 1966 an unexpected event occurred. The venerable St. Louis Award Committee, composed of principal civic, business and educational leaders, persuaded Edgar Queeny to accept the prestigious award for that year.

People who knew Queeny said, "Impossible; Edgar Queeny doesn't accept awards. He'd never show up for a public ceremony."

But he did. He showed up at the historic Old Courthouse in downtown St. Louis, almost a mile north of the place where Monsanto had been founded, and he sat somewhat impatiently while the chairman extolled his contributions. His acceptance speech was courteous—and brief.

The following two years he looked older, walked slower, and surfaced less frequently. Sensing he'd not be around much longer, he gave the following order to the Monsanto public relations department: "If you write anything about me after I've gone, for God's sake don't make me a Prince Charming."

It was part shock and part no shock when on July 7, 1968, he died at his home in suburban St. Louis.

His wife, Ethel, died February 10, 1975. In one plot at Bellefontaine Cemetery in north St. Louis are the graves of Edgar, Ethel and the baby son who died shortly after birth.

There are no known families left using the name Queeny. A hundred or two hundred years from now, perhaps only a small number of people will ever recall that the name existed.

Yet the word Monsanto—borrowed from John F.'s wife's and Edgar's mother's maiden name—is not so transient. It will grow in usage as the company grows, worldwide. Ironically and inescapably, as more people encounter the word Monsanto in the years ahead, fewer will remember the Queenys who founded and built the empire.

Realizing the respect and affection the father and son had for their wife and mother, Olga Monsanto Queeny, it can be safely surmised they'd not wish it any other way.

CHAPTER V

Expansion in a Perilous Era

W HEN Edgar Queeny took over as president in 1928, he and his colleagues were convinced Monsanto's growth would best be assured if the company concentrated on being a fountainhead of technology for industry. There was no plan to enter the consumer goods field.

The Annual Report of 1930 and several that followed gave due attention to the tremor of the Great Depression and its consequences. But they also gave due attention to the company's growth as a supplier to such pivotal industrial markets as food, paint, apparel, pharmaceuticals —and that prestigious industry called petroleum.

Significantly, Monsanto had pointed out the "revolutionary changes resulting from the utilization of petroleum products" as raw materials rather than a reliance on coal tar or vegetable sources for feedstocks. The petroleum industry thus became a big *supplier*. The company also pointed out that the petroleum industry was "developing into a large potential *customer* for our organic chemicals." (And not too far in the future, it would point out that the petroleum industry was becoming a major *competitor* in chemical manufacture.)

Even though Monsanto was in a business where technology was setting the pace, it often found that purchasing agents and other decision-makers at customer companies were nontechnical, or at least nonchemists. Also, Monsanto was beginning to notice that its ability to land a new order was often directly dependent on demonstrating to a customer or potential customer precisely how and why a certain chemical would provide for the customer company a competitive advantage in the marketplace.

Sales literature and old-time salesmanship were not enough.

It was unsurprising, therefore, that in 1928 Monsanto established a development department under a tireless chemist, Lynn A. Watt. He had come aboard in 1919 and was well versed in all the company's operations. He reasoned: "We will succeed only to the extent we can provide for each customer the kind of technical assistance he needs in order to make our products do his job."

73

Yet Edgar Queeny was not content with the mere challenge of serving industries better. He wanted to serve more industries. The rubber industry had a promising potential, so Queeny decided to become a supplier for it.

In June of 1929 Monsanto acquired, for $3,500,000 in stock, the Rubber Service Laboratories of Akron, Ohio, and Nitro, West Virginia. This was a company which had been started in 1922 by four former Goodyear men who were convinced they could succeed if their group could serve as technical consultant and supplier for the many small independent rubber companies in the Akron area. The large rubber companies were able to take care of their own technical requirements, but the smaller companies needed additives to make rubber do a better job.

Today's old-timers may recall that in the twenties and thirties Sunday-afternoon voyages in the family car were often interrupted by tire failure. Tire companies, going all out on programs to prevent this, found that a variety of chemicals could come to the rescue in vulcanization and curing processes, giving tires greater strength and abrasion-resistance. These were natural rubber tires, of course.

Queeny saw rubber additives as a market of long-term promise—a view borne out almost 40 years later when rubber chemicals became the company's first product group totally organized on a worldwide basis.

The 1929 transaction not only gave Monsanto an Akron laboratory and a group of people familiar with the needs of the rubber industry. It also gave Monsanto an additional manufacturing plant at Nitro, West Virginia, in the Kanawha River Valley near Charleston. Rubber Service Laboratories had purchased this plant as war surplus in 1922—a plant where Monsanto made new capital investments and got seriously into the business of manufacturing accelerators, antioxidants and other specialized proprietary products for the rubber industry.

RSL, as it was called, was not a major acquisition by 1977 standards. But it was an important one in that it gave Monsanto an appropriate entry into a field which has mushroomed ever since. RSL did not restrict its technical service to small companies for long. As its technology blossomed, the "biggies" began to lean on Monsanto for products and services, initially for additives for natural rubber and subsequently for additives for synthetic rubber. In 1977 Monsanto rubber chemistry technology is hidden to the average eye, but it is omnipresent in such brand names as Goodyear, Goodrich, Firestone, Pirelli, Dunlop and Michelin.

MERRIMAC

The "big leap" also came in 1929, when Monsanto purchased Merrimac Chemical Company, with offices and a plant at Everett, Massachusetts, three miles north of the Boston Common, and with a second plant at Woburn, Massachusetts, also in the Greater Boston area.

Merrimac's price tag, $4,500,000 in Monsanto stock at the then-current market value, was only $1,000,000 greater than the cost of acquiring Rubber Service Laboratories. Yet Merrimac was to have a more profound influence in far-reaching ways on Monsanto's future affairs.

Merrimac brought new markets, which was the reason for the acquisition. In addition, it brought new strengths and new weaknesses. And it brought into Monsanto two men of exceptional leadership qualities, who would wind up in the presidential chair—Charles Belknap and William M. Rand, who became No. 5 and No. 6, respectively (following John F. Queeny, Gaston DuBois, Beverly Harris and Edgar Queeny).

Merrimac also subsequently became a divisional headquarters and sent into St. Louis many other executives who would be in charge of such functions as engineering, purchasing and marketing. Two notable executives who started in St. Louis, Charles H. Sommer, a future president and chairman, and John L. Gillis, a future senior vice president, took their turns on their way up as general managers at Merrimac. (Sommer is still a board member today. Gillis was killed in an automobile accident in Jamaica early in 1976.)

Edgar Queeny called Merrimac "our first big step." He often smiled a small smile when he recalled "The son is much older than the father." A free translation of this inside joke is: Monsanto was only twenty-eight years old when it added Merrimac; but Merrimac traced its roots to 1853, six years before the founder of Monsanto, John F. Queeny, was born.

Supplying chemicals needed by the New England region's textiles, leather, paper and other industries, Merrimac Chemical Company had grown and flourished with them. But by 1929 it had ceased to grow.

Merrimac President Belknap and Vice President Rand knew that much of their manufacturing and laboratory equipment was obsolete and many of their processes were outmoded. In addition, there was wasteful duplication between the plants at Everett and Woburn. Earlier, Belknap and Rand had wanted to consolidate and modernize at Everett at a cost of $2 million. But the board of directors was wary of the risk.

Bill Rand, in 1977 still fit and hearty at ninety years of age and greeting each new morning with delight at his home in Lincoln, Massachusetts, remembers well the "exciting old days" before and after Merrimac's affiliation with Monsanto. And he chuckles over the fact that both he and Belknap were called "the skipper" in the presidential seat of Monsanto, back to back. His comments:

> I knew Charlie Belknap during World War I. We met in the Office of the Chief of Naval Operations in Washington, D.C. A man named Richard S. Russell was also with the Navy in Washington and, as it developed, his organization, called the Russell Company, managed Merrimac Chemical Company for a period following the war. My

shipmate, Charlie Belknap, and I were both introduced to Merrimac by Dick Russell. Belknap joined Merrimac first, in 1919, to be followed by me in 1920—Belknap initially as chief executive officer (with a man named Salmon W. Wilder as president), and then I went in the following year as treasurer.

Old-timers will recall that for many years the Merrimac plant at Everett was sort of a landmark. Its big pile of dry, yellow sulfur at the Mystic River dockside could be seen for miles around. I've been told that even airplane pilots used it as a checkpoint into the Boston airport. The pile was later abandoned when molten sulfur was introduced, but the old dry stuff was there in a very large quantity when I came aboard—and for many years thereafter, as a matter of fact.

In the early twenties the various Merrimac department heads had their own cubicles. In the old New England tradition, each man had a tenacious hold on his job. I'll never forget the director of purchasing I met. He refused to communicate with anyone, even people in his own department. I once asked him, "What will happen if you become injured on your way home?" People were reluctant in those days to accept the principle of delegation of authority.

Charlie Belknap was great to work with. He had been the U.S. Navy's commander in charge of the greatest concentration of shipping—troops, supplies and ammunition—in world history up to that time.

But this chemical business was new to both of us. Merrimac's sulfuric acid process was in pretty good shape, but our other processes were old-fashioned, even for serving the limited demands of New England industry. Particularly in nitric acid, acetic acid and muriatic acid, our techniques were time-consuming and inefficient.

Charlie Belknap and I were in sound agreement on three fundamentals: 1) there was no need to be making identical chemicals in plants only 14 miles apart (Everett and Woburn, Mass.); 2) we needed more modern processes; and 3) we foresaw that shortly our company would not even earn enough to make our dividends.

Naturally we didn't wish to preside over the demise of the company. Estimating we'd need about $2,000,000 in addition to the $1,500,000 cash and securities we had on hand, the board was reluctant to approve funds for modernization and it asked us to see if we couldn't sell the company outright to some company looking for a New England manufacturing outlet.

So in the late twenties we went shopping for a savior. Salmon Wilder went to see DuPont. Charlie Belknap went to see American Cy. I was asked to contact Allied and Penn Salt. The search wasn't too productive. Sure, there were a few companies which expressed preliminary interest, but we knew the first thing they'd do would be to come in and shut down a lot of operations and put most of our employes out of work. This was unacceptable. We knew there had to be a better way to get out of our dilemma. But we weren't sure what the better way was.

While the search for a savior was continuing, who should walk into the Merrimac office one day but Edgar Queeny of Monsanto! Totally unannounced! Had I met him earlier? Indeed I had. Actually, I had met him at several industry meetings. I distinctly remember two rather unique encounters with Edgar Queeny.

The first came at Greenbriar, White Sulphur Springs, West Virginia. Edgar Queeny had heard a man named Billy Thom, of Westvaco, was supposed to be a fast sprinter. One night after dinner he bet Billy Thom five dollars that Thom couldn't run as fast as Bill Rand of Merrimac Chemical Company. Queeny proposed a race down one of the hotel's wide corridors. Both Thom and I accepted the challenge. Before the race started, I took off my coat and handed it to Edgar and also gave him, for safekeeping, my watch with a gold medal on the chain. Soon the two of us were off. As it so happened, I touched the further wall ahead of my competitor and was back at the starting line a good five yards ahead. At the end of the race Edgar not only claimed his reward but he also showed my competitor a gold medal dangling at the end of my watch chain, a medal that was given by New York City to me and other members of the victorious 1908 Olympic track team. Queeny commented to the loser, "How about that?"

The second occasion was even more unusual. I was having dinner with Edgar Queeny at an elegant New York restaurant when he told me he wanted to introduce me to someone nearby but was disappointed that I wasn't adorned in my Navy uniform. Rather than suffer through the tedium of introducing an inauspicious-looking guest, Edgar called over the waiter and complimented him on his resplendent, decorative, braided jacket. He purchased the jacket off the back of the astonished waiter for ten dollars and persuaded me to put it on briefly so that I'd look properly proper in uniform. I still have that jacket somewhere in my closet.

Anyway, the 1929 negotiations with Monsanto went smoothly. It was obvious from the start that Monsanto very much wanted to have a manufacturing base in the northeast. It was equally obvious Monsanto could use Merrimac to extend its reach. And, happily, it was also obvious Monsanto was not about to move in and fire a lot of people. We had that commitment from the start.

In 1931 more than $2 million was spent to rebuild and consolidate Merrimac at Everett, and the Woburn operation was closed down.

In 1935, when Edgar was kicked by a horse and suffered serious injury to his right eye, to the degree he ultimately lost the eye's usefulness, Charlie Belknap was summoned to St. Louis to run the company as executive vice president during a period of several months when Edgar had to be out of action. Belknap did well in St. Louis—and he stayed. After Charlie left Everett, I moved in as Merrimac president. Subsequently, when the New England company was redesignated as the Merrimac Division of Monsanto, and when I became the division manager as well as a corporate vice president, I had some of my most interesting Monsanto experiences.

I can think of two special "case histories."

While serving as general manager at Everett I learned the corporate controller in St. Louis wanted a daily report on the "in and out" carboys in which we shipped sulfuric, acetic, nitric and muriatic acid to our New England customers. The glass carboys, holding fifteen gallons each, were returnable. We were constantly dealing with charge-outs and credits for the carboys. And St. Louis wanted a daily—repeat daily—report. This was too much. A few weeks later, during a meeting in St. Louis, I was the lone division general manager speaking out against what I thought was an unnecessary bit of corporate regimentation—plus a cost-creating intrusion into my own business. Edgar heard us all out. I wasn't sure how he'd react to my feeling that the new corporate regulation would be a burden for all of us at Everett. After each had had his say, Edgar commented, "It looks like everyone is out of step except Bill Rand." Keeping in mind that this comment could very well be interpreted as indicating my lack of cooperation, he went on to tell me to stick to my convictions and to run my shop the best way it seemed efficient.

Yet later on I had a more serious problem to contend with. I had again taken a rather strong and different position on a matter of corporate policy, largely because I thought it was my job to speak out for the good of Merrimac Division, which had some unique problems. My reward, it develops, was a rather stinging rebuke from Edgar in the form of a brisk and scolding memorandum.

I worried. I really worried. My wife, Lucy, God bless her, worried, too. I had several sleepless nights. Finally, after several days of brooding, I called in my secretary and dictated a note tendering my resignation from Monsanto.

Knowing I'd be out in St. Louis again within a few days, I asked my secretary not to mail the letter but instead to give it to me so that I could at least have the respect and dignity of personally handing it to Edgar Queeny. I felt this would be a warmer thing to do than to simply send something this crucial in the intercompany mail.

Several mornings later, I visited Edgar Queeny's office and delivered the letter. After he read it in my presence, I added: "Edgar, you can't have a successful company when you've got one fellow like me pulling in the opposite direction. I'll be happy to stay on at Merrimac until you decide on a replacement."

Edgar's reaction was: "Bill, you damn fool. When things are important for the corporation I know you always want to do what's best for all of Monsanto. But when you feel your division is being disadvantaged for small corporate gain, you speak up. Please understand when I write you a memo like that it doesn't mean we're not friends; it doesn't mean I don't want you to speak up. To show you how I feel, I want you to come to St. Louis and become a member of the Executive Committee."

I'll never forget that experience. I'll never forget Edgar. He was something else.

SWANN

In two steps (in 1933 and 1935), Monsanto took an even bigger jump—this time into almost $9,000,000 (mostly stock) worth of expansion and diversification.

Earlier reaches for diversification and growth had been across the Mississippi River (Commercial Acid, 1918); and to Graesser-Monsanto in London and Raubon, North Wales (1920 for 50 percent and 1928 for the remaining 50 percent); to a caffeine intermediate plant in Norfolk, Virginia (1925); to Akron and Nitro (1929) and to New England (1929).

The new jump was "down South"—to Birmingham and Anniston, Alabama, for, initially, the controlling stock equity of the Swann Corporation and, two years later, the full acquisition of Swann.

This was a larger milestone than Monsanto realized at the time. It involved the introduction into the Monsanto family of new products, new technology, new customers and new people, many of whom would in the years ahead take over positions of commanding importance—up to and including chairman of the board (Edward A. O'Neal), executive vice president (Robert R. Cole), senior vice president (John L. Christian), vice president (Felix N. Williams) and even a president (Edward J. Bock).

Ultimately the Swann group would become known within Monsanto as the Phosphate Division and, later, as the Inorganic Division. It would bring a unique kind of "school spirit" to affairs of the company in what was called "the era of the 'sand and gravel' boys." Why "sand and gravel"? This was a group accustomed to making heavy chemicals, dealing with large volumes of solids, gases and liquids, often under conditions of small but important profit margins. John L. Christian once bragged, "No bulk is too big and no volume too great to discourage me and my boys." In trying to find one word to sum up the attitude of the group sired by the Swann Corporation, Edgar Queeny once decided that "swashbuckling" might come near the mark.

Earlier acquirees into the Monsanto family had not been exactly prim and prissy. Granted, the New Englanders brought with them their northeast idioms and figures of speech and an unusual way of pronouncing certain words. But, by and large, they were not garrulous people.

Many in the early Swann crew, on the other hand, were a bit on the extrovert side. Also they brought bits and pieces of Southern culture and tradition into the Monsanto mix, along with a rather extreme divisional pride and an occasional tendency toward cronyism. Retrospective comments range from "the greatest morale and team spirit in the history of the company" to "the Inorganic Mafia."

The word most frequently used to describe the Swann-rooted people is "unorthodox." In the late thirties, forties and fifties there were instances when Phosphate (and, later, Inorganic) Division people went to such extremes in expressing pride in their own performance and "example" that they'd often be tempted to be a bit condescending toward the rest of the company, to "tolerate" others—with some Southern charm and politeness, to be sure.

Edgar Queeny had, one might say, asked for it. He not only wanted diversification into new business but he wanted diversification into new people. He couldn't stand yes-men, and on occasion he'd tell those who specialized in subservience that they were limiting their personal careers by not airing their convictions.

The Swann-rooted crowd had few yes-men. Under encouragement from some of its divisional leaders, and to some degree the encouragement of Queeny himself, they practiced what Mae West once suggested: "When you got it, flaunt it."

They were not only proficient in phosphorus- and phosphate-related product lines. They also developed a singular expertise in poker and gin rummy and the ability to cope with copious quantities of non-watered-down Jack Daniel's Black Label Tennessee whisky. One young Phosphate Division plant manager once said, "I have to be good in running my plant and I better also be good in the extracurricular requirements, too."

There seems to be general agreement that the Swann/Phosphate/ Inorganic group was not particularly inhibited by the formalities of a corporate infrastructure. The group's attitude seldom reached the point of noncooperation or revolt and never reached the point of secession, but it did involve a certain sense of unbridled spontaneity. In large measure, the pluses loom more conspicuously—or at least more memorably—than the minuses, particularly since this group had an outstanding record in contributing to growth, to profitability and to the art of developing new managers. Indeed, after Edward J. Bock, an Inorganic alumnus, moved into the Monsanto presidency in 1968 and when he presided over the reorganization of 1971, his principal lieutenants were those who had cut their teeth somewhere along the line on the policies and practices of Inorganic's "sand and gravel" traditions.

The roots of the Swann Corporation trace to World War I days, when an energetic promoter named Theodore Swann began to manufacture ferromanganese and other steel-making chemicals at Anniston. In the early twenties Swann began manufacturing phosphoric acid, importing phosphate rock from Florida and Tennessee for the purpose.

Phosphorus—a major element and "gift from the earth"—and its compounds were seen by Theodore Swann to hold exceptional promise. Further, he realized phosphoric acid was a door opening into a growing market for phosphates in foods, drugs and detergents.

As his company grew, it branched into calcium carbide, abrasives and lampblack. As entrepreneur behind this mushrooming enterprise, Swann had an office in Birmingham and a principal plant at Anniston. In addition, he had smaller manufacturing units in South St. Louis (Carondelet) for the manufacture of monocalcium and dicalcium phosphate for baking powders, and another small plant at Camden, New Jersey, for making lampblack and bone ash.

Owner Swann's managerial capabilities had limitations. Even when his company was soundly in the black, his personal finances were shaky, due in no small measure to his investment in a "million-dollar home" on Red Mountain overlooking the city of Birmingham, an edifice his associates called—somewhat sarcastically—"the palace."

By 1933 he had involved his company in a $700,000 debt. When several New York banks became insistent, he turned northward for help—and to Monsanto to "bail him out," to use Edgar Queeny's language.

With high transportation costs and with sources for phosphate rock running out, the Swann organization's fortunes were marginal at best in 1935, when Monsanto acquired it and embarked upon a path to make Swann, ultimately, the world's largest producer (at Columbia, Tennessee, and Soda Springs, Idaho) of elemental phosphorus, one of the most versatile of all chemicals, and of many derivatives of elemental phosphorus.

A graphic picture of pre-Monsanto Swann and Monsanto Swann is painted by Felix N. Williams, seventy-six, now retired and living the life of a Southern gentleman at Boca Raton, Florida. Williams, who was a Monsanto vice president and member of the board when he took early retirement in 1964, recently expressed the following recollections:

> My family was living in Anniston in 1923, when I received a chemical engineering degree from the University of Virginia. I decided I ought to try out my technical talents in the local area—and I very well remember the day I went rolling out to Swann's plant in my red Stutz Bearcat to see if I could get a job.
>
> I was all dressed up in my white flannel trousers, eager to make a good impression and to show them what a chemical engineering graduate from the University of Virginia looked like. I was told right promptly they didn't need any chemical engineers but they were taking on a few laborers.
>
> I was in no position to be choosy so I signed on as a laborer. Without ado, they handed this dandy dude a shovel and pointed to a wheelbarrow and told this upstart to get to work. My pay was twenty-five cents an hour, which wasn't bad considering the standard schedule was eighty-four hours a week and included all seven days of the week.
>
> It was my job to dig crystallized ammonium phosphate out of a big drying pan and to wheel chunks of crystal over and dump them in a centrifuge. In the process, some of the "mother liquid" bounced out and got on me. The first night when I got home and took off my flannel trousers and tossed them into a corner, I had to laugh when I noticed the trousers were so stiff they stood up by themselves.

Shortly after Monsanto took over and started its Phosphate Division, I was told it would be my job to go to Columbia, Tennessee, and help build the elemental phosphorus plant. I'll never forget when Edgar Queeny brought his directors down to Tennessee for the first time—on a private L&N parlor car which was shunted into the Columbia plant site on a new spur. There were no roads into the plant then. We had just started to build.

Everyone knew it would be impossible to show the distinguished visitors the soggy phosphate fields by automobile. In the soft Tennessee clay, an automobile would bog down. Theodore Swann and his principal assistant, Rush Cole, had the idea of giving the visitors a royal welcome, and accordingly they had ordered that a big wooden sled be built for the occasion—with benches and even with seat belts. That was the first time I ever saw the meticulous Edgar Queeny—sitting there on a bench on a sled while a bulldozer pulled him through the rich and gummy fields of phosphorus ore he had just purchased.

Later I became plant manager at Columbia, Tennessee, and subsequently became production manager for the Phosphate Division before moving up to Springfield, Massachusetts, to learn about plastics.

Why did Phosphate contribute so many leadership people into Monsanto ranks? It developed people by the way it treated people. We gave people a job and let them do it. Give Rush Cole a lot of credit for this.

Rush didn't make a lot of noise but he made a lot of common sense. When he'd give someone a job to do, if that someone would ask "how?" Rush would say, "That's your business. If I didn't think you could figure out the 'how' of it I would not have assigned you to the task in the first place." He didn't withhold advice if it would be needed, but he'd never hold his people on a tight rein and he'd never nag them with a lot of do's and don't's.

It didn't surprise me at all when Ed O'Neal became chairman in 1965. He really flowered when he went to England in 1946. Ed's an ideal example of someone who started down South and became an international figure for Monsanto.

John Christian was the most vocal of the Phosphate group. He was an unusual fellow. I once told John Christian and Ed Bock if they didn't shape up I'd fire them. But they both came around.

Edward A. O'Neal, former chairman, who retired as a Monsanto board member in 1975, divides his time between residences in England, the Pennsylvania Poconos and Skinker Boulevard in St. Louis. He earned an A.B. degree in physics ("You can't hardly get that degree any more") at Davidson College, and in 1926 he knocked on Swann's door at Anniston, in search of a job. He remembers the early days, to wit:

Rush Cole was in charge of operations at Anniston and Dr. John N. Carothers was in charge of research. Nobody told me the day I was hired, but later on Rush Cole told me that he and Dr. Carothers had flipped a coin after seeing me for the first time. It seems the loser was to take O'Neal. Poor Dr. Carothers, he lost—so he brought me into the control lab, where I washed beakers. About six months later someone down there noticed the lab job didn't seem to be my turn of hand, so I was given a few odd jobs in the plant, and then I progressed to foreman, supervisor and superintendent of the abrasives operation. Pretty soon I was plant manager. And then I was sent to Trenton, Mich., to run the start-up there.

Looking back on the Phosphate days, I surely give Rush Cole a lot of credit for the spirit of the group and for developing so many good people who went upstairs within Monsanto.

THOMAS AND HOCHWALT

The 1936 Annual Report contained the following demonstration of Edgar Queeny's ability to make a terse, on-target statement: "The substance from which our industry obtains its growth is research."

Queeny added: "A fundamental and long-range research program is necessary to attain leadership. Toward this objective, the well-known Thomas and Hochwalt Laboratories of Dayton, Ohio, were acquired early in the year. Having evaluated their talent and experience through several years' use of their services, the staff and facilities of these laboratories were well-known to us, and compatibility of our organization and theirs, as to both executive and laboratory personnel, was assured. We believe that a fresh point of view can be obtained by a group of research workers not directly attached to any manufacturing unit and who, therefore, can concentrate without distraction on fundamental and long-range research."

The text went on to say Monsanto was at the threshold of such new fields as "synthetic resins and other derivatives of petroleum ... and synthetic detergents, wetting agents, wood preservatives and insecticides."

That sums up the so-called "Dayton acquisition" and one of the major reasons behind it: a fresh point of view.

If one would pick the "top ten milestones of Monsanto's 75 years," much as one would select the top ten motion pictures of the year or the top ten rock records, it would be difficult to omit the acquisition of the Thomas and Hochwalt Laboratories. The significance may have been somewhat appreciated in 1936, but in fact this acquisition was only the firming up of an R&D foundation upon which Monsanto later built a body of new technology that Messrs. Thomas and Hochwalt could scarcely have dreamed of in the thirties.

In 1977 much of Monsanto's proprietary and patented chemical know-how traces back to Dayton, but even more to the succession of researchers nurtured in the spirit of Thomas and Hochwalt.

Friends have called Thomas and Hochwalt by such names as Damon and Pythias. The two were, in fact, collaborators in science even prior to their official partnership.

Their story goes back to 1923, when Monsanto was struggling with post–World War I woes. It was in this year that two young chemists—Charles Allen Thomas and Carroll A. (Ted) Hochwalt—met in the laboratories of General Motors Research Corporation, Dayton, and became close friends. To be more precise, lifetime friends.

The General Motors research director at the time was the renowned Charles F. "Boss" Kettering, the man who several years earlier had headed up a team of scientists to develop the Delco self-starter for a new ignition system for automobiles.

Charlie Thomas and Ted Hochwalt, eager young chemists, worked directly under Thomas Midgley, Jr., who had been assigned by "Boss Ket" to develop anti-knock gasoline—the breakthrough which would revolutionize the automobile industry by permitting the introduction of high-compression engines.

Ted Hochwalt developed the synthetic process and chemistry of tetraethyl lead. Charlie Thomas worked on what was known as the "scavenger project."

Tests showed that tetraethyl lead deposited lead oxide on an engine's valves and spark plugs. This was bad.

Thomas found that adding ethylene dibromide to the fuel would scavenge the unwanted lead residue and blow it out of the exhaust system. This was good.

In 1925 General Motors decided to move its research laboratories to Detroit. But Charlie Thomas and Ted Hochwalt decided not to go along. Three years earlier, Hochwalt had married a young lady named Pauline Burkhardt and was immensely satisfied with Dayton as a place to raise a family. Thomas was freshly in love with a stunning Daytonian named Margaret Talbott and most definitely didn't want to move to another city. Subsequently they were married—in 1926.

With their General Motors jobs moving out from under them, Thomas and Hochwalt decided the best thing to do was to go into business as scientific entrepreneurs. They formed the Thomas and Hochwalt Laboratories in 1926 and opened their first lab in an attic in downtown Dayton. Two years later they moved to a "respectable laboratory" on Nicholas Road.

The Thomas and Hochwalt lab had a wide variety of industrial clients from its inception until the time it was acquired by Monsanto ten years later. Among these was General Motors. And Monsanto.

In the early days, the lab worked on phosphorus derivatives, chemicals from brine, hydrocarbon chemistry, oil additives, synthetic rubber, carbon paper and the aging of bourbon whisky.

That last item always raises eyebrows. People generally inquire, "bourbon whisky?"

The story goes like this:

In 1932, expecting Franklin D. Roosevelt to be elected President and anticipating he would bring about the repeal of Prohibition—which occurred in 1933—Thomas and Hochwalt paused to contemplate the plight of the American whisky industry, which would surely be faced with an unprecedented, pent-up demand. And it was widely known that the distillers' inventory of whisky was extremely low—almost non-existent.

There would be no time, the Dayton scientists reasoned, for people to sit around and wait for whisky to age through traditional processes. Americans would want whisky pronto—not four or eight years later.

Thomas recalls: "We figured out a way to beat the clock and to bring about rapid aging, and were about to take our findings into the industry at large when people at National Distillers, somehow or other, found out what we were doing. We signed a contract with them forthwith. Once Prohibition was repealed, about three million bottles were produced at a pilot plant in Louisville, giving National Distillers a head start in the suddenly legal marketplace. It wasn't very good bourbon. But it was pure, wet, alcoholic and available."

Call it opportunistic science, if you will, but it added to the revenue of the Dayton laboratory.

Ted Hochwalt also recalls: "Charlie and I did some interesting work in the twenties for the FyrFyter Company of Dayton. We developed the ingredients for a fire extinguisher which operated successfully at forty degrees below zero. Prior to this time, all soda-acid fire extinguishers had to be kept indoors. Now they could be established in lumber yards and anyplace it might be prudent to put them—all over the world. We received royalties from FyrFyter for seventeen years, in the form of quarterly payments. Lynn A. Watt, a research executive from Monsanto, somehow learned that we were purchasing a Monsanto product for the new fire extinguisher and he visited our Dayton lab to find out what we were up to. Mainly, he was curious. And he was always on the lookout for someplace where Monsanto could find a way to sell more chemicals."

This was the first contact between Monsanto and the Thomas and Hochwalt lab.

The second contact came a short time later, under precisely the same circumstances. Hochwalt explains: "We developed a liquid called Carbosol, a carbon-removing agent, for the Alemite Corporation. Here again we used a Monsanto chemical in our ingredients, and here again we had a visit from Lynn Watt, who wanted to know what we were doing."

Hochwalt adds: "He kept an eye on us thereafter, and it is my understanding he gave Edgar Queeny a fill-in on the goings-on in our Dayton lab."

Before long the Thomas and Hochwalt shop began to handle some farmed-out research for the fast-growing St. Louis chemical company.

Charlie Thomas remembers a visit from Monsanto executives in 1936 and recalls Edgar Queeny's comment verbatim: "Your bills are so high it would be cheaper for Monsanto to buy you out." The Thomas and Hochwalt staff had by then grown to fifty. Queeny said he wanted to buy "the whole stable."

And he did—for $1.4 million in Monsanto common shares. They called it the Thomas and Hochwalt Laboratories Department of Monsanto—later to become the company's Central Research Department.

At that time, most of the company's research was in areas related to the various product groups at Merrimac, Swann, Rubber Service and at St. Louis headquarters. Research teams at these locations pressed hardest to find new processes and new markets related to their traditional product lines. Some new horizons were occasionally explored, but there was no overall corporate planning for such exploration. Such a job was handed to Charlie Thomas and Ted Hochwalt and their Dayton staff.

Ted Hochwalt recalls Edgar Queeny putting the assignment in nine words: "To develop and expand the technical proficiency of Monsanto."

The contract between Monsanto and Thomas and Hochwalt was signed in St. Louis on Easter Sunday, 1936. Hochwalt remembers: "I went to mass with W. W. Schneider, head of Monsanto's law department, after which we all went down to South Second Street and signed the contract."

Both Thomas and Hochwalt repeat over and over how fortunate they were to encounter a man named Queeny—a man who was willing to take a risk and who understood the relationship between research and growth. Queeny loved new things. He knew Monsanto's competitors were pressing ahead vigorously in all functions—in manufacturing, marketing and, indeed, in the laboratory.

Thomas says, "It wasn't simply that Queeny didn't want to be outdistanced. He wanted Monsanto to take a leadership role in science."

Shortly after coming into Monsanto, the Dayton scientists began working on surface-active agents (detergents for removing dirt and stains from fabrics) and on phosphate builders (for keeping in suspension in wash water the dirt removed from fabrics). This research not only led Monsanto to becoming a major supplier for the detergent industry but also, in the forties, to the invention of the world's first low-sudsing detergent, subsequently to be christened by Monsanto as "all" and to cause a bit of a stir in the hitherto high-sudsing marketplace, dominated by such important Monsanto customers as Procter & Gamble, Colgate and Lever Brothers.

A wide range of new products was destined to be born at Dayton. Quite often the new technology was unexciting in the layman's view, particularly when it simply led to better ways to make old products. Much of Monsanto's patented and proprietary technology is "simply" in the area of "better ways," but those better ways have often involved revolutionary processes, proprietary technology and important patents. Such technology plus the engineering it required have perhaps added more to profitability over the years than the exciting, totally new final products—like the detergent "all."

Charlie Thomas and Ted Hochwalt recall that Queeny was not only an ardent supporter of technology but sometimes an impatient supporter, eagerly waiting for the results—or profits—to come pouring "out of the pipe." They remember that Queeny very well understood the time lag of at least seven years from test tube to marketplace. On the one hand he understood. Yet on the other hand, particularly when corporate earnings were only so-so, Queeny kept insisting that his researchers "shorten the gap."

Today Charlie Thomas, at seventy-six years of age, has an office on the ninth floor of the Pierre Laclede Building in suburban Clayton, Missouri, and Ted Hochwalt, at seventy-seven, has an office on the eleventh floor. It is the same office building to which Edgar Queeny "escaped" in 1962 and Ed O'Neal in 1968. Pundits call the Pierre Laclede Building "the Valhalla of Monsanto executive alumni."

Thomas and Hochwalt can now, in retirement, sit back and relax while recalling the pressures of those earlier, nonrelaxing days when Edgar Queeny kept an anxious eye on what was coming "out of the pipe."

FIBERLOID

Plainly, Edgar Queeny was on the move for more diversification.

In March, 1938, Monsanto completed arrangements of the acquisition of the Fiberloid Corporation, a plastics company on the banks of the Chicopee River at Indian Orchard, Massachusetts, a suburb of Springfield. Monsanto had purchased a 14-percent interest in the company five years earlier and had kept its eye on Fiberloid from then on. In addition, Fiberloid had been an important customer for Merrimac's nitric acid (for cellulose nitrate) and was the largest customer for plasticizers from the Organic Division. As a result, Fiberloid's products and people were rather well known to Monsanto.

Almost $11 million in Monsanto stock was involved in the various stages of the transaction. To further sweeten the situation, Monsanto also acquired, at about the same time, a 50-percent interest in Fiberloid's next-door neighbor, Shawinigan Resins Corporation.

Fiberloid's story had involved a substantial measure of pioneering.

In the late 1880s a group of Springfield businessmen who had been manufacturing collars and cuffs out of stiff white paper found themselves facing technical obsolescence. The source of the threat was a substance invented in 1869 by an Albany, New York, tinkerer named John Wesley Hyatt—a cellulose nitrate compound which Hyatt trade-named Celluloid. (Actually, Hyatt had introduced Celluloid not for collars and cuffs. He had heard that a billiard ball manufacturer was looking for a substitute for ivory and was offering a $10,000 prize. So he entered his Celluloid as a candidate. But he won no prize.)

Celluloid was the first man-made plastic.

In 1888 the Springfield collar-and-cuff people contributed both their capital and their marketing experience (with paper products) to a joint venture with a Newburyport, Massachusetts, manufacturer of Celluloid. The new venture was called Lithoid Mfg. Co. In 1904 its management people decided to move to Springfield and they renamed the company the Fiberloid Corporation.

As new uses developed for the plastic—toiletware, cutlery handles, automobile curtains, piano keys, toothbrushes, spectacle frames, watch crystals, fountain pen parts and so forth—Fiberloid grew. It even developed, in the mid-twenties, cellulose nitrate plastic for a safety glass interlayer for automobile windshields. Chiefly because cellulose nitrate discolored with age and was weakened by both heat and cold, it was far from ideal as the "middle of the sandwich" in safety glass. Nonetheless, it was the first substance to make safety glass possible and, as such, was hailed as a technological breakthrough.

With the coming of the Great Depression and its domino-effect consequences, and with the rise of new competitors developing newer plastics, from the late twenties through the mid and late thirties, Fiberloid faced a rough uphill fight. By the time Monsanto entered the picture as the new owner, cellulose nitrate was no longer being used for windshields. Cellulose acetate, instead, had become the material for the safety glass interlayer. It was better than cellulose nitrate but still left much to be desired. Later on, it would be displaced by polyvinyl butyral, the ideal plastic interlayer—and 1977's plastic interlayer.

Monsanto's entry into plastics "with both feet" in 1938 was based on a plan to go both deep and wide—deep into technology and broadly into a wide variety of plastics materials. Shawinigan added to the product mix with its vinyl acetate resins. To further round out its line, Monsanto lost no time in acquiring the Resinox Corporation of Edgewater, New Jersey, in order to be able to bring into Springfield an operation to manufacture phenolic resins.

Fiberloid was not, nor did Monsanto want it to be, a molder or fabricator of finished products. It was a manufacturer of sheets, films, rods, tubes, crystals and powders—a supplier to companies wanting to make things out of the wondrous new materials.

For a time Monsanto considered adding its own substantial line of plasticizer chemicals to the Fiberloid catalogue. (A plasticizer is a liquid which adds flexibility to certain plastics.) Yet prudence suggested that developmental work on a wide variety of plasticizers be continued in St. Louis. Plasticizers were, after all, another family of chemicals. Monsanto decided to develop them separately—and independently—apart from its newly acquired Springfield company.

John C. Brooks, Fiberloid president, who came along as an important part of the deal, moved into the job of general manager when Monsanto took over. He was promptly elected to the Monsanto board.

And whereas the Monsanto 1938 Annual Report contained several references to Fiberloid per se, the corresponding document of the following year took up the nomenclature Plastics Division. Both the 1938 and 1939 Annual Reports left no doubt that Monsanto had embraced plastics in a big way. On the cover of the 1938 publication a color photo appeared at the upper left showing a cluster of orchids. Covering the flowers was a 3- by 4½-inch piece of rigid transparent Vue-Pak film, the new packaging material from Monsanto. In the 1939 Annual Report Edgar Queeny quite plainly could not contain his enthusiasm. Noting that Vue-Pak could protect everything "from blankets to bonbons, from shoes to stogies," he had a full-page-size sheet of the Springfield protective product inserted in the book, superimposed over photos of appropriate products.

Felix N. Williams, who was quoted earlier in this chapter, recently related a few memories of his arrival at the Plastics Division in 1944, when he succeeded John C. Brooks as general manager:

> When President Charlie Belknap asked me to leave the Phosphate Division and move to Springfield, I told him, "Hell, Charlie, I don't know anything about plastics." He replied, somewhat facetiously, "Hell, neither does anyone else." Fact of the matter was a lot had been accomplished by Fiberloid and a lot had been added by Monsanto. But we were still on the threshold. There was a lot to be learned.
>
> The phenolics were the only heavy-tonnage item, and the Bakelite Corporation had a big lead in that field. We called our product Resinox. It was used for telephone housings and other staple items. But it was an unglamorous, commodity-type product with limited potential.
>
> One of the biggest advances had to do with Shawinigan bringing in resins for polyvinyl butyral for the interlayer for windshields. Shawinigan made the resins and Monsanto made the sheeting. Here, finally, was a proprietary product which we knew would be a winner. We called it Saflex.
>
> Initially the product was clear and transparent. However, we knew there would be a market for tinted material to protect motorists against the rays of the sun. Also, we knew the ideal sheet for a windshield would be one that was somewhat darker on the top to protect the driver's eyes against glare. So we developed what we called variable density Saflex interliner. For a while we hand-dipped plastic sheeting into dyes. But this was primitive. Then one day Carl T. King, production manager, got the idea of asking his son, who was in the printing business, to see if the dye process couldn't be handled on a rotogravure press. This experiment showed us the way to go.

Saflex is one of the most profitable products the company has ever made. Later on we added production units at Trenton, Michigan, and Ghent, Belgium.

There was a little experimenting with polystyrene during World War II, but not much. After all, styrene monomer was needed for synthetic rubber. Yet when the war ended, polystyrene went to town as a general-purpose molding compound. We called our first products Lustron and Lustrex resins. I'll never forget the experts said that someday polystyrene molding compounds would sell up to 10 or 12 million pounds a year, industrywide. What a silly prediction. Monsanto got to over a billion pounds a year all by itself.

It took a while to work out a precise coloring process for all the hues of polystyrene and to keep the colors consistent. There has been a lot of upgrading since, of course. ABS (acrylonitrile, butadiene and styrene) is now the No. 1 molding compound and Monsanto is very much the leader in the development and marketing of this sophisticated and versatile member of the plastics family.

WHEN Edgar Queeny started his first full calendar year as president— in 1929—he had his hands full. The ensuing decade was to be one of the nation's most violent economic periods. The Monsanto 1939 Annual Report demonstrated the distance of the ten-year progression.

The following "roll call" for 1939 situates the various principals and units of Monsanto as they moved along—into a new war period.

Edgar Queeny was chairman and president. The rest of the board consisted of Charles Belknap, executive vice president of the company and chairman of the Executive Committee; John C. Brooks, general manager of the Plastics Division; G. Lee Camp, co–general manager of the Organic Chemicals Division (the basic, "parent" division, which sired the company); Gaston DuBois, member of the Executive Committee; John W. Livingston, co–general manager of the Organic Chemicals Division; Lloyd F. Nickell, managing director of Monsanto Chemicals Limited, London; William M. Rand, general manager of the Merrimac Division; Theodore Rassieur, general counsel; and Walter W. Smith, outside board member who served as financial adviser.

The Executive Committee and the operating divisions were supported by the following general staff departments: Accounting, Advertising and Monsanto Practice, Central Research (Dayton), Development, Engineering, Legal, Patent, Purchasing and Traffic, and Treasury.

In 1929 sales had been a bit above $17 million. In 1939 they were almost $43 million.

But figures don't tell the story. Monsanto in 1929 had a limited product line. Monsanto in 1939 had a greatly expanded product line, plus an impatient Central Research Department at Dayton.

Yet even in 1939 the food and pharmaceutical industries remained the No. 1 and No. 2 customers. Then came (in this order) manufacturers of glass and vitreous products, plastics, rubber, paint, color and dyestuff, soap, petroleum, paper and printing—and so on.

In turn, many of the above industries had the automobile industry as one of their chief outlets.

Monsanto's days as a major supplier for other basic industries—notably housing, agriculture and textiles—were still ahead. But, importantly, the Terrible Thirties were beginning to dissolve into history and the rainbow ahead, called the Fabulous Forties, beckoned. Especially in 1939 it seemed advisable to look forward rather than backward. Despite the clouds of a still-simmering new war, all systems seemed go.

CHAPTER VI

World War II and Its Aftermath

A new organization plan established by the company in 1939 was sound—and was destined to stay rather firmly in place until January 1, 1954, when a more sophisticated, though not necessarily more lasting, concept would be introduced.

During this 15-year interim, two new operating divisions would be added (Western and Texas)—bringing the total to six. Also, there would be adjustments to the nomenclature and alignment of general staff departments. Yet, by and large, the basic "divisional arrangement" determined at the dawn of World War II long served as the foundation of a rather decentralized superstructure.

In the sixties Monsanto would carry the format to the point where there would be as many as nine divisions and thirteen corporate staff departments. But the record shows that important and hard homework for organizational efficiency started in 1939.

Even though the British-based Monsanto Chemicals Limited was designated an "operating division" in the 1939 organizational plan, largely as an interim convenience, the fact remained that domestic Monsanto became divided into four major profit centers: the Organic Chemicals Division, the Phosphate Division (later to be renamed Inorganic), the Merrimac Division and the Plastics Division.

The motivation was to divide Monsanto into manageable segments and to delegate authority and responsibility as far downward as was deemed realistically possible, thus making each divisional general manager accountable for his share of the company's substantial investments.

Even in 1939 and 1940 there was good-natured joshing about the "maharajas" who would rule the divisional roosts—two in St. Louis and one each at Everett and Springfield, Massachusetts. The "little kings" were forerunners of a larger hierarchy of division general managers and, later, operating company managing directors who would have something approaching—approaching but not quite reaching—autonomy in their line responsibilities.

As the company moved into the forties, to be tested severely by the war years and by a shattering tragedy at Texas City, Texas, Edgar Queeny served in two capacities, as presiding officer of the board of directors and as president of the company. Charles Belknap, who had been summoned hastily from Everett in 1935, when Queeny was kicked by a horse and permanently injured his right eye, served as executive vice president.

There was an Executive Committee assigned to long-range planning and matters of corporate policy. Administrative responsibilities were placed with the operating divisions, with support from corporate staff departments.

Monsanto was better prepared for the war years than it would have been had it not undertaken its organizational readjustments. The company had not only digested its new bites into new businesses in the late twenties and in the thirties, but it had worked with some intensity to integrate the new people, new plants and new product lines into the total operation. Edgar Queeny was not the sole architect of the 1939 plan. All his senior officers were involved in putting it together. Queeny's appraisal: "It tidied us up."

The year 1940 had its special strains.

On the political front, Edgar Queeny was not the only businessman who believed President Franklin D. Roosevelt's two terms in office were a plentiful sufficiency.

Queeny became fascinated by Wendell L. Willkie, a colorful, semi-conservative (compared to FDR) dark horse for the Republican presidential nomination. Up to and during the national convention in Philadelphia, Queeny was an ardent Willkie supporter. But the infatuation was short-lived. Shortly after Willkie was nominated as the Republican standard-bearer, Queeny found several of Willkie's "One World" platforms unsuitable and he ducked out of the political arena faster than he had entered it.

Until Pearl Harbor Day, December 7, 1941, many Americans—perhaps responding to their hearts and hopes more than to reason—kept saying, "It's not our war." Even after Hitler moved into Czechoslovakia and Poland, there were Americans who insisted the war clouds over Europe would simply remain war clouds over Europe.

In the June, 1940, issue of *Monsanto Magazine* Queeny wrote: "If the United States is to produce all that is necessary with the greatest speed, every American must give both loyalty and cooperation."

A few months later, the realities were driven home when the officers and staff of Monsanto Chemicals Limited moved from London to a safer "temporary headquarters" in rural England. This relocation was only a hint of the drama and disruption that all of Monsanto—and much of the world—would shortly be facing.

The 1940 Annual Report stated: "Due to the uncertainties created by the conflict abroad and the exchange restrictions, we have eliminated

our British subsidiary from all our consolidated accounts and statements."

Production-related milestones for the year included the establishment
of a new synthetic nitric acid plant at Everett; a new Resinox plastic
plant at Springfield; a fourth electric furnace for elemental phosphorus
at Columbia, Tennessee; a new contact sulfuric acid plant at Monsanto,
Illinois; and the start of construction of a plant at Trenton, Michigan,
near Detroit, for the production of phosphate salts.

A non-production-related milestone ranked equally high, or perhaps
higher, in lasting importance: In 1940, Monsanto shareowners approved
a farsighted pension plan covering all employes.

But it was not a "business as usual" year.

Nor was 1941.

"American industry geared itself to full war production" was the way
the 1941 Annual Report started. A subsequent paragraph read as follows: "Approximately $8,500,000 was expended for improvements and
extensions of plant facilities. All major expansion was in directions
whereby we could be of more service in the preparedness program and
for which we were granted Certificates of Necessity permitting amorti-
zation over a five-year period. Capacity was increased for production of
phthalic anhydride, important raw material used in the manufacture of
special paints for Army and Navy equipment. Production facilities were
provided for an increased supply of plasticizers for synthetic resins and
synthetic rubber. Broader use of sulfanilamide and related sulfathiazole
intermediates and salicylic acid, aspirin and acetophenetidin caused us
to increase production facilities of these important pharmaceuticals."

Other products identified were tetryl, "a high explosive," and oleum
"for TNT."

Immediately after the Japanese bombed Pearl Harbor on December 7,
Edgar Queeny ordered a dispatch to all Monsanto locations, calling on
the company's total resources. He later confided to a friend, "We had the
illusion that, somehow, we were ready. But there was a lot of catching
up to do."

At the close of 1941 Monsanto had four major war plants under
construction or on the drawing boards—two for the Chemical Warfare
Service, one for the Army Ordnance Department, and one for the Rubber Reserve Company, a government agency.

The 1941 Annual Report used this language: "Shutting off of rubber
imports and the subsequent demand for rapid increases in the manufacture of synthetic rubber brought Monsanto a request by the Rubber
Reserve Company, a government agency, to design, construct and operate a plant to manufacture an important raw material for synthetic
rubber. We have acquired a site ... on which the plant, government
financed, will be erected."

No mention of the product: styrene monomer.

No mention of the location: Texas City, Texas.

Obviously and understandably, Monsanto felt under wraps. Security was a constant consideration in wartime.

Yet styrene monomer had been no secret product in prewar Monsanto. Dr. Charles A. Thomas and Dr. Carroll A. (Ted) Hochwalt, up at Dayton's Central Research Department, had been working since 1938 with styrene monomer, in conjunction with the research department of the Plastics Division at Springfield, Massachusetts. They had viewed styrene monomer as a raw material of great potential in plastics. They had even set up a small pilot plant using styrene for plastic compounds.

Styrene monomer thus was no newcomer to Monsanto. Yet in the 1941 Annual Report, with styrene monomer looming as the key to the government's all-out effort to mount a synthetic rubber program, prudence indicated that the words styrene monomer not even be mentioned. Instead, Monsanto confined its language to "an important raw material for synthetic rubber." A new day of restricted disclosure had dawned.

The same Edgar Queeny who in the early thirties was eager to provide shareowners with more detailed information now found himself in a corner, confined by the constraints of national security. Indeed, he knew the Germans had developed their own synthetic rubber, buna-S. He knew the Germans and Japanese were aware that "an important raw material for synthetic rubber" was inevitably and inescapably styrene monomer. Yet he chose not to identify the end-product in his report to shareowners.

Several people who worked closely with Edgar Queeny at that time express the belief that it was difficult for "Mr. Monsanto" to restrain his enthusiasm—for he very well knew that America rolled on rubber, that the war would roll on rubber, and that Monsanto styrene would become a crucial necessity of the wartime synthetic rubber program.

Governmental restriction piled on governmental restriction the following year.

Monsanto's 1942 Annual Report faced a new inhibition head-on, as follows: "It is with regret that we abandon our past practice of transmitting to our shareowners an informative and interpretive Annual Report on our operations. Two causes dictate this course. The necessity of secrecy imposed by our national interest surrounds much of the activities upon which the company has been engaged. The other cause—to which we yield with reluctance—is the result of new proxy provisions prescribed by the Securities and Exchange Commission. We have been advised that these new rules make an annual report a part of proxy soliciting material. Therefore, they may have the result of imposing severe liabilities upon the directors and officers of the company in the event of misstatement or omission of material fact. Honest expressions or interpretation of operations or prospects by company officials might,

The Monsanto Chemical Works telephone switchboard shortly after World War I.

Edgar M. Queeny en route to England in the mid-twenties.

A container for the company's first product, saccharin, made for use in the China market during the twenties.

A dinner at the Chase Hotel in St. Louis following a sales meeting in 1924.

An early vehicle used by Graesser-Monsanto Chemical Works, Ltd., in Ruabon, North Wales, in the twenties.

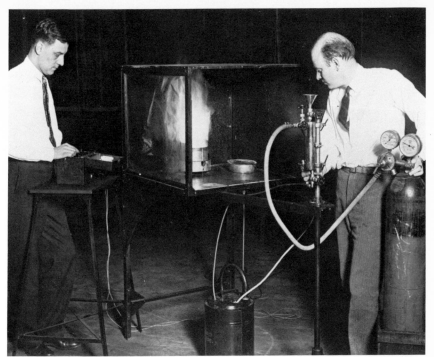

Carroll A. Hochwalt (left) and Charles A. Thomas working on an improved fire extinguisher at the Thomas and Hochwalt Laboratory in Dayton, Ohio, in 1930.

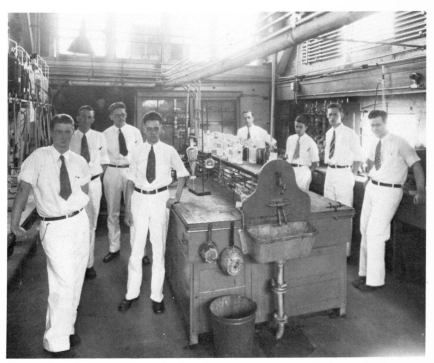

The laboratory on South Second Street in St. Louis in the early thirties.

The accounting department in the late thirties.

In 1943 President Charles Belknap (right) presented a safety trophy to Vice President William M. Rand, who was general manager of the Merrimac Division at Everett, Massachusetts, and who in 1945 succeeded Belknap as president.

An Army-Navy "E" pennant presented to Edgar M. Queeny, Gaston F. DuBois and R. R. Cole during World War II.

During 1946 approximately 4000 employes were off the job for almost four months during a strike of the Chemical Workers Union (AFL).

in the light of subsequent events, prove incorrect. . . . Company officials cannot be infallible."

The message added: "Until the import of these new regulations is established or clarified . . . no prudent course seems open other than limiting Annual Reports to terse statements of fact, verified at the time by independent auditors."

In the guarded era which followed, Monsanto Annual Reports, heretofore brimming with information to help shareowners understand the full and open facts of their company, became sparse, digital and—to quote Edgar Queeny—"dull."

Interim reports were a bit more open. Comments at Annual Meetings were much more open. And *Monsanto Magazine* all of a sudden began to contain more stories of substance regarding the operations of the company. Queeny wryly observed, "No penalty is as yet attached to human errors that may appear in company publications." He added, "Our magazine is our forum; let's use it to the fullest."

When he was asked how he felt about the new SEC regulations and the handcuffs they imposed on Monsanto and other public companies, Queeny chose one honest word: "bitter."

A close associate said, "Edgar felt the medicine was worse than the disease. He had no reservations at all when it came to prudence in national security. When in doubt, he chose not to divulge information which might be sensitive. But he regarded the SEC regulations as more unnecessary Big Brotherism from Washington, impeding a corporation's obligation to disclose material information to its owners. He was already sufficiently opposed to government interference. The SEC handcuffs made him even more obstinate."

Most businessmen who had observed Queeny as an opponent of the New Deal and as an insurgent in the wake of newly imposed SEC policies were inclined to understand—because the shoe that pinched Queeny also pinched them. However, there were also a few who misinterpreted Queeny's motives and who said, in the light of the era of patriotism of 1942, that Queeny had gone a bit too far at a time when all Americans should be standing together.

The 1942 Annual Report of Monsanto ended with these words: "The Monsanto organization gave to the nation its best in a difficult year. Faced with dislocation and losses of markets, interruptions in the flow of raw materials, staffing and bringing new plants into operation, and the meeting of production requirements with many of our personnel in the armed services, Monsanto men and women gave to the fullest of their ability. The Army-Navy 'E' flies over the executive offices and five of our plants. . . . Ninety-eight percent of our personnel have subscribed for war bonds."

Francis J. Curtis, a sensitive and articulate chemical engineer who had come into Monsanto via Merrimac, sensed the strain besetting

Edgar Queeny in 1942. He remarked, "Above all, Edgar was an American. I would call him a Fourth of July American. But few people knew
this. And he was not about to sing 'The Stars and Stripes Forever.' His
fervor for America and for Monsanto was so deep that he simply could
not tolerate any Washington edicts which he thought were wrong. As a
consequence, he was often in a position where he felt he had to speak
out against the policies of the country he loved. I am sure he weighed
the possibilities of his positions being misconstrued. But he had convictions—and he insisted they be aired."

And that was the uncomfortable position of Edgar Queeny and Monsanto in 1942.

This same Frank Curtis became a vice president the following year
and stepped promptly into a singular niche in Monsanto history. A
Harvard-trained scholar, Curtis had an influence—especially in the
company's technical community—that far transcended the formal nature of his job. His official function was to serve as director of Monsanto's program of long-range development in the U.S. and abroad,
including general research and sales development. This was an assignment he tackled with gusto, but it represented only a portion of his
contribution to the company.

A bachelor and proud of it, Frank was a warm and jovial "Friar
Tuck" who had an easy rapport with people. He became one of Monsanto's early champions of the role of chemical engineer. His pink
cheeks would flush pinker when he heard people relegate the engineer to
second-class status.

Many industrial chieftains use the tired old expression about their
doors always being open—but Curtis didn't have to, for it was widely
known that he was, in fact, available as father confessor to those in
search of counsel, solace or encouragement.

In 1943 the biggest news on South Second Street's "Peacock Alley,"
or executive suite, was the elevation of Charles Belknap from executive
vice president to president, Edgar Queeny having relinquished this latter
post while continuing as chairman.

(In its 75-year history, Monsanto has used the executive vice president title rather sparingly, and Belknap was the first. In the late forties
Charles A. Thomas had this title before moving along to the presidency.
In the mid-fifties Robert R. Cole was given the title prior to his retirement, primarily as an expression of gratitude and respect. In 1959
Charles H. Sommer was elected executive vice president before taking
over presidential responsibilities the following year. It was not until
1975–1976 that others—Edmond S. Bauer, H. Harold Bible, Louis Fernandez and James J. Kerley—were honored with this high title.)

There have been vice presidents and group vice presidents and senior
vice presidents and regional vice presidents in the course of executive
realignments, but that special designation executive vice president was
particularly fitting for Charlie Belknap, Navy alumnus and Merrimac

alumnus, who weathered many of the major storms of the period of acquisition and of the early days of World War II. Back in World War I he had been credited by a high government official as the man who brought shipping out of "chaos and confusion" to "organization and efficiency." His elevation from executive vice president to president met with widespread internal acclaim.

Edgar Queeny, in his continuing role as board chairman, may have inadvertently misled a few outsiders when he insisted on taking a cut in salary for relinquishing the presidential chair. Without offense to the leadership qualities of President Belknap, the overpowering reality was that Edgar Queeny's influence was not dramatically diminished by the 1943 change of command. Queeny was still Queeny, titles notwithstanding.

William F. Wendt, longtime handyman in the service department, had an appropriate comment about 1943, plus a little anecdote comparing Edgar Queeny with his father.

Wendt said, "I'll never forget the time in the early twenties when I went to a wholesale hardware house downtown to take advantage of a sale. One broom was forty cents and the second broom cost only twenty cents. When John F. Queeny saw the sixty-cent invoice he reprimanded me harshly and told me, 'This is a one-broom company and when I think it has become a two-broom company, Mr. Wendt, I will so inform you.' I felt chastised. There was no doubt about who was the boss in those days. Equally, there was no doubt about who was the boss even when Edgar Queeny vacated the job as president. It really didn't make any difference what you called him. You could have called him an office boy, but he still would have been Edgar Monsanto Queeny."

In 1943 there wasn't a Monsanto employe who didn't know what Bill Wendt knew. And, to be sure, Charlie Belknap knew—and he knew there was a lot of work to be done. He also knew his new credentials would enable him to exercise greater leadership responsibilities in concert with Queeny during an era that all in Monsanto found challenging and fatiguing.

So now Monsanto had a man known as "the skipper" on the bridge. He had a look of the sea about him. He was distinctive. He even had bushy eyebrows. And he had the honor of being the first import from another company (Merrimac) elected to occupy Monsanto's presidential chair. All prior top corporate officers had been affiliated with the parent company, which was now, in 1943, called the Organic Chemicals Division.

Perhaps Monsanto's proudest day of 1943 came on March 10, when the first tank car of styrene monomer left Texas City for Akron, Ohio, where in a Goodyear plant it was mixed with butadiene to become synthetic rubber for the first U.S. Army Jeep tire in history—styrene from a $17-million plant designed and built by Monsanto, a plant that had come under construction March 17 of the previous year. Before

1943 ended, Monsanto received the Chemical Achievement Award for its round-the-clock scurrying to bring the government's first styrene plant on stream.

Sticking with colorful, tempestuous 1943 . . .

Sales were up over those for 1942, but earnings were down. Queeny commented, "In light of all we've tried to do, what an epitaph!"

The 1943 Annual Report was again eloquent with his feelings. It led off: "It is with regret that we again refrain from publishing an interpretive report of our operations. . . ."

It continued: "In view of prevailing criticisms of industrial earnings, it seems desirable to call attention to one statement of important fact obvious itself from the company's reported net income—*Monsanto Chemical Company is not profiting from this war!* On the contrary, 1943 net profit was less than that of 1942, which in turn was less than that of 1941. Earnings are less now than immediately preceding the war, although wartime sales are the greatest in our history. *Our operations are making no war millionaires.*"

In the same vein, Queeny went on to say, "Realizing the owners of Monsanto Chemical Company are entitled to a fuller report than management is willing to hazard under prevailing circumstances, its officers plan to review in detail the various phases of our company's operations at the forthcoming annual shareowners' meeting." This was part bite, part bark. Queeny was upset.

But he did add this in the Annual Report narrative: "In the past year, Monsanto gave its best to the nation. Approximately 1800 of our men and women have entered the armed services (out of 11,000). Despite this serious drain on our personnel, operations continued at a high rate. Monsanto's substantial contribution to the production of vital war materials is attested by 19 Army-Navy 'E' Awards for excellence in production."

Frank Curtis, sensitive to the things that make people react as people, was a friend who could "read" Edgar Queeny—one who could comprehend what he called "Edgar's mix of pragmatism and idealism." He commented, "This was an era when Edgar had a tug-of-war in his mind and heart. Somehow, he felt the chemical industry's obsession with serving the government during the time of war should have been recognized by a more responsive reaction from Washington lawmakers. The more Edgar pressed on, the more he felt he was being turned off. He didn't really care about glory or recognition. He had the old-fashioned notion that, at a time his country was fighting for freedoms, a few freedoms should be accorded to the business system which was helping the nation in war. He hated bureaucratic interference—and he was not about to be talked into hiding his feelings. Not everybody understood. And I know he knew this. But he would not be dissuaded. He had never figured life as a popularity contest, anyway."

By 1944 Monsanto-watchers had learned not to count on anything beyond a "bare bones" narrative and a heavy sprinkling of digital, tabular material in the Annual Report. But the company was much more outspoken at the Annual Meeting on the fourth Thursday of March, at which time shareowners were provided with some glimpses backward into 1943 and also were offered a view into the present and immediate future.

Among the Annual Meeting speakers was Vice President William M. Rand from Merrimac, who uncorked a stunning statistic when he announced, "It is costing Monsanto $225,000 a year to answer government questionnaires and to fill in federal forms." Bill Rand, still healthy and hearty in retirement at Lincoln, Massachusetts, would no doubt agree that this expense was petty cash compared to the staggering amounts of dollars and manhours spent in subsequent years.

A rather major event involved the acquisition of I. F. Laucks, Inc., Seattle, a customer company which had developed a strong line of plywood glues, along with a wood sealer and primer trade-named Rez and a variety of related products. Laucks would ultimately become the nucleus of what for a brief time Monsanto called its Western Division. Compared to Merrimac, Swann and Fiberloid, Laucks was not a major affair. It commanded 25,000 shares of Monsanto stock, worth $2 million, in June, 1944. The Rez line was marketed by Monsanto for a short period through paint and hardware stores and ultimately sold to Pittsburgh Paint. Laucks adhesives, involving Monsanto resins, remained profitable but unspectacular. But Laucks did help strengthen Monsanto's market position and identity on the West Coast.

Particularly insofar as Monsanto employes were concerned, the warmest story of 1944 involved a major and long-overdue award for one of the "original Swiss," Gaston F. DuBois, who was presented with the prestigious Perkin Medal by the Society of the Chemical Industry before an audience of 500 industry leaders at the Hotel Commodore in New York. This was a year before his retirement, and those who knew him felt the high honor could not possibly have gone to a more worthy recipient. The "fox terrier of research," who had been one of the founder's early lieutenants, was probably tempted in his acceptance speech to look back upon the day when he arrived in St. Louis, shortly after the turn of the century, and to recall how the city was a maze of telephone poles. He could have recalled the adventures of the early days when John F. Queeny was trying to start a new company with one product. Yet instead medalist DuBois gave a humble address, citing the future opportunities of the chemical industry. Despite his opportunities for nostalgia, he looked in one direction—forward.

Monsanto's principal tie with the old Fiberloid Company, John C. Brooks, general manager of the Plastics Division at Springfield, Massachusetts, had become one of DuBois' firmest admirers—perhaps because DuBois, for his part, had become the self-advertised champion of phenolic resins. A sad event of the year was the sudden and unexpected loss of Brooks, who died on a train en route from St. Louis to New York.

Brooks was succeeded at the Plastics Division helm by General Manager Felix N. Williams, who moved from the corresponding job with the Phosphate Division in St. Louis. Williams, in turn, was succeeded at Phosphate by another executive on the way up, Edward A. O'Neal.

The year 1944 also saw Monsanto establish a textile chemicals department at Merrimac. Its principal new products were Resloom, for reducing shrinkage and adding wrinkle-resistance in wool; Resproof, a water repellent for cotton, rayon and wool; and Syton, a sizing agent for nylon and natural fibers. Chemicals for fireproofing and mildew-proofing were also introduced by this department. It was not known at this time, however, that Monsanto's big success in the wide and wonderful world of textiles would not be confined to fiber-treating chemicals but would, in a few short years, be in the exciting and competitive arena of actually manufacturing fibers—through chemistry.

Several high-level changes marked 1945. When Dr. Lloyd F. Nickell, managing director of Monsanto Chemicals Limited, London, retired from the board of directors, he was succeeded by Charles S. Cheston of Philadelphia, former senior partner of Smith Barney & Company. When Gaston DuBois said farewell as a vice president and member of the Executive Committee 41 years after coming over from Switzerland "to see the World's Fair," he was succeeded in these positions by Dr. Charles A. Thomas, director of Central Research at Dayton.

And in September, one "old salt" was succeeded by another when President Charles Belknap retired from that post to be succeeded by Vice President William McNear Rand. The two had been shipmates in the Navy and colleagues at Merrimac. No one applauded more enthusiastically for the new president than the "older skipper," Charlie Belknap.

Rand brought to the presidency a brisk sense of leadership, the genuine respect of Monsanto employes everywhere, and a determination to carry on in the spirit that had made the company so successful in meeting wartime production challenges. Tall and forceful, Rand was every inch a president. If Central Casting in Hollywood had been told to find a symbol of the way an eminent chemical industry president should look, Central Casting could not have found a better embodiment than Bill Rand. But Bill Rand ran deep—in character, integrity and humanity. Of many exemplary qualities, warmth was Bill Rand's trademark. He radiated a genuine sense of concern for employes and others —but employes in particular.

Of course the big news of 1945 was the cessation of hostilities. Shortly after V-J Day the Chemical Warfare Service and the Army Ordnance Department promptly canceled the Monsanto contracts, but the company continued to operate the styrene plant at Texas City, a major installation it would take over from the government at the purchase price of $9,500,000 the following year.

In 1945 it was disclosed that during the war Monsanto had developed for the Army a lightweight armor material for actual wearing by military personnel. It was called Doron and was named for Brigadier General George F. Doriot of the Quartermaster Corps. The product was made of glass cloth and resin, a forerunner of reinforced plastics typified by the famous Fiberglas.

War's end also enabled Edgar Queeny to report that Dr. Charles A. Thomas had led the group of scientists (in 1943 and 1944) who refined the 94th element, plutonium, preparing the way for the development of the atom bomb.

This story is best told by a letter written to Edgar Queeny on August 15, 1945, by Major General L. R. Groves of the War Department:

"With the advent of V-J Day and the realization of the United States and the world that the atomic bomb played a major part in bringing about peace at an earlier date than could otherwise be expected, I wish to personally thank you for the work done by Monsanto Chemical Company.

"A detailed description of your efforts must still remain undisclosed because of security requirements, but I want you to know that Dr. C. A. Thomas and his associates made a major contribution to our success. Dr. Thomas personally coordinated a very important phase of the chemical research pertaining to the project; he also completed vital research and solved production problems of extreme complexity without which the atomic bomb could not have been. . . .

"I also appreciate your taking over the contract for the operation of Clinton Laboratories (near Oak Ridge, Tenn.). . . . Your recognition of the need for industrial management of Clinton Laboratories showed your continued confidence in our prospective success at a time when success had not yet been achieved or even assured.

"I am sure Monsanto Chemical Company will continue to give aid to the nation in carrying on future development in the field of atomic energy."

This was prophetic. Within a few years Monsanto would indeed be busily engaged in researching peacetime uses of atomic energy as a contractor for the Atomic Energy Commission at a large installation called Mound Laboratories at Miamisburg, Ohio.

The message from General Groves was reproduced in *Monsanto Magazine*. In addition, a letter went to all employes saluting them for all they had done to help their nation during World War II.

No one seemed happier in 1946 than Josiah B. Rutter, Merrimac alumnus and now director of corporate engineering, when the company purchased from the government the Texas City styrene plant. Rutter had been the construction boss when the gleaming towers of Texas City were installed in seven days less than a year during the pressure-cooker strain of war's demands. He called the plant his "pride and joy." And he reveled in the company's postwar plans to expand and modernize, to add polystyrene molding compound as well as several petroleum-based intermediates. More than $140 million was ticketed to be spent for this expansion.

By August of 1946 this transfer—from "Uncle Sam to Uncle Edgar," as the joke went—was effected and things looked bright on the sunny Gulf Coast of Texas.

Things had less of a sheen on the labor front. The Chemical Workers Union (AFL) had demanded a closed shop agreement along with a master contract covering Monsanto's St. Louis area plants. Monsanto said no. As a result, three major locations—the John F. Queeny plant in St. Louis, Plant B near East St. Louis, Illinois, and the plant at Everett, Massachusetts—were struck. For almost four months operations were restricted while 4000 workers stayed away from their jobs. When the strike was settled the union gained a tidy package of benefits—but not a closed shop and not a master contract.

President Rand's sights were high as the company moved ahead into other product expansions and into new markets, at home and abroad. His 1946 comments about exports reflect the surge of the times:

"The world demand for products is in excess of our ability to supply. The rate of our current exports is even greater than that of our lend-lease shipments during the war. We are furnishing supplies to European markets. We have resumed shipments to the Philippines. We are increasing our sales to South America. Our representatives are at work in the Far East, South America and India."

He also mentioned that Monsanto had its own production facilities in England, Canada and Australia.

In London, Edward A. O'Neal, who had gone steadily up the ranks in the Phosphate Division, moved in as managing director of Monsanto Chemicals Limited in 1946. The story is best told by O'Neal:

> During the previous year, I had been sent on a special assignment to London to investigate a rumor that the postwar Labour Government in England was considering nationalizing the chemical industry. My most reliable source for checking this out was Lord McGowan of Imperial Chemical Industries, who was high both in industrial and political circles. He assured me there was no such government plan. I reported this to the Monsanto board at its meeting during Christmas Week of 1945.
>
> Then when I was sent to London on a permanent assignment in 1946, employes were just beginning to trickle back from Ruabon, where they had been able to work during the war at their hideaway headquarters, safe from German bombs. MCL had about 50 headquarters employes at the time.
>
> The Ruabon plant very much needed repairs and new processes after the long period of wartime demands in production. The other MCL plant, at Sunderland, on the North Sea, had been demolished by German bombs. Nothing was left but rubble and twisted metal. There was no choice other than to abandon this location.
>
> The job ahead for the British subsidiary was clear—to mold a

stronger company. MCL very much needed an accounting department and an engineering department. But there was insufficient room at Victoria Station House. Granted, we had a long-range plan to build our own office building in the heart of London. But that was a bit in the distance. The only solution was to split up into several locations, awaiting the time we could regroup and occupy our own Monsanto House on Victoria Street near Westminster Abbey.

The overpowering need after the war was plant modernization and maintenance. St. Louis decided we should be responsible for our own financing and encouraged us when we decided to raise $15 million in sterling by placing a third of MCL's shares on the public market.

In retrospect, this was a master stroke. It made Monsanto more a part of the country at a time when British concern about Britain was very important to the national morale. Our parent was known to be American—and it was up to us in the subsidiary to be a part of the place where we lived. The British public now had a piece of the action. This was all to the good.

Throughout Monsanto, in that upbeat year of 1946, optimism prevailed. Consolidated sales were almost $100 million and earnings were $10 million—despite the effects of the four-month strike. Both numbers were all-time records. And capital expenditures were a then-massive $25 million.

One of the major capital expenditures initiated in 1946 was for a $3 million production facility at Plant B, for Santomerse, a "soapless soap." This became the company's first major entry into the dawning era of synthetic detergents. Monsanto had been making Santomerse on a small scale at Nitro, West Virginia, and by 1946 was aware that it had a product which could be an important factor in putting an end to the soap rings around the nation's bathtubs.

Two other important new products—both highly innovative—also came onto the scene during 1946. One, like Santomerse, was an entry in the field of detergents. It was called Sterox low-sudsing detergent. The other was Skydrol nonflammable hydraulic fluid for aircraft.

Each was a "specific remedy for a specific ailment." Each was a Monsanto invention.

The Sterox detergent product was still two years away from being manufactured in commercial quantities in Trenton, Michigan. Yet even in its introductory period it was attracting attention. It had been developed at the Central Research Department in Dayton as an outgrowth of research into phosphate builders and surface-active agents and water softeners.

Central Research staffers, working with many varieties of automatic washing machines in the testing of various phosphate-based detergent compounds, had noticed that high-sudsing detergents were somewhat inefficient when used within the confines of certain kinds of automatic washing machines, mainly the so-called front-loading makes.

Westinghouse Electric Corporation deliberately and specifically called to Monsanto's attention the shortcomings of high-sudsing detergents in the front-loading Westinghouse washers and asked Monsanto if it could come up with an efficient detergent which wouldn't create a heavy mass of suds. Voilà—Sterox low-sudsing detergent!

A dilemma.

On the one hand, the Phosphate Division's No. 1 customer was the detergent industry—"the soapers." Companies like Procter & Gamble, Colgate and Lever Brothers were crucial to Monsanto's present and future. These companies were busily and profitably advertising their high-sudsing detergents all over the land, high-sudsing detergents which were doing a heroic job in a wide variety of household and industrial uses, affording a dramatic improvement over the earlier era of soaps made from animal and vegetable fats.

On the other hand, here came Monsanto with a low-sudsing detergent which would work more efficiently in front-loading automatic washing machines with a water level lower than that in top-loaders.

It was a good-news-and-bad-news situation.

Monsanto's technological breakthrough was the good news. But a bit of a customer relations problem began to loom on the horizon, and this of course was the bad news.

What, Monsanto wondered, will the soapers say about low sudsing at the very time they are trumpeting, via millions of dollars' worth of advertising, the virtues of high sudsing?

Procter & Gamble's late-forties advertising campaign for the general purpose household detergent Tide showed how a small amount would fill a railroad boxcar full of suds. Monsanto was totally in cahoots— and ran its own ad captioned "The Day Niagara Falls Flowed Over," an ad that depicted an overpowering cascade of cleansing suds. Monsanto was, after all, a principal supplier for the high-sudsing phenomenon.

The new low-sudsing product thus developed into a mixed blessing for Monsanto, which had traditionally avoided head-on competition with its major customers. After all, the company's slogan was "Serving Industry Which Serves Mankind."

Here was a company which was the world's largest manufacturer of acetylsalicylic acid, selling this product to drug houses, which packaged it by its more popular name, aspirin. But Monsanto would never dare to compete with those drug houses by taking aspirin tablets straight to the corner supermarket. Here was a company making plastic raw materials, but one which would never dare to compete with the manufacturers of plastic countertops, toys, toothbrushes, appliance parts. Here was a company calling itself the world's largest in the mining and general technology of elemental phosphorus, and a company basic in phosphate raw materials, which would never dare to alienate a major segment of its industrial phosphates market, namely: the soapers.

The product called Sterox low-sudsing detergent—later to be christened "all" detergent—brought Monsanto to the crossroads. Introduced in 1946 and manufactured in large quantity a few years later, this turned out to be one of the company's most exciting products and it became, for better or worse, one of the reasons why Monsanto decided later—in 1952—to "go retail." The chain-reacting consequences are discussed in detail in Chapter IX.

But the low-sudsing detergent was not the only big postwar news from the laboratory. Skydrol nonflammable hydraulic fluid for aircraft was also a subject of special attention.

Keeping in mind 1946 was still a bit prior to the jet age, it is useful to remember that in piston-powered aircraft with reciprocating engines, vibration was an omnipresent factor. Hydraulic lines carrying fluid to various parts of the aircraft—for the control of such essentials as flaps and landing gear—were much like the arteries in a human body. Vibration was a constant problem to cope with—vibration which could cause joints in a hydraulic system to rupture, and could result in a leak spraying liquid under pressure—flammable liquid. When such liquid was sprayed onto hot metal, a fire could result. Even sparks could ignite such a liquid.

The need, plainly, was for a nonflammable hydraulic fluid—one which could bring a new measure of safety to aircraft operations, which could remain stable, could withstand pressure, could flow easily, and could provide sufficient lubricity for use within the pumps powering the hydraulic systems.

The call to Monsanto came from Douglas Aircraft Company, manufacturer of commercial and military aircraft operating around the world. Monsanto's research mission was announced early in 1946 and by 1948 Skydrol was available in commercial quantity. Douglas Aircraft had not only sounded the alarm but had cooperated at every inch of the two-year research road. The problem-solving product Skydrol was precisely tailored to fit a need—to do a specific job and to do it effectively.

Monsanto had been saying all along its products were in the public interest. Here was another piece of evidence to back up the claim. Skydrol would not even ignite in manifold tests when it was sprayed onto a surface at 1300 degrees Fahrenheit.

Its use subsequently continued on into the jet age—around the world. Jets would have less vibration but an even greater number of arteries carrying hydraulic fluid through their airframes.

Edgar Queeny was especially proud. An aviation enthusiast and a member of the board of directors of American Airlines, he liked the whole idea of having Monsanto associated with aircraft safety. More than once he pointed to the sky and commented, "You'll find Monsanto up there."

CHAPTER VII

Texas City, April 16, 1947

T HE year 1947 began as a period of promise. Progress seemed assured by momentum alone. The mood was *grow*. A new Western Division was announced, to accommodate the acquisition of I. F. Laucks, Inc., and a Texas Division was formed to provide an adequate setting for the high styrene towers that served as the proud focal point of the company's newly acquired engineering gem at Texas City.

At the March Annual Meeting, optimism prevailed.

Then came April 16, 1947.

It was a bright day in St. Louis, befitting the company's general mood. Chairman Edgar Queeny was in New York attending a morning meeting of the board of directors of American Airlines. President Bill Rand was aboard a train en route from Boston to Springfield, Massachusetts. Vice President Charlie Thomas, six weeks away from his step up to executive vice president, was in Atlantic City attending a meeting of the American Chemical Society, of which he was president-elect.

The only officer on Executive Row on South Second Street was cool, experienced, wiry Vice President Osborne Bezanson, self-styled "operating man's operating man" who had cut his teeth in the Merrimac part of the Monsanto family.

Turning now 800 miles south, to the Gulf Coast . . .

There, too, the day dawned with flawless clarity and brilliance over Texas City, Texas, and the curving coastal plain around it. Later on, an observer commented on the cloudless sky and recalled that two small planes had been buzzing in the otherwise unoccupied blue over the glistening Monsanto styrene plant.

At ground level all was quiet.

Within the Monsanto plant, employes had checked in for another day. All was routine.

Construction workers employed by contractors had also moved in for a day of work, adding new hardware to the massive installation.

The Monsanto plant was an industrial city in itself, making styrene around the clock, and workers were trying to get the bugs out of a new polystyrene manufacturing unit sputtering its way to the state known as "on stream."

There was, it should be mentioned, one unusual circumstance in the neighborhood—quiet but unusual. A French freighter, the S.S. *Grandcamp*, which was tied up at a pier at the Seatrain docks, adjacent to newly established railroad spurs, was sending up a curious, orangish-brown column of smoke from one of its cargo holds. The ship was 270 feet from the Monsanto boundary, a few blocks from the heart of the small community of Texas City, 8 miles from Galveston and 40 miles southeast of Houston.

Many of the 574 people in the Monsanto plant were about to die.

Many of the 18,000 inhabitants of the then-little-known town of Texas City were about to die.

The pilots of the two small aircraft—circling in curiosity around the unusual plume of smoke—were about to be blown out of the sky to their deaths.

At precisely 9:12 A.M. it happened.

The S.S. *Grandcamp* blew up.

The ship had taken on 2500 tons of ammonium nitrate fertilizer sent from U.S. government ordnance plants in Nebraska and Iowa for an ultimate destination in South America.

But the cargo in the hold had ignited and exploded.

An unparalleled disaster.

People who survived later described that moment as "a flaming end of the world" and "the most horrible sound mixed in with the most horrible sight."

The incredible news was initially relayed to Monsanto's St. Louis public relations department by a soft-spoken, diligent United Press reporter named Stanley Mockler. He phoned, almost routinely, to inquire if Monsanto could confirm a freshly arrived, Teletype bulletin that said the giant Monsanto plant at Texas City had blown up and was in flames.

The stunned silence in response no doubt told the reporter something of Monsanto's shock and surprise.

Disaster planning notwithstanding, no company is ever ready for a phone inquiry like that.

A routine check, St. Louis to Texas City, was out of the question because of a national telephone strike. Vice President Oz Bezanson was equally stunned when the United Press inquiry was passed along to him. His response: "Let me check it out; keep cool."

Bezanson, self-composed and orderly by instinct and habit, asked his secretary to get Joe Mares, the Texas Divisional general manager, on the telephone fast. But no southbound call got through. "Don't worry. Someone down in Texas will find a way to reach you," he said.

Bezanson's anxious wait was fruitful because Joseph R. Mares was able during this daytime nightmare to initiate, on his own, a northbound telephone report to headquarters. He had informed a Texas telephone operator that it was an emergency of the highest order.

The Mares incident itself was unusual. One might wonder why he was not at his office in the plant at 9:12 A.M. "Why was the captain not upon the bridge?" was a frequent query.

Here's why: Joe Mares had been up until about 3:30 A.M. the night before. He had stayed on at the plant, where effort was being pressed to coax the new polystyrene operation into production. It was about three o'clock in the morning when he left the plant. A half hour later he turned in at the Galvez Hotel in Galveston, dog tired.

With his family still in St. Louis, scheduled to move to Texas at the end of the school year in June, Joe Mares was "batching it" at the Galvez.

Mares recalled last year, "I slept in a bit. I had left the hotel a little before nine A.M. and had driven over the causeway to the mainland. Between the causeway and the Texas City cutoff, the first indication I had was the physical jolt. Then, looking to the right, I saw our plant was in flames."

He tried to disbelieve but couldn't.

His heart urged him to race to the plant. His head told him to get word to St. Louis.

Somehow he found a public phone in the town of Texas City and insisted his call was urgent. When he finally got St. Louis and talked to Oz Bezanson, all he knew was that the magnificent styrene plant was an inferno. And he so reported.

Mares didn't know then about the earlier telltale plume of smoke, about the ship, about the ammonium nitrate. He knew only what his ears and eyes had witnessed. The plant was a holocaust. He knew his employes, his friends, were somewhere in that maelstrom.

A pale, tense, trembling Oz Bezanson summoned several appropriate people for a meeting in President Rand's office. He sorted things out, best as one can in a state of shock. He kept repeating, "We've got to get down there. We've got to get down there."

After breaking the news to his colleagues, he asked for suggestions. Someone asked, "Who'll tell Edgar Queeny and Bill Rand? Where's Dr. Kelly? Shouldn't we alert all our employes?"

Effort was already under way to reach Queeny and Rand. One of the secretaries nearby was asked to try to reach Dr. R. Emmet Kelly, head of the medical department, who was at Oak Ridge, Tennessee. The public relations man in attendance phoned the personnel department to discuss setting up a system to keep employes informed. A secretary was asked to phone the Monsanto flight office at the airport and to get several planes ready for immediate departure.

The first plane to take off, a twin-engine Beechcraft, carried Bezanson and the public relations staffer. It was en route south within an hour. Pilot George Myers kept switching to commercial radio stations to pick up the news bulletins. He passed the earphones to his passengers. It was during this interval that the group learned the Monsanto plant had not exploded but that the S.S. *Grandcamp* had. When the public relations man suggested that the facts be set forth promptly upon arrival, Pilot Myers shrugged his shoulders and commented, "I'm sure that's what you'll have to do, but what has happened has happened and the cause seems sort of secondary." He was thinking of the tragedy, which was ongoing, irrespective of the nature of its origin.

No flight could ever have been more tense.

Smoke over Texas City was visible a half hour before landing.

The "bright year" for Monsanto was transformed into the saddest episode in the company's annals.

To this day, no one has capsulized the tragedy of Texas City more movingly than Edgar Queeny. His April 30 letter to shareowners, employes and friends was his idea, his language. Business observers were later to call it a classic. It was Pragmatist Queeny/Idealist Queeny under stress. The Texas City story is best told as he told it:

To Monsanto Shareowners, Employes and Friends:

As soon as we learned of the crushing misfortune that overtook Texas City, Mr. Rand and I, who were in the East, flew to the scene. Before landing, we circled the holocaust. You have heard it described in the press and over your radio. The reporters did not exaggerate. Exaggeration would have been impossible; our language is too inadequate.

The French liner *Grandcamp*, burdened with 2500 tons of ammonium nitrate, was berthed at a quay immediately opposite our own. More ammonium nitrate, which has an explosive power about one-half as great as T.N.T., was on the dock at which she was loading. About half past eight on the morning of April sixteenth, fire was noticed on the *Grandcamp*. Soon after her crew abandoned her, and the nitrate exploded, subjecting portions of our plant to an impact we believe to be equivalent to 250 five-ton blockbusters exploding simultaneously. Because the atomic bombs were exploded high above Hiroshima and Nagasaki, the blast beneath them we believe may have been less severe than that suffered by parts of our plant.

Our warehouse—a steel and brick structure—was flattened; not a splinter remained upright. The main power plant was similarly crushed. As the blast fanned out, walls of manufacturing buildings fell, windows of the plant office and laboratories shattered, roofs were ripped off, and pipe lines carrying inflammable liquids were torn apart. A huge wave, rushing in from the basin where the ship had rested, inundated the area while the explosion's heat ignited the benzol, propane and ethyl benzene pouring out of the ruptured pipes and storage tanks. Savage and cruel fires, feeding on these inflammable liquids, scalded those who had fallen, and melted and twisted steel supports and girders.

Preventing effective rescue, these fires raged two days, sending up a mile-high Vesuvian wick which joined the titanic smoke columns arising from the nearby storage tanks of oil refineries, forming a pitchy umbra over the racked and grief-laden community.

Because our payroll records were kept in the plant and were scattered by the blast, we are without an accurate list of those on duty at the time. We employed 658 persons in this plant. After most careful checking, we believe that 451 were on duty at the time. Of this number, 154 were either killed or are missing and believed dead; more than 200 required hospitalization; and 95 of the more seriously injured are still in hospitals. Some of them are not expected to survive. While there were many miraculous escapes from death, few escaped without the proverbial scratch! Almost all those not requiring hospitalization needed some medical aid.

In addition to our own casualties, 123 employes of outside contractors were engaged on construction in our plant. As most of them were working in areas of greatest exposure, their ratio of death and injury was greater than our own. Of the combined forces in our plant, the dead, missing and believed dead total 227—more than one-third of the whole area's total.

While Fate usually plays no favorites, our technical staff suffered the heaviest proportion of casualties. J. R. Mares, General Manager of our Texas Division, was fortunate; he did not reach the plant until a few minutes after the *Grandcamp* exploded. But glass was blown into the brain of H. K. Eckert, our Plant Manager. Although he remained for a few days in a critical condition, he is expected to recover. Charles Comstock, the Division's Technical Director; B. F. Merriam, Chief Plant Engineer; R. E. Boudinot, Production Manager; R. D. Southerland, Safety Engineer; and F. A. Ruecker, Chief Power Engineer, and all his staff, are dead. Robert Morris, Assistant Plant Manager survived, although the plant jeep in which he was riding, seeking a tug to pull the *Grandcamp* into the bay, was hurled high in the air and overturned. He was saved by the giant wave which covered him. With punctured eardrums and painful bruises, he rescued many trapped office workers.

Of seventeen young and promising chemists who were supervising production in different departments, sixteen perished, leaving behind many young widows and families of tiny ones. To this list may be added other technical men who are still in critical condition.

Several other company officials came to Texas City to help, organize and plan. Among the first arrivals were Dr. Emmet Kelly, our Medical Director, and some of his staff. A plane-load of nurses and medical supplies was also flown in.

Friday, Mr. Rand and I accompanied Dr. Kelly on his round of the hospitals. As we visited with our own stricken and saw the conditions of others, it was impossible for us to contain emotions. But we heard not one word of recrimination nor any attempt to fix blame. Each accepted his anguish stoically as the lot which Fate had cast for him. We attempted to solace wives sitting beside husbands whose lives were in the balance. Their manner was brave but their eyes betrayed the torment of their souls.

A young girl, shattered and barely conscious, who had been in charge of payroll records, seemed to be worried only about the loss of her records. Another girl, bandage-swathed and disfigured forever by flying glass, touched us to the quick by saying softly, "Oh, I'm so sorry for Monsanto, losing so many fine men." Many evidences of unselfishness, heroism, pluck and courage were unveiled to us!

By Friday morning, except for the benzol storage tanks which continued to burn, most fires in our plant had subsided. We visited the ruins. Fires still raged in both Humble and Republic Oil companies' nearby tanks, raising a huge Bikini-like pillar of pall 3,000 feet into an otherwise clear sky, where it was joined by the gray of our own benzol. There, both plumed and stratified, forming a gloomy awning of darkness which drifted on southerly winds. Monsanto pilots flying to St. Louis that afternoon reported that these clouds stretched to Missouri's southern border.

The smoldering rubble in our plant still hissed as fire boats played streams upon it. Squads of Red Cross men were engaged in the dangerous work of removing bodies. Bulldozers had cleared pathways through the rubble, along which we passed stretcher after stretcher bearing the charred organic remains of employes. It was heartbreaking and gruesome; memories of it will haunt us forever.

Attempts to assuage the grief of the victims of such a disaster are ineffective, this being within the province of Time alone. But Mr. Rand and I believed that our shareowners would approve alleviating the financial problems attending the changed circumstances of so many of our employes. Hence we offered immediate payments of $1,000 in case of each death to each widow or nearest dependent. Almost all employes of over three months' Monsanto employment were covered by our Group Insurance Plan, and as accidental death doubles the payment, the beneficiary of an insured hourly employe will receive $6,000 to $8,000 in insurance. Since insurance payments increase in ratio to salary, the widow of a man who earned $7,500, for instance, will receive $17,500. Our Treasurer and a representative of the Metropolitan Life Insurance Company began making payments forty-eight hours after the blast.

In addition, Texas law requires in such fatality cases the payment to the widow or beneficiary of $20 a week for 360 weeks—$7,200. Our legal liability in this respect is covered by Liberty Mutual Insurance Company, who will make the payments.

We requested all cases of special hardship to make known their needs to our Texas City Personnel Officer, who was granted authority to deal liberally with them.

We also announced that hospitalization costs of our injured employes and their dependents, not covered by the employes' Blue Cross scheme, would be borne by the company and that full base salaries and wages would be guaranteed to them during both hospitalization and convalescence; and further, that all who suffered permanent injuries preventing re-employment would receive individual and liberal consideration beyond compensation for which we are legally liable.

Our hastily established housing group has made temporary repairs to the homes of 148 employes, and more are being cared for as rapidly as material becomes available. We are surveying all housing damage and other losses suffered by our people, and our Texas Division officers are instructed to do all possible to alleviate hardship.

We arranged to pay for the transportation of the remains of employes whom we had moved into the area and for the transportation of their families and household goods to their former homes, if they desired. We also guaranteed widows of those we had moved into Texas City against any loss of the equities they had acquired in their homes, in the event they desired to move away.

Hourly employes who are able to work were guaranteed their wages through April twenty-seventh. Thereafter, we hope to find employment for most of them in the work of clearing the site and reconstruction.

To provide for the cost of these payments which are beyond our legal liabilities and to reward outstanding cases of heroism, our Board of Directors has appropriated $500,000. All of our legal liabilities will be discharged by our insurance companies. We hope our shareowners will approve the use of this part of their profits to alleviate the misfortunes of the men, women and bereaved families of those who worked for them.

But the contribution Monsanto as a company is offering is not the whole story. Monsanto employes are also showing their feelings for the sufferers in the disaster area. Various Monsanto plants have started voluntary collections, a spontaneous personal expression of their sympathy.

At Oak Ridge, where Monsanto operates the Clinton Laboratories, a number of employes are giving the equivalent to a day's pay. At Trenton, Michigan, donations have been coming in with cooperation of the Union. Seattle and Vancouver employes of Monsanto's Western Division are contributing. The Phosphate Division sales office in Birmingham, Alabama, the Western Division sales office in San Francisco, California, the main office at St. Louis, Missouri, and the Central Research Laboratories at Dayton, Ohio, all sent in generous donations. At Carondelet, Missouri, and Anniston, Alabama, plans are under way to assist employes of the stricken plant. By no means can this be the entire story for it will be weeks before all the facts are known, all the stories told of sacrifice, sympathy and understanding of the multitude who gave in the time of need.

Due to the magnitude of the disaster and the anxiety for news, some erroneous statements were circulated. We should like to correct some of them.

The ammonium nitrate aboard the *Grandcamp* did not originate in any Monsanto plant; Monsanto does not manufacture ammonium nitrate. Nor was it being loaded at our dock, nor was it destined for any of our plants. We do not use it.

Our Texas City plant did not use or manufacture *any* explosives. Several inflammable products such as benzol and propane consti-

tuted its raw materials. It manufactured monomeric styrene and polystyrene; the former is inflammable but the latter will only support
combustion like wood—the distinction between an explosive and an
inflammable being that the former can be detonated on impact and
the latter bursts into flame when ignited.

There were no major explosions in our Texas City plant. None of
the minor ones, described by our surviving staff as "puffs," was
great enough to cause any damage outside our plant area. The main
fires in our plant were in the storage tanks and tank cars of benzol,
propane and ethyl benzene, an intermediate in the manufacture of
styrene.

Our Texas City operation was not considered a hazardous one—
no more so than oil refining, which it resembled. It carried the same
insurance rates as oil refineries.

An irresponsible criticism of the plant's design by an employe of
a contractor who had been engaged in its construction received wide
publicity. Unfortunately, a repudiation of his statement by the president of that company was not widely publicized. There were no
construction faults accountable for even a part of the disaster. In
rebuilding, we expect to utilize the same type of construction. No
manufacturing plant is designed as a fortress, nor could many for-
tresses withstand a blast such as came from the *Grandcamp*. The
plant also contained fire protection approved by our insurance companies; it was adequate to cope with any foreseeable contingency.

There were rumors in financial circles that our insurance coverage
was inadequate. The plant and its contents were insured for $14,-
750,000, which covered the plant inventory of approximately
$1,000,000 and the depreciated value of its buildings, machinery
and equipment on a 90% co-insurance clause. As we have no estimates of reconstruction costs, we do not know how far our insurance
receipts will fall short of them. In addition, the plant was covered
by $7,500,000 of Use and Occupancy insurance and $2,500,000 of
Public Liability insurance.

Of course, the loss of such an important unit will have adverse
effect on future profits, although Use and Occupancy insurance will
compensate during the coming twelve months in large degree. But
the greatest loss will be in the potential profits from several derivatives of styrene which we planned to manufacture and which must
now await either the rebuilding of the Texas City plant or supplies
of styrene monomer from other sources. We are actively exploring
every avenue. We are hopeful of securing a substantial supply but
it is not likely that we can purchase enough to carry on with our
recent program.

Our plant was the first to produce styrene for the manufacture of
synthetic rubber so desperately needed after Pearl Harbor. It is now
gone and with it many of the men—chemists and engineers who
contributed to perfecting the process in the laboratory and in the
pilot plant stages. Working literally day and night in the dark days
of 1942, their ideas and designs took shape in the mass of pipes,

apparatus, columns, mortar and bricks at Texas City. The physical part of the men and the plant have gone, but not the products of their minds. These will live on. Based on their contributions and that of others, we will build again at Texas City on their foundations. The results of their work will continue to serve their fellow men.

The company has many friends. Hundreds of messages of sympathy and offers of assistance poured into our offices from customers, competitors, individuals and suppliers. Many came from far corners of the earth. All were comforting and appreciated.

I should like to pay tribute to the splendid work of those remarkable organizations, the Red Cross, the Salvation Army, the Volunteers of America, the Boy Scouts of America, the United States Army's medical staff, the staffs of the hospitals in the area, and the officials of both the State of Texas and the City of Texas City, for the way in which they responded to the challenge of the emergency. The manner in which the Monsanto staff overcame the initial shock and established an effective organization to command a most difficult situation—they immediately planned for the future—was gratifying in the highest degree.

Sometimes it takes a tragedy to bring forth the better qualities of human beings. Our visit to Texas City made us proud to be Americans and especially so to belong to the exceptionally able group of them making up Monsanto.

April 30, 1947   Edgar M. Queeny

To complete the record on Texas City, the digital recap follows:

The total death toll in the region was 512 people. This included 145 Monsanto employes.

Almost 3,400 residences in Texas City were damaged or destroyed. Total damage attributable to the disaster was in the range of $90 million.

Monsanto's insurance claims totaled $22,317,937. The claims were settled for $17,312,000—then the largest sum ever paid for a single loss.

Yet the numbers tell only part of the story.

The heroic part dealt with the response of people helping people, with the town's ultimate re-emergence—and with Monsanto's.

During late 1947 work was pressed to clear away the debris at the plant. By early 1948 new construction was underway.

Companies after deaths are like families after deaths. Life moves on.

ON April 16, 1949, precisely two years after the explosion and fire, Monsanto executives from St. Louis went to Texas City to honor the living and the dead—and to dedicate the new plant that had risen on the ashes of the old. Styrene monomer was still the dominant product at the new and sparkling installation. Polystyrene—the molding compound based on styrene monomer—was also involved in the new product lineup. In subsequent years Texas City would come on stream with such products as acrylonitrile for synthetic fibers, vinyl chloride, plastic resins, acetylene (for acrylonitrile), low-density polyethylene, methanol (wood alcohol) and ethylene (for many uses). Texas City had been a "pride and joy" before the tragedy in 1947. It would become a more important major installation in the new era.

Yet product groups were not the item of discussion April 16, 1949. The most poignant event of the day was the dedication of a granite memorial bearing the names of the 145 men and women of Monsanto who had lost their lives two years earlier.

The inscription on the memorial: "The physical part of the men and the plant have gone, but not the products of their minds. These will live on"—words from Queeny's April 30, 1947, letter.

The brief memorial ceremony at the plant was attended by appropriate Monsanto personnel and by a liberal sprinkling of citizens from the still-rebuilding town of Texas City. There had been a company/city partnership prior to the tragedy. The partnership was continuing. It was the key to the rebirth. The ongoing involvement, each with the other, was compelling.

Following the ceremony at the plant—under the same kind of clear skies as had been the cover for the horrors just two short years earlier—there was a dinner in Houston that evening, at the then-new Shamrock Hotel. In attendance were citizens of Texas City, Monsanto officials and a generous representation of Houston-area businessmen. The principal speaker at the dinner was Karl T. Compton, chairman of the Research and Development Board of the National Military Establishment and chairman of the Massachusetts Institute of Technology.

The most memorable thoughts of the evening were expressed by President Bill Rand of Monsanto. He said:

"Since the initial plant was built at Texas City, none of the reasons that brought us here have changed—raw materials, transportation facilities and the friendliness of the people. When the question of whether or not we should rebuild arose, however, these things did not assume the importance in comparison to an overwhelming reason. We had lost many of the men who had built the plant. We had lost some of the men in whose dreams today's better plant had been formed. Their friends and associates, who still lived, shared those dreams. Could a company abandon such a force? Our decision to rebuild was immediate and spontaneous."

A financial editor from the *Houston Chronicle*, attending another meeting that night at the Shamrock Hotel, quietly moved into the back of the room where the Monsanto post-dinner program was being held. After hearing Bill Rand's comments, he remarked to a friend, "I don't think I have ever heard an American businessman who has more earnestly meant every word he said."

He was right.

Bill Rand had said it all. Monsanto had both its heart and its head in the rebirth of Texas City. Both the idealism and pragmatism of Edgar Queeny had been served.

CHAPTER VIII

The Birth and Growth of Chemstrand

IN May, 1949, a company announcement said, "Monsanto Chemical Company and American Viscose Corporation have joined in the formation of a new company to engage in research and development work in the field of synthetic fibers. The corporation, as yet unnamed, will be headed by Dr. Carroll A. Hochwalt of Dayton, a Monsanto vice president, and will pursue its research and development work through the laboratories of Monsanto and Viscose."

The announcement also identified the composition of the board of directors for this new joint venture.

What, one might ask, was the significance of this deliberately wooden, fractionally informative disclosure?

Was such an unobtrusive little item in fact the start of something big?

Answer: This was the door to a new era for Monsanto, the entry into a new world—the wide and wondrous world of synthetic fibers, in which DuPont had already staked out an enviable claim.

Prior to the mid-thirties, the world had been clothed in wool, cotton and silk—and animal hides. Rayon from cellulose had been destined to make something of a small mark. But the big news was yet to come.

Man-made fibers began to move into the picture in 1928, when Dr. Wallace H. Carothers and a team of DuPont scientists started the study of polymerization. In the early thirties they were able to produce a clear, molasseslike polymer which, when molten, could be drawn into a fiber. They were working with compounds called polyesters and polyamides.

The polyesters were shunted aside, at least for the time being, and attention was given to a polyamide made from hexamethylene diamine and adipic acid. The first satisfactory results were announced and the product emerged in 1935, although some patents had been registered all along, during the research and development countdown.

They called it nylon.

Actually, it was Nylon, with a capital N, at the start, a product protected not only by a broad series of patents but also by a registered trademark for Nylon fiber.

No one knew in 1935 that trademark-protected Nylon would become a generic word, nylon. And no one knew that this man-made fiber would create a revolution in fabrics, in apparel, in tire cords and in industrial usages for which natural fibers had never even been considered.

Dr. Hochwalt had a "layman's recipe" to explain how nylon was made: Take 2½ tons of water, 80 pounds of steam, 43 pounds of air, 1¾ pounds of cyclohexane, 5 pounds of natural gas, ¾ pound of ammonia and indefinite amounts of 27 other materials—and sprinkle generously with large amounts of skill and patience.

By the forties DuPont's nylon was a household word, and DuPont had also begun to work on an acrylic fiber, to be called Orlon.

Starting in 1942, at Monsanto's Central Research Department in Dayton, work was pressed on the chemistry and, subsequently, on the spinning of a highly sophisticated kind of acrylic fiber. The raw material acrylonitrile was nothing new to the Dayton scientists, but the processes they invented were new—processes which involved polymerizing acrylonitrile into a white powder and dissolving it into a syrupy liquid to be pumped through a device called a spinnerette. Once the material was forced through the spinnerette it could be dried and formed into staple fibers, somewhat resembling natural wool.

Just as DuPont had protected its chemistry and spinning techniques by patents for its fibers, Monsanto similarly began to protect its know-how by patents through the mid-forties.

By 1949 Monsanto was confident it had a bright new technological wonder at its Dayton labs—a proprietary fiber made from acrylonitrile.

When the announcement was made about the joint venture with American Viscose, J. R. (Rusty) Wilson, director of Monsanto's patent department, was intensively searching for two trademarks—one for the acrylic fiber and one for the newly announced company. Shortly thereafter, Wilson was confident he had come upon two words which would not conflict with previously registered trademarks and which would therefore become assets in themselves for the years ahead: Acrilan acrylic fiber for the product, and Chemstrand Corporation for the 50-50 company.

It was fitting that Ted Hochwalt should become Chemstrand's first president, largely because so many of the day-and-night hours of research had been literally under his nose at the Central Research Department in Dayton.

When Charlie Thomas, the executive vice president in St. Louis, and Ted Hochwalt lyricized Acrilan's potential for Chairman Queeny and President Rand they found enthusiastic encouragement. And when the Monsanto board was advised that the company could be on the threshold of a rewarding achievement in a field new to the company, the board was willing to commit a major investment of dollars and manpower in what Bill Rand called "the bouncing new baby from our Dayton labs."

Why did Monsanto tie in with Viscose instead of going it alone? Two principal reasons: The investment was, of course, cut in half, and Viscose, as a fibers company (mainly rayon), knew the market. Monsanto's only related experience had been in making and applying various chemicals to improve the properties of natural fibers. This experience in fibers and in textiles, alongside Viscose's, was meager.

Rusty Wilson recalls: "All of a sudden we were hearing a foreign language containing such words as throwsters, dyers, converters, cutters and griege goods."

Monsanto didn't have time to get educated from scratch, particularly in light of DuPont's head start with nylon and Orlon. The latter fiber, also from acrylonitrile, was more woollike than the silklike nylon. Monsanto's Acrilan was also woollike. But it was not just a "me too" fiber. Its Dayton inventors were convinced that it had unique properties, that it could be made as a staple or as a filament, and that it would lend itself to a wide variety of uses, including apparel but—importantly —beyond apparel.

As things turned out, Acrilan had—in addition to its unique advantages—one surprising and unique disadvantage in its early years. The fiber misbehaved; it did something called "fibrillating."

In point of fact, the fiber showed no signs of serious misbehavior within the limits of its small-scale production at Dayton. Even when it was moved to a pilot plant owned by Viscose at Marcus Hook, Pennsylvania, the dimensions of its shortcomings weren't sufficiently appreciated. Not until it was made in quantity at Chemstrand's first plant in Decatur, Alabama, did Acrilan reveal its basic flaw: susceptibility to fibrillation.

What's fibrillation? Well, the fibers scaled; they ruptured. When used in, let us say, a dark-blue sweater, the fibers would break down at a crucial point, such as the elbows. When the fabric ruptured—as though its components had been too brittle—the white core of each individual damaged fiber would become exposed. The sweater's elbows would no longer be blue. A bit of white would peek through.

This was disconcerting—and embarrassing.

Also, the product wasn't as soft and woollike as DuPont's Orlon. It was somewhat rougher and fuzzier. Its "hand," or "feel," left something to be desired. An anecdote that didn't seem too funny to Monsanto at the time went as follows: A man with the National Cotton Council at Memphis, who had encountered an Acrilan fiber product somewhere, sent a small bottle of ointment to a Monsanto friend with this note: "Suggest rubbing your skin with this salve, containing some good, old-fashioned cottonseed oil, to eliminate the itch caused by that scratchy Acrilan, which reminds me of shredded wheat."

So it was back to the drawing board, under stress and duress, at the Dayton labs. Ultimately a process improvement materialized, using steam to eliminate the old devil, fibrillation. But, meantime, the giant new Acrilan plant at Decatur had been closed down.

Naturally, neither the Monsanto board nor the Viscose board nor the Chemstrand board was happy. For almost two years the "bouncing, new baby" gave every indication of remaining a delinquent—requiring more research, more testing, more time, more dollars, more patience.

The problems went beyond fibrillation and were accentuated by the fact that Chemstrand was a new entity in the marketplace, trying to make a mark and find its way. Both Charlie Thomas and Ted Hochwalt still shake their heads when they remember those "long days." In retrospect it's easy for them to look back and say, "We knew we'd lick the problem and be on our way." Yet their colleagues were inclined to be a little impatient during Chemstrand's early years.

The trial period for Chemstrand was not all tribulation. There was a bright side as well. This was briefly hinted at in the Monsanto 1950 Annual Report: "The company is negotiating with E. I. du Pont de Nemours and Company for a license to manufacture and sell nylon."

At the Annual Meeting of shareowners on South Second Street in March of 1951, the nylon license was referred to when President Rand mentioned that negotiations with DuPont were "nearing their final stage."

At that time no one knew or even guessed the extent of the costly delays Acrilan was about to encounter. No one knew or guessed that fibrillation, plus start-up problems at Decatur, Alabama, plus delays in market penetration would ultimately result in Acrilan's causing Chemstrand a $20-million loss over a period of nearly ten years. Edgar Queeny's high-noon comment: "A nightmare."

When viewed in such perspective, the pursuit of the nylon license— or, better stated, pursuit of rapid profitability for Chemstrand—looms all the more heroically. In fact nylon turned out to be one of the most dramatic heroes in Monsanto history. Viewed in the context of melodramas of the old days, nylon was the gallant savior rescuing Nell from the fibrillating Acrilan rope which bound her to the railroad tracks.

Rusty Wilson tells the pursuit-of-the-DuPont-license story in a slightly more detached way than Charlie Thomas or Ted Hochwalt, who still wince when the word "fibrillation" is spoken in their presence. Rusty Wilson is more wince-resistant. In addition, he had the advantage of viewing the quest for nylon from a slightly different position. His version goes like this:

> In 1950, an antitrust suit had recently been filed against DuPont by the Department of Justice, alleging DuPont and ICI [Imperial Chemical Industries of London] had an agreement under which they would not compete against each other in nylon.
>
> DuPont wanted an arm's length arrangement with an American licensee for nylon for two reasons: 1) It wanted a competitor to remove the sting of having a U.S. monopoly on nylon, and 2) it wanted a yardstick to measure what DuPont should rightfully charge for know-how, if and when the day would ever come when an

antitrust decree would require DuPont to make nylon know-how and patents available to others.

During the forties DuPont had been contacted by many companies, each requesting to be considered if the day might ever dawn when DuPont would be willing to discuss licensing its nylon know-how and patents. Monsanto was on such a list and so was American Viscose—long prior to the Monsanto-Viscose association in Chemstrand.

Yet DuPont initiated its first contact with Eastman Kodak. And Eastman said no. I should add at this point that later on President Bill Rand was puzzled as to why Eastman said no. Upon investigating he learned that Eastman declined to negotiate with DuPont not because of the potential of nylon but because Eastman had a policy of not incurring a debt of the magnitude which would be required to get into the nylon business.

Considering Monsanto and Viscose were both on the DuPont list, and considering these two companies were now united in the Chemstrand venture, it is easy to see how DuPont was able to kill two birds with one rock in agreeing to enter into preliminary discussions with Chemstrand.

Thanks to Charlie Thomas's long friendship with Hank DuPont [Henry B. DuPont] and Crawford Greenewalt, several DuPont representatives, including President Greenewalt, agreed to come to Monsanto's Central Research Department at Dayton for the initial and super-secret meeting with the Chemstrand board—in 1950.

And that, says Rusty Wilson, is how the nylon discussions got under way—on Monsanto's home ground, at the same Dayton laboratory where Chemstrand's founding fiber, Acrilan, was invented.

"Did the Chemstrand board members seem interested when DuPont laid out its preliminary proposal at Dayton?" was a "does a cat like milk?"–type question for which Rusty Wilson found a prompt answer in St. Louis when Chemstrand President Hochwalt called him in and knighted him as the ad hoc chairman of a team to work with DuPont in setting forth a fair and equitable formula. The time: May, 1950. The priority: very high.

Before looking at the negotiation period, it is appropriate to look at the man who spearheaded the urgent task. Rusty Wilson was (and is) a special sort of hybrid—part lawyer, part patent expert, part chemist, part chemical engineer. He had received his bachelor's degree in chemical engineering and his master's degree in organic chemistry before getting his law degree. Then he served for three years as a patent examiner in the U.S. Patent Office. He joined Monsanto as a member of the patent department in 1938 and became director of the department in 1946. He qualified for the job of negotiating with DuPont not just because of his formal credentials but also because he had two other relevant strengths: 1) He had a substantial knowledge of existing patents on the chemistry and know-how for making synthetic fibers, and

2) he was well on his way to becoming a bona fide international expert in negotiating business contracts, particularly those involving sophisticated technology.

His 1950 assignment from Ted Hochwalt—to head up a small team of cost accountants and engineers—turned out to be a responsibility that lasted almost a year before final agreement on nylon was reached between Chemstrand and DuPont.

The job took skill and perseverance, of course. But it took more than that. It took a touch of diplomacy. And patience.

It was important for Wilson to maintain the respect of people at DuPont. It was equally important for Wilson to keep in close touch with the Chemstrand board (populated with both Monsanto-related and Viscose-related gentlemen). On certain occasions he would also check things out with the Monsanto and Viscose boards. Additionally, non-board officials of Chemstrand, Viscose and Monsanto ducked in and out of the details as negotiations developed.

Not surprisingly, when Wilson reported, "Here's how things stand at the moment," the reactions and counsel he received from his various high-level constituencies were not always neat, tidy and uniform. He was the man in the middle, determined to try to "satisfy everybody."

For the first few months everything went rather smoothly. It was a fact-finding expedition of unusual complexity. All parties cooperated nicely. But by early 1951 the road became rocky. At one point, negotiations were terminated. On that occasion a DuPont team came to St. Louis and said flat out that Chemstrand's proposed offering was woefully inadequate and that DuPont would "now go out and beat the bushes elsewhere." This downturn in an erstwhile upturn situation was particularly distressing to Monsanto Executive Vice President Charlie Thomas, whose reflex reaction was to contact DuPont's Crawford Greenewalt and suggest that this was no time for either party to back away. Although Greenewalt was in Europe, Charlie Thomas reached him by phone. During that trans-Atlantic call the negotiations got back on the track.

In June of 1951 a complicated formula for payment, acceptable to both Chemstrand and DuPont, emerged. It provided Chemstrand payments to DuPont based not only on the cost of manufacture of nylon but also on such factors as inflation, labor rates, raw materials prices, pretax return on investment, construction costs and selling prices.

DuPont wanted—and got—about $120 million for its know-how and for establishing the operation of a Chemstrand nylon plant geared to make 50 million pounds a year. This was paid over a 15-year period. As it turned out, during the period of licensing Chemstrand got its nylon plant up close to 200 million pounds a year. Even so, the know-how payments to DuPont remained in the $120-million range.

There are several reasons why it turned out this way, the chief one relating to the "product mix" at the Chemstrand nylon plant, which went into operation at Pensacola, Florida, in 1953, one year after the start-up of the acrylic plant at Decatur, Alabama.

When the DuPont-Chemstrand contract was signed in mid-1951, nylon was being used in apparel, women's hosiery and a wide variety of industrial applications. At that time nylon had not invaded the automobile tire market. Rayon had been used for tire cord, but not nylon. Viscose, experienced in rayon, had the foresight to suggest that nylon would have a bright future in tires.

When the Chemstrand Pensacola plant started production in 1953, general textile fibers accounted for 43 million pounds, and the heavier-denier nylon for tire cord accounted for seven million pounds. Almost immediately Chemstrand decided to expand rapidly in the heavier-denier continuous filament for the tire industry. Because it was a less-expensive product to make and sell, Chemstrand gained under terms of the DuPont formula.

The 1951 pact, based largely on the complicated formula, made Du-Pont responsible for actually setting the Pensacola plant into operation. There was also a patent license involved—a license for a wide variety of 17-year DuPont patents. Some of the patents were about ready to expire in 1951, while others, also licensed, were newer. More than 300 individual patents were involved. The agreement even gave Chemstrand a license on those DuPont nylon patents which would be issued for the ensuing five years after 1951. Royalty fees for patent licensing ranged from 4 to 6 percent over a 10-year period. Yet this was not totally an "extra fee" beyond the know-how formula, since a part of the royalty payments was covered in the know-how agreement.

When the acrylic plant went into operation at a 700-acre site in Decatur, Alabama, in 1952, moving headlong into problems of fibrillation, fuzziness and market-resistance, the nylon plant was halfway up at a 2000-acre site at Pensacola, Florida. It was an interesting "race." In terms of success and profitability, the later-starting Pensacola plant won handily. Chemstrand nylon—and particularly Chemstrand nylon tire cord—was an immediate hit. Acrilan was more of a miss. Nylon was ready. Acrilan wasn't.

By this time Osborne Bezanson, the veteran Monsanto production man who was reared at Merrimac, had taken over Chemstrand's presidential reins from Ted Hochwalt, who returned to Monsanto. When start-up day finally arrived at Decatur, Bezanson had proudly proclaimed, "I'm tending bar."

A sober and serious man, Oz Bezanson was fated for less levity when fibrillation of Acrilan became an intense problem and the plant had to be temporarily closed down. After his period of service as Chemstrand president, he retired at the end of 1953 and handed the reins to a Viscose production man, Henry H. Bitler, a diligent introvert who was proud of his slogan, "I take no chances."

Meantime, down on the sunny Gulf Coast at Pensacola . . .

In 1953 Chemstrand cranked up what would become—and still is—the world's largest integrated nylon plant combining both chemical and fiber manufacturing operations. In 1954 capacity went from 50 million to 58 million pounds. With gratifying smoothness.

In perspective, Acrilan straightened itself out—and went ahead with dispatch once it had shaken off its infant ills. And it didn't simply move ahead in the footprints of DuPont's Orlon. It moved in the direction of its own singular strengths.

By 1955 Chemstrand's faith in the soundness of its acrylic property was restored, as evidenced by the fact that Chemstrand took its first big step abroad—to England, where it formed a wholly-owned subsidiary, Chemstrand, Ltd., to make and market Acrilan. It should also be noted that in August of 1955 Chemstrand turned the corner and finally got into the black, thanks mostly to nylon, of course.

From there on, the record book is not unlike that of a winning sports team—on and on and on. And upward. Once the momentum was established, based on success and sophistication in both early-blooming nylon and late-blooming Acrilan, it was a surge too impelling to ignore.

Chemstrand had grown up.

The other partner, Viscose, had had sleepless nights. It hadn't reckoned on the foibles of fibrillation (neither had Monsanto). Nor had it perceived how nylon would take care of its "sick little sister," Acrilan. Viscose needed Chemstrand's success. Viscose had nothing of substantial promise in its labs; its 50-percent stake in Chemstrand was its principal asset.

Edward A. O'Neal, who became an international figure as managing director of Monsanto Chemicals Limited, London, from 1946 to 1953, and as head of the parent company's Overseas Division from 1953 to 1956, succeeded Bitler as the fourth president of Chemstrand. It was necessary for him to resign from the Monsanto board and to give up his Monsanto vice presidency when he stepped into the top Chemstrand slot. O'Neal's 1956–1964 reign at Chemstrand was marked by a sense of flair, not just because of his own personality but also because this was the era when the Chemstrand organization began to strut.

O'Neal recently recalled: "Each parent had the same number of representatives on the Chemstrand board. The bylaws provided the president would vote in the case of a tie. During my whole period as president, I never had to cast a vote to break a tie. I probably spent as much time keeping peace among the two parents as in running Chemstrand.

"It was apparent shortly after I arrived at Chemstrand that Viscose wanted out. And, of course, that's what happened in 1961, when Monsanto acquired Viscose's 50-percent equity and turned Chemstrand first into a wholly owned subsidiary and then into an operating division.

"During my whole time at the Chemstrand offices in the Empire State Building, there was a hands-off policy to which both parents had agreed. We ran our own show. Chemstrand even had its own Annual

Reports in 1957, 1958 and 1959. Quite often I'd make appearances before security analyst groups. Granted, Chemstrand had only two stockholders, but we were a major presence on the financial scene with our own set of fiscal responsibilities. For several years Chemstrand's profits were greater than those of Viscose."

During the O'Neal era, an acrylic plant was built at Coleraine, Northern Ireland; a nylon plant was established at Greenwood, South Carolina; an acrylic plant was built at Ashdod, Israel; and plans were started for polyester at Decatur, for a major nylon installation at Echternach, Luxembourg, and for a research center in North Carolina's Research Triangle Park.

In 1959 the fifty-eight-year-old parent company's consolidated sales were over $800 million. Net income was almost $62 million. Chemstrand, now ten years old, had sales of almost $200 million and net income of $24 million, 14- and 31-percent increases, respectively, over the sales and net income for the preceding year.

In that buoyant year of 1959 Chemstrand sold more than 130 million pounds of fiber. Its employe head count was almost 9000, a 100-percent increase over the Chemstrand population of 1954.

There were people at Chemstrand who were saying, "At this rate we'll outdistance the rest of the company."

The so-called Soaring Sixties got off to a good start when Monsanto and Viscose came to an agreement that Monsanto would acquire the Viscose 50-percent equity in Chemstrand for 3,540,000 shares of Monsanto common stock. The agreement was approved by Monsanto and Viscose shareowners at separate, special meetings on January 16, 1961.

Up until that time no one had suggested that the fast-moving Chemstrand organization should in any way act like a regular player on the Monsanto team. It had been set apart not only by its involvement in the unique world of textiles, but also by the plain fact that it had been a 50-50 associate company and therefore not a regular part of Monsanto.

Moreover, even during 1961, when Chemstrand joined the Monsanto family as a full-fledged member, it showed no signs of wanting to behave like the other, more traditional and "staid" units of the company. For a brief time it operated as a wholly owned subsidiary and then it became an operating division—but was still called Chemstrand. It had its own esprit de corps, its own traditions, its own loyalties, and its own bristling brand of independence.

Some of its people had come in from Monsanto, notably its smooth bossman and Southern gentleman, Edward A. O'Neal; others had come from Viscose. But most had signed on as Chemstrand employes—not Monsanto or Viscose. Chemstrand was their flag. This was their company—their successful company. And they didn't want it tampered with by some non-textiles strangers "out in the prairies of St. Louis."

Particularly in the Empire State Building office, the people who laid out big plans in marketing, merchandising, promotion and advertising were, by and large, imports from the world of textiles. "We're non-chemists," they proudly proclaimed.

Some of the engineering staff and production staff had in prior years worked long and hard bringing in new processes at Decatur and at Pensacola. During tense and fatiguing start-up periods, side by side with colleagues equally intent on "making the damn thing work," a special breed of Chemstrander was born, loaded with spirit and with pride in this brand-new company.

Monsanto to most Chemstranders was another company, somewhere out in the Midwest. Granted, Monsanto had invented Acrilan, had spearheaded the nylon negotiations with DuPont, and had helped bankroll the entire enterprise; but the Chemstrand breed had meanwhile developed its own set of loyalties. These went deep—and were not about to be transferred casually to the parent company by the mere formalities of several boards of directors.

Plus, Chemstrand was doing nicely!

Veterans in Monsanto saw this attitude as a repetition, on a larger scale, of the time in the late forties when the Plastics Division, headquartered at Springfield, Massachusetts, was flexing its muscles and suggesting to the rest of the company, "We're the wave of the future, and we're in a different business. So leave us alone." However, the time would come when plastics would be a less heroic commodity in the profit column, and this then tended to neutralize some of the bombast.

Similarly, it was likely that the time would come when chemical fibers would suffer from overcapacity and low prices, and that some of the cocky strut would slip from Chemstrand's gait.

But in the early sixties the world was aglow at the Empire State Building and at Chemstrand's manufacturing and research operations. The inbred sense of autonomy didn't budge a bit when Chemstrand changed from a 50-percent associate to a wholly owned subsidiary to a regular Monsanto operating division.

After all, this was a group which a short while earlier had operated with a free-wheeling OK from Monsanto and Viscose. Chemstranders liked their freedom, particularly as they were convinced that that old-fashioned company out in St. Louis, specializing in industrial chemicals, wasn't sufficiently sophisticated to sponsor a luncheon at "21" for apparel manufacturers, stylists and fashion editors.

Ed O'Neal was firmly in command at Chemstrand during this tricky transition. He felt his first and foremost responsibility was to make Chemstrand grow in size and profitability. But the internal sensitivities were not to be ignored.

Chemstrand had its own policies, its own accounting practices, and had even developed its own pension plan (involving a "variable" Part B plan permitting the option of "fixed and risk investments," several years before the parent company even considered such a modification).

The differences between "textiles" and "chemicals and plastics" were

—and are—many. The somewhat conservative parent company, which had come along nicely "Serving Industry Which Serves Mankind," had never tried to be glamorous. Its relationship with consumer products had been limited. In its approaches to the public and shareowners, it had tried to be more of a statesman than a showman.

But showmanship was the mood at Chemstrand. Network television, with big-name performers like Frank Sinatra, Elizabeth Taylor and Barbra Streisand, became standard fare for Chemstrand in the sixties. If the TV viewer looked fast he may even have seen the word "Monsanto." The big identity went to the division picking up the tab—Chemstrand.

During the early sixties Chemstrand intensely developed many markets that were opened in the late fifties—including the basic and beckoning world of carpets, served both by Acrilan acrylic and nylon fibers.

Thanks to some innovative executives, the Monsanto division, which was No. 2 to DuPont in both acrylic and nylon fibers, decided to try for No. 1 in creative marketing. The philosophy of pull-through merchandising was introduced in all product lines—"pull-through" meaning that Chemstrand would pay to exploit end products in order to assure public recognition and acceptance of sweaters, blankets, dresses and carpets made by customers of Chemstrand fibers. This system was not only a master stroke in customer relations but it brought national attention—via TV, magazines and newspapers—to customers' products and thus broadened the market for Chemstrand fibers.

The rest of the company had done little in so-called "horizontal" mass media. The parent company's corporate advertising campaigns—rising and falling with the largesse (or lack of largesse) extended by budget-conscious Executive Committees—had been conservative and spotty. The St. Louis rationale was, "Why should we spend a lot of money in the mass media, considering we're not a consumer goods company?"

The parent company and its non-textiles operating divisions were not sitting back and pouting during the period of Chemstrand's metamorphosis from an associate to a subsidiary to an operating division. Perhaps in a less flamboyant manner, they were making tracks in their own far-from-Broadway, less-glamorous industrial worlds.

In 1960 the parent sired an Agricultural Division—based largely on fertilizer, herbicide and pesticide products taken from Organic and Inorganic—which would someday become more golden in profitability than Chemstrand. But in 1960 Ag was more of a promise than a fulfillment. In 1961 a Hydrocarbons Division came into existence—another forerunner of future glories, but seemingly less spectacular in concept than Chemstrand, which was sponsoring 60-minute TV specials. The Hydrocarbons Division's raw materials and intermediates would nourish Chemstrand. But the new division didn't have Chemstrand's sheen and flourish.

The other operating divisions—Organic, Inorganic and Plastics—

were progressing solidly. But by now they were rather old hat, measured against the glitter, glamour and growth of Chemstrand. They had deeper roots, but less brilliant foliage.

Monsanto's 1962 Annual Report lost no time in reporting nylon and Acrilan were up substantially in sales. Profits, likewise, were increasing. This was the year when the corporation's total sales exceeded one billion dollars for the first time; the year that the pioneering Chocolate Bayou plant was established at Alvin, Texas; and the year Monsanto's equity in the Plax Corporation went from 50 to 100 percent. (Plax was the seed of the Packaging Division, and the Packaging Division was the seed of a revolutionary new plastic container for beverages to be known as the Cycle-Safe bottle for Coca-Cola and other refreshments. And the Cycle-Safe plastic bottle—which, of course no one realized during the early days of Plax—was ultimately fated to receive a stunning blow by being banned by the Food and Drug Administration many years later— in 1977.)

Yet the razzle-dazzle of 1962 resided with the Chemstrand Division. The Red A for Acrilan, which had been popularized in advertisements starting in the mid-fifties, leaped into new prominence, aided by a massive promotion of quality standards for carpets containing Acrilan. Nylon didn't sit in a corner. A "Cumuloft" brand of nylon for carpeting burst upon the national scene, and a Blue C joined Acrilan's Red A—C for Cumuloft, by plan, but C for Chemstrand in the eyes of many Chemstranders.

The parent company, meantime, was putting fresh dollars behind its block M. (Chemstranders didn't like the block M. They said it was too ponderous and "too masculine.")

In some respects, Monsanto had two different sorts of companies— an old one making chemicals and plastics, and a new one making fibers. Complications were inevitable.

For instance, appropriations requests for the board agendas came from two different sources. The Monsanto Executive Committee reviewed chemicals and plastics projects before sending them along for board actions, and the Chemstrand Committee reviewed fibers projects before they were sent to the board.

It was an interesting era.

The year 1963 also marked the first all-out campaign for perhaps the most inventive plan ever to be born and bred at Chemstrand—the Wear-Dated warranty program. Actually the program had been announced late the previous year, but its big impact came in 1963.

Created by Robert H. Born, an intense, extremely creative and somewhat high-strung promotion man in the Empire State Building, the Wear-Dated program proclaimed that for certain apparel Chemstrand would provide a guarantee protecting the merchandise for a full year of normal wear. Consumers were assured they would receive the full purchase price if a garment failed to give normal wear for one year and was returned to Monsanto with the Wear-Dated tag and sales receipt.

This program was—and is—a winner. It was precedent-setting. It placed Chemstrand in the rather daring position of guaranteeing products it didn't make. And it resulted in the establishment of quality-control standards that fiber customers were happy to comply with in exchange for the power of the Wear-Dated tags and other promotional pluses.

Nothing could have been more appropriate for the oncoming era of consumer movements. The Wear-Dated concept stands solidly and squarely on the principle of assuring the purchaser: 1) You'll find value in this product, and 2) if you don't feel you've had satisfactory wear, the fiber maker—not the apparel maker—will be responsible. A mid-seventies survey showed that approximately 46 percent of the women in the United States were aware of the Wear-Dated concept—a noteworthy outcome.

The Wear-Dated program is now operating in 18 nations. While its principal emphasis is on apparel, in recent years it has also been applied to blankets, rugs and upholstery fabrics. In 1976 approximately 100 million tags were printed for domestic use alone.

A phenomenal outcome for a consumer-conscious Chemstrand (now called Monsanto Textiles Company) profit center? Of course.

The internal rivalries involving chemicals and plastics vs. textiles presented a serious dichotomy for an extended period. Until 1971 each unit had its own separate office location in New York. At one time, in London, there was absolutely no communication and no relationship between the offices of Chemstrand, Ltd., near Piccadilly Circus, and Monsanto Chemicals Limited near Westminster Abbey. The former was the synthetic fibers company. The latter was the chemicals and plastics company. An often-told story concerns a visit to London by the chairman of Monsanto, Dr. Charles A. Thomas, in the early sixties. When he and his wife were the honored guests at a dinner given by key Monsanto employes, the Chemstrand employes and their wives were in dinner jackets and long gowns; the Monsanto Chemicals Limited employes and their wives were in plain, ordinary daytime apparel. No one had bothered to coordinate the British "Hatfields and McCoys" in a temporary truce in honor of the visiting Monsanto chairman.

The twain since have, to a large degree, met. Corporate efficiencies have required certain company-wide standards.

The old Chemstrand pride was punctured a bit—but only a bit—when financial analysts would inquire, "Why were you all so late in getting into polyesters?" Ed O'Neal has a quiet response. He says, "We were so busy trying to keep up with opportunities in Acrilan and nylon we didn't react promptly to the chance and challenge of polyester." Outsiders suggest Monsanto misread the market in the early sixties. O'Neal admits, "When we did get in, we got in in a hurry with the wrong product. And we had to back out and start all over again." Not Chemstrand's finest hour.

A St. Louis invesment banker summed it up nicely when he observed, "Chemstrand has been an invaluable but not infallible part of Monsanto."

CHAPTER IX

The Perils of Consumer Products

COZILY tucked into a security blanket of doing what comes naturally—namely, selling chemicals and plastics to industry —why did Monsanto "go retail" all of a sudden?

Why did it stray from the comfortable wonders of its industrial existence and venture into the perils of an uncomfortable unknown?

It is difficult to put a precise fix on where and why the company decided to establish a division to explore the strange world of consumer products. The influences were many.

Some finger-pointing, in retrospect, is inevitable as the ill-fated experiment of the fifties is analyzed. Life's (and Monsanto's) successes have many fathers; life's (and Monsanto's) failures tend to be orphans.

There is ample evidence that Edgar Queeny always had a hankering to see what would happen if he could have some of his company's products tiptoe into the consumer marketplace, ideally without stepping on the feet of his industrial customers in the process.

From the chronology alone, a case could be made that the company was past the point of no return when it developed the low-sudsing detergent Sterox at Dayton in 1946 and established facilities at Trenton, Michigan, in 1948 to make and package the revolutionary product that would be nationally distributed to supermarkets under the trade name "all," in direct competition with Monsanto's principal industrial customers, "the soapers."

Sticking to chronology, the year 1950 also said something about the company's subliminal itch to get into the consumer marketplace, for this was the year Monsanto blossomed in New England with highway billboards trumpeting the glories of Eskimo antifreeze, made at Everett, Massachusetts. The product never went national. Shipping costs precluded that. In fact, it never went very far in the New England states, for two reasons: 1) Profits were difficult to pull through because of the expense of promotion, and 2) it was a commodity-type product with no distinct advantages. It stayed on the market for two years, until Mer-

135

rimac General Manager Charles H. Sommer decided to lower the boom.

Then there was a retail line of Rez paints and sealers that came into Monsanto through the acquisition of I. F. Laucks, Seattle. Yet these were not "Monsanto inventions," and they presented no case for urgency. Granted, they were quality products, but their market was limited to a modest number of paint and hardware stores.

There was also that pestiferous product called Krilium soil conditioner, introduced late in 1951 and marketed in 1952.

If the villain that tipped the scales must be identified, Krilium gets the nod.

The 1952 Annual Report walked both sides of the street. On its back cover it carried the perennial corporate slogan "Serving Industry Which Serves Mankind." But page 19 carried a telltale paragraph: "The advent of Krilium soil conditioner provided Monsanto with a long-sought opportunity to move Monsanto trademarked products to the retail counter. For its entire history, the company has sold nearly all its products to other industries; seldom had the customer bought a Monsanto trademarked product in a retail store."

In May of 1952, the Merchandising Division (later to become known as the Consumer Products Division) was formed. It remained alive—not healthy, but alive—until 1958, when its elective vice-presidential general manager became an appointive regional vice president in California.

Because "all" (nee Sterox) detergent came first, this—rather than that pestiferous Krilium—is the best product to look at initially in tracing the adventures and misadventures of the company's formal entry into the consumer products arena.

In 1946, when the Central Research Department at Dayton had developed its revolutionary, non-ionic, low-sudsing detergent, Sterox, Monsanto found itself in an unusual situation. In an era when the soapers were equating sudsiness with cleanliness via many millions of dollars' worth of advertising for Tide and similar general-purpose detergents, Monsanto was sitting on an invention that was based on the opposite proposition: namely, that suds interfere with cleaning efficiency within the confines of front-loading automatic washing machines.

Westinghouse Electric Corporation, in Pittsburgh, Pennsylvania, was overjoyed. Its front-loading (as compared with top-loading) automatic washing machines had had problems with high-sudsing detergents. To begin with, clothes weren't getting clean enough; furthermore, the foaming suds would tumble out onto the floor when a housewife decided to open the hatch and insert an extra pair of socks in the middle of the washing cycle.

Westinghouse was so overjoyed by the availability of a low-sudsing detergent in fact that it put a box of Monsanto's "all" in the basket of every new automatic washer, an endorsement which gave the new detergent an auspicious merchandising boost at the outset.

In the late forties a detergent tailored for use in front-loading automatic washing machines was a specialty product compared to the high-volume, high-sudsing, all-purpose detergents made and marketed by Procter & Gamble, Colgate, Lever Brothers and other soapers—all important Monsanto customers for such detergent raw materials as surface-active agents and phosphate builders.

Monsanto lost no time in approaching the soapers to find out the nature of their interest, if any, in its low-sudsing discovery. At the time, the regular detergents were moving heroically in the marketplace. Understandably, the soapers weren't too impressed by Monsanto's "novelty" product. None wanted to take it over. None wanted to champion the "contradictory cause" of a low-sudser against the popular high-sudsers.

The people in Monsanto's Phosphate Division, notably the outspoken John Christian, were cool on "all" from the start. Executive Vice President Charlie Thomas and Vice President Ted Hochwalt, from whose Dayton laboratory the product had sprung, were inclined to take the opposite view. "You can't stand in the path of scientific achievement" was their attitude. President Bill Rand had apprehensions but in the final analysis was inclined to go along when serious discussions got under way to explore the possibility that "we might have to take this to the consumer market ourselves." And when Edgar Queeny cast his vote the same way, the fork-in-the-road problem ceased to be a problem. It was full steam ahead to find the right way to market the low-sudsing detergent at the consumer level.

Monsanto had initially decided to sell "all" through an erstwhile small customer, Detergents, Inc., of Columbus, Ohio. This company had some advantages as the vehicle for marketing.

A few (though not many) observers thought Monsanto was picking a straw party to handle "all" in order to hide its new consumer-oriented strategy from the soapers. This was not the case, for two reasons: 1) The detergent manufacturers had been informed about "all" by Monsanto early in the game and were aware of Monsanto's quandary; 2) the manufacturers had pretty good avenues of commercial intelligence and would not be easily fooled by something as simple as the name of a Columbus company, Detergents, Inc., on a box of Monsanto detergent.

Such matters notwithstanding, Monsanto's entry into consumer marketing with "all" began with Monsanto making the product and Detergents, Inc., marketing it. Perhaps the most noteworthy idea contributed by Detergents, Inc., was a massive advertising campaign involving full-page, semi-monthly exposure for "all" in almost 100 major metropolitan markets. The Columbus merchandisers suggested that the impact of high-exposure advertising would be necessary to successfully launch the daring new detergent. A multimillion-dollar advertising program was as revolutionary to Monsanto as its entry into consumer goods.

The Trenton, Michigan, plant's production capacity for the low-sudsing product was strained as early as 1951, and shortly thereafter Monsanto decided it should take over marketing custody of "all" from Detergents, Inc., and permit "all" to become a front-running product for Mother Monsanto. Anyway, Detergents, Inc., had rung up a large due bill with Mother Monsanto and had to be bailed out by the sheer force of a Monsanto takeover.

When in 1952 Monsanto formalized its consumer marketplace intentions by establishing a Merchandising Division, it brought in from Ralston Purina Company a man with longtime experience in distributor-dealer relations, Roy L. Brandenburger, as the new division's general manager.

Brandenburger had his hands full.

By the time he arrived, the "all" situation was in full bloom and the Krilium situation was approaching crisis proportions.

Krilium also traces to the Thomas and Hochwalt cradle, Central Research in Dayton.

Krilium soil conditioner was an exciting and technically successful product. It achieved worldwide acclaim overnight. But it never made a dime.

Its story goes like this:

Charlie Thomas had been curious early in 1949 when he noticed that on his farm, on the outskirts of Dayton, two side-by-side sections of land were quite different. One had loamy soil; the other had heavily compacted clay. Crops grew easily in the former but not in the latter. The contrast prompted Thomas to think anew about the relationship of soil condition to growth potential.

"What can chemistry do about such a problem?" was a question that always went through Thomas's mind, and in this instance he voiced it to Ted Hochwalt, his longtime friend and colleague, who was serving in 1949 as director of Central Research.

Equally unwilling to shrug off a tantalizing question, Ted Hochwalt strolled into a lab at Dayton just prior to Thanksgiving and gave out a new assignment. He announced that he wanted some of his top chemists to drop everything and start an intensive program of research into soil structure.

Hochwalt recently recalled: "Our researchers had no preconceived ideas about what might work and what might not work. Obviously they didn't consider natural products such as peat moss or compost, where great quantities are needed to condition the soil. They were looking for a synthetic soil conditioner. They were sure the right product had to be a polymer, but beyond that they had an open mind. Quite early during the course of their research they bumped into an acrylonitrile formulation that was ideal for a copolymer powder which could embody precisely the benefits they were looking for. It was all very fortuitous. And quite sudden. Within a few months we found the winner."

Acrylonitrile was a household word at Dayton, this having been the raw material used for experiments in making acrylic fibers at the same laboratory in the early forties.

After Hochwalt's principal research colleagues found the right kind of polymer, other chemists in the lab were brought into the project, and various formulations were made in small quantities and tested as soil conditioners.

At the outset the Dayton scientists knew that nothing they'd invent would change the structure of soil. The knew that compacted soil would have to be manually or mechanically broken into pealike bits and then, once the soil was properly aggregated, it would be the new chemical's job to maintain the loose consistency and not permit the pealike particles to compact together again in a nonporous mass.

In essence, the Dayton scientists were not asked to invent something to compete with a Rototiller, a pneumatic drill, a shovel, or a hoe. They were asked to invent something that would maintain ideal consistency of soil, not cause ideal consistency. (This may seem like a small point, but it's one of many factors that led to the ultimate downfall of Krilium.)

Initial lab tests involved stirring various quantities of an acrylonitrile copolymer powder into well-aggregated soil. Tests were made with various kinds of soil at various temperatures, under various moisture conditions and at various depths—and at various rates of application.

Vegetables and flowers were grown in side-by-side test plots in Dayton, in treated and untreated soil.

Because the synthetic product did in fact maintain soil aggregation, moisture and nutrients became rapidly available for root structures—and plants emerged rapidly, in healthy condition and larger-than-expected size. Also, root growth was facilitated, and seeds didn't send up shoots destined to break their little necks against a wall of bricklike clay. The seedlings shot up easily in the aggregated soil.

Quite plainly, the product worked. Monsanto had a new invention on its hands.

Not only did Krilium work as a soil conditioner. It also could be broadcast on the surface of soil and then watered down to become a weblike agent to retard erosion. But that was a secondary consideration.

Ted Hochwalt and Charlie Thomas lost no time in advising their executive colleagues about the promise of the new product. It was agreed in mid-1950 that: 1) There should be no premature announcement; and 2) there should be tests conducted at university experiment stations and at other facilities in various regions of the country so that Monsanto would have reliable data on results under diverse conditions with different crops.

No difficulty was encountered in persuading ag schools, county agents and research-oriented farmers to test the new product. The "strings attached" involved keeping accurate records in control and noncontrol test plots, keeping Monsanto advised, and keeping mum.

That last item was the one that caused the difficulties. It wasn't because the cooperators, as they were called—and there were 80 of them—wanted to violate an agreement. It was simply that they couldn't contain their enthusiasm when their own tests demonstrated the Monsanto soil conditioner caused extremely favorable and almost startling results.

By summertime of 1951 field results showed that Monsanto had a highly successful new product.

Then the phone began to ring.

Example: An editor from the *Des Moines Register* and *Tribune* phoned to advise he had been told by a county agent that on a nearby farm "the greatest corn in history" was being grown. When the editor asked, "Is it true that a Monsanto chemical is making all this happen?" the company simply had to tell the truth. (Some editors asked, "Is it true a new Monsanto *fertilizer* is making all this happen?")

Actually Monsanto had a formal procedure for such inquiries. The procedure provided that the people calling in should be told Monsanto did, in fact, have an experimental product being tested and that no details were available on plans to take the product to market.

It would have been folly to try to persuade editors they had no story and greater folly to suggest they not publish information about "the greatest corn in history" growing nearby. If news means something unique, this was, inescapably, news.

In Dayton, meantime, data from the 80 cooperators were being analyzed in rather orderly fashion—data leading to the conclusion "the product really works."

By Labor Day the product had been christened Krilium synthetic polyelectrolyte. A Public Relations Department staffer barged in on Patent Director J. R. Wilson and pleaded, "I heard about the name you picked and, please, Rusty, please say it isn't so."

"Whaddya mean?" Wilson inquired. "'Krilium' has to be adjectival, as any proper trademark should, and like all good adjectives it should modify a noun. Of course, there's a second adjective, 'synthetic.' And that noun's the right noun because the product is, after all, a polyelectrolyte."

"You can't spring a name like that on the American public!" the public relations fellow protested. "Not one in a million knows what a polyelectrolyte is."

But Rusty Wilson held his ground. He was somewhat proud of the trademark Krilium, mainly because it had a nice ring and it hinted at the raw material acrylonitrile. In addition, Rusty Wilson was a chemist (and a chemical engineer) and he knew the product was a synthetic polyelectrolyte. (In fairness, Rusty Wilson softened a few months later and grudgingly permitted the product to be called Krilium soil conditioner. He chuckles today as he recalls how he relented in the face of pressure from "laymen" for simpler language.)

It was early September when the principal executives of Monsanto met head-on with the problem of whether to keep the lid on or to announce Krilium.

By this time a number of cooperators had achieved press coverage on their own. In some cases this was accurate and potentially helpful to Monsanto. In other cases it wasn't. The cooperator experimenting with tomatoes, for example, talked only about the abundant yield of tomatoes. That's all he had worked on. Understandably, Charlie Thomas and Ted Hochwalt didn't like this. After all, they had discovered the world's first synthetic soil conditioner, not the world's first synthetic soil conditioner for tomatoes.

The September decision—"Okay, let's announce it"—was expedited by the overwhelming amount of data on many crops that had come into Dayton, mostly favorable.

It was Charlie Thomas who insisted from the start, "We'll announce this in a dignified sort of way, in a scientific environment." Upon checking, he found it wasn't too late to get a spot on the program at the annual convention of the American Association for the Advancement of Science, which would be meeting during Christmas week in Philadelphia.

Once this was locked in, the company had a calendar countdown to deal with.

In Dayton technical papers were prepared, based on data accumulated there and data from cooperators. Also in Dayton an employe named Sally Alabaugh was assigned to make a motion picture showing how plant growth was accelerated in treated soil. As an added touch, she shot some spectacular time-lapse scenes showing brilliant flowers bursting into bloom in vivid colors.

In St. Louis it was generally agreed that there was one principal booby trap to avoid: namely, overstating Krilium's advantages by even a fraction in news releases and other materials. "Heaven help the person who contributes the slightest exaggeration," was Charlie Thomas's party line. And by now, it should be added, his party line was not ignored because by this time Charlie Thomas was president.

Somehow there was a feeling even before the product was announced that Krilium could get out of hand. The feeling was supported by the fact that Monsanto would not be starting commercial production until the spring of 1952—several months after the planned announcement.

The various news releases and technical papers prepared during November, 1951, were read by a large internal jury. Whenever any "blue sky" or "sell" sentences were detected, out came the sentences.

Because of the significance and sensitivity of the product, it was decided to have news conferences in Dayton and New York prior to the official unveiling December 29 at the AAAS meeting in Philadelphia. The reasoning went this way: "We are as much interested in accuracy as we are in recognition. If we permit reporters to ask questions, we'll wind up with more accurate material in the media." There was one other pressing reason: It was a rather complicated and technical story to explain.

To begin with, Krilium was not a fertilizer. This had to be stated. Secondly, it did not cause soil to disperse into fine particles. It simply maintained the crumbly condition after—repeat after—the soil was previously conditioned.

But the complications didn't end there.

Krilium would not be readily available in quantity for quite some time.

Retail price? Monsanto was unsure—all the way down to the starting line. Distribution network? "We're working on it."

Any special problems about mixing it into the soil? Yes. If the soil happened to be too moist, the Krilium powder would turn to a Jello-like substance and become ineffective. In plain terms, this meant that users would not only have to be sure their soil was churned up properly in the first place, but they'd have to be sure the soil was not too moist when Krilium powder was introduced via a thorough mixing process.

Any other problems? A few. How much Krilium to cover how many square feet? How to disperse it evenly?

The Dayton researchers had the answers to such questions, but getting all this material together in lay language was quite a task. Depth of treatment was a challenge. Once water percolated down a few inches and hit solid clay, this became a problem all by itself, called the "bottom-of-the-bucket problem."

It was emphasized that using Krilium involved many separate considerations—and the weakest link in the chain of considerations could, of course, spoil everything, in farm or back yard.

The information kits covered all bases. At the news conferences Drs. Thomas and Hochwalt and their principal Dayton colleagues patiently fielded all the questions. Sally Alabaugh's color film, entitled *Soil Condition: Key to Productivity,* helped dramatize the various points. It all added up to a massive job of communicating a total story composed of innumerable parts.

How did it all work out?

Perhaps only one example is needed—an all-too-typical example.

In attendance at the New York news conference and at the AAAS meeting was William L. Laurence, Pulitzer Prize–winning science editor for *The New York Times* and one of the most distinguished journalists of the day. His stature can be best appreciated when it is noted that he was the only journalist in America permitted by the U.S. government to sit in on every step of the development of the atomic bomb—with the understanding, of course, that he'd not utter or write a word about the project until given permission, after Hiroshima.

Here, one would have thought, was a journalist who would surely handle such a story with discretion, especially considering the safeguards Monsanto had built into its material.

Page-one headline in *The New York Times*, December 30, 1951: SYNTHETIC RESTORES SOIL PRODUCTIVITY IN HOURS INSTEAD OF USUAL YEARS. The Laurence by-liner that followed ran almost a thousand words.

Two choice sections of his story included the following:

"Tests . . . indicate the new chemical . . . will mark the beginning of a revolutionary era in agriculture, in which man-made deserts may be turned in a short time into blooming gardens and green acres."

And: "Scientists attending the symposium expressed the view that the new synthetic soil conditioner might prove to be an even more powerful weapon against Communism than the atomic bomb, since Communism thrives among peoples who live on soils that no longer produce enough food to support their increasing populations."

That did it. Monsanto now had an anti-Communist secret weapon in its arsenal.

Early in 1952 the famed Edward R. Murrow of CBS came to St. Louis to originate a network telecast from Monsanto. After putting up Krilium like a golf ball on a high tee, Monsanto could not pretend its very visible new product didn't exist. All it could do was continue to cooperate with the media and take every opportunity to "drag its feet" by explaining the problems of availability and the multiple cautions of application.

To be sure, Monsanto was not shy about being identified as the inventor, and there was somehow also the feeling that the sudden acclaim for Krilium might be sufficiently sustaining *until* the company could turn out the "wonder powder" in commercial quantities.

There was one other little ripple . . .

Keeping in mind that the era under discussion is late 1951 and early 1952, mention should be made that Monsanto had a new issue of 400,000 common shares of stock in February, 1952. This issue, which brought in $37,900,000 for construction projects and other corporate purposes, had in fact been planned long before Bill Laurence of *The New York Times* sat down at his typewriter and sang Krilium into heroic proportions. Yet there were a few observers who suspected the Krilium "theatrics" were part of a strategy to make the new stock issue an instant success. The timing, one analyst commented, was "both good and bad."

In 1952 Krilium had an additional hurdle to clear. It faced spirited competition from other soil conditioners, which had sprung up all over the nation in short order. Some were mostly sand. Most were hasty compounds rushed opportunistically onto the market in an attempt to ride the coattails of Krilium's exciting entry. Not many of the competing products remained on the market very long, but they compounded public confusion about the use and nature of a synthetic soil conditioner.

Krilium not only hung in there in the face of competition, but it grew. By mid-1952 it was being manufactured at five Monsanto plant sites.

The various Krilium-related complications, plus the challenges of marketing the increasingly popular "all" detergent, provided a full plate for the embryo Merchandising Division, formed for the purpose of putting Monsanto consumer products on Main Street.

There were several fundamental problems:

1) Monsanto wasn't steeped in consumer merchandising experience.

2) It had a limited line of merchandise.

3) Krilium and "all" didn't lend themselves to the same marketing techniques or outlets.

At least two regular operating divisions were involved in supporting the Merchandising Division. The Organic Division developed a program to license formulators under Monsanto's Krilium patents. The Phosphate Division developed, at considerable speed, a concentrated, water-soluble, 20–20–20 fertilizer, Folium, to round out the Merchandising Division's so-called agricultural line.

Subsequently, the Laucks-developed Rez brand of wood primers and sealers was also added to the new division's product catalogue to provide breadth.

In the hurry and scurry to give the new division a more comprehensive array, Monsanto reached deep into its resources and considered a wide variety of supplementary retail products. It test-marketed a liquid starch product, called "all starch," and learned—among other things—that bottling the liquid with a screw-on cap made it virtually impossible to remove the cap from the bottle.

To demonstrate that there was no loss of humor during those tense days, Sam Ballard, Gardner Advertising Company's longtime account executive for Monsanto, had a creative solution to the problem of the stubborn bottle cap. "Let's put a Stillson wrench in each box with the bottle of starch," was Sam's contribution.

During 1953 and 1954 "all" saved the day for the brave new division. But Krilium, despite heroic production and marketing efforts, continued to have problems. At one time the division general manager was so desperate he wondered out loud whether it might help to add the word "miracle" to the Krilium label. A colleague reminded him, "It's a good product but unrelated to Lourdes."

To begin with, Krilium was expensive, partly because at the start it was made in small quantities. The full-strength powder cost $3.45 a pound and would treat only 50 square feet of soil to a depth of 6 inches. A blend called the "Merloam formulation," 20 percent Krilium and 80 percent inert powder, cost less and was easier to handle. It was ideal for use around the home—around shrubbery beds and in flowerpots. The Merloam product didn't gum up as fast when used in moist ground, and this too was a distinct advantage. It was almost foolproof.

A homeowner seeking the benefits of Krilium for his lawn (assuming he had an established lawn, and most homeowners did) had to begin by having his lawn area Rototilled or otherwise churned up. Not everyone wanted his lawn so destroyed. After such churning up, the proper amount of Krilium had to be mixed in—evenly and carefully. Afterward the ground had to be raked into a condition for seeding or sodding, then fertilized. When these various steps were undertaken properly, an exceptionally fine lawn resulted. Grass flourished (and so did weeds) in the aggregated soil. Particularly for new lawns, Krilium was ideal.

The product really worked!

Yet millions of homeowners, aware their lawns were something less than those pictured on grass seed catalogues, were unwilling to undertake all the advance work required. They were unwilling to pay the high price for having their lawns churned up. Their lawns were a problem— but not their highest-priority problem.

Krilium was relatively easy to use in flower beds. And that's where much of it went in the home market.

In 1954 the Merchandising Division was rechristened the Consumer Products Division, but this didn't seem to help. In Monsanto's 1955 Annual Report the company said, "During the past several years, we have mentioned developments which, at the time, seemed promising. These included . . . titanium, Krilium soil conditioner and atomic power. They have not borne fruit." It added, "We have not yet been able to develop applications which will take full advantage of properties of Krilium or reduce its cost to the point where large-volume uses would be economical. Sales effort has been curtailed but not abandoned."

However, the low-sudsing detergent "all" was prospering, having been joined in 1955 by a companion product, "Dishwasher all."

The 1956 Annual Report noted that "all" continued to reflect profitability, but it added, "We face the reality that our consumer products line is not now broad enough to support a completely competitive merchandising organization."

And the following year the company announced, "Lever Brothers purchased from us the trademark and franchise to market the detergent 'all' and 'Dishwasher all.' We have contracted to manufacture these products for Lever Brothers and, for an interim period, to package them. This agreement permits Monsanto, in the detergent field, to devote all of its energies to the development and sale of its chemicals to detergent manufacturers."

A few years later the Rez line of wood primers and sealers was sold to Pittsburgh Paint (now PPG Industries, Inc.).

This, then, is how Monsanto "went to market" in consumer goods during a brief, exciting period in the fifties.

Charlie Thomas, who was president during the period, says the company "learned a lot of lessons, many of which proved invaluable in subsequent years."

The Krilium experience, despite the chain-reacting problems, at least did not involve stepping on the feet of major industrial customers. That at least is one headache Krilium did not produce. It may, indeed, have been the only nonheadache in the short but tempestuous life of Krilium.

Charlie Thomas recently recalled, "As president, I took the rap for Krilium—and I should have. It wasn't handled right. It was an example of taking something that was 'half-baked' and pushing it prematurely. The newspapers took hold and got excited. Normally, no product should be forced. When the timing is right, a meritorious product will bloom. With Krilium I wound up with egg on my face, particularly with security analysts who kept asking, 'Where are the profits?' Inventions have to be shepherded quietly and not exploited prematurely."

Thomas added, "I am surely glad we never tried to market aspirin the same way. But don't forget it's a changing world. You'll find today there is practically no field in the consumer business where we'd not collide with the interest of some of our industrial customers. It's not as much of a shock today when basic industrial manufacturers decide to try their wings in the consumer field. However, the same old basic cautions still have to be reckoned with."

When the Consumer Products Division folded its tent following the 1957 sale of "all" to Lever Brothers, no epitaph was discussed.

Yet by now Monsanto had dropped its slogan, "Serving Industry Which Serves Mankind," even though the experiment with consumer goods had served to confirm that "serving industry" should, more than ever, be the company's policy.

Fewest tears during the Consumer Products Division's requiem period came from Phosphate (renamed Inorganic) Division General Manager John L. Christian, who had continuously objected to the company's competing with his division's principal customers, the soapers. Christian had continued to hammer away at Edgar Queeny and to assert, "We ought to get out of this damn foolishness while the getting's good." Both Christian and the events, as they occurred, were persuasive.

With Charlie Thomas convinced that the ground was getting shakier all the time under the Consumer Products Division, it was Edgar Queeny, no less, who finally pulled the plug.

And in those days, when Edgar Queeny pulled the plug, a certain air of finality was involved.

And so the rest of Monsanto, which had in the meantime been doing nicely, inherited the benefit of top management's total concern. The distraction of the consumer products era was gone, but not forgotten.

CHAPTER X

Meanwhile, Back at the
Rest of the Company...

WHILE side issues such as "all" detergent and Krilium soil conditioner were taking the spotlight in the early fifties, the other parts of the company—the traditional operating divisions—were progressing in an orderly manner, broadening their customer lists and product lines and, in general, moving ahead at a rapid rate. The company's controller remarked, "It takes a lot of profits from the established segments of the company to underwrite the noble experiments."

The year 1950 brought external waves which caused a bit of boat-rocking within. Chief among such influences was the government's imposition of an excess profits tax applying to the last six months of the year, making for a major adjustment in the earnings picture. Sales of $227 million were 37 percent above the previous year. Earnings were $5.37 a share compared with 1949's $3.74, but they would have jumped to $6.58 if there had been no excess profits tax to reckon with.

At the 1950 Annual Meeting, in March, shareowners approved the company's first comprehensive and enduring bonus plan, designed to provide incentives and to reward eligible employes contributing to the company's progress.

One event mentioned in the 1950 Annual Report that did not necessarily call for a 21-gun salute—the start-up of a polystyrene molding powder manufacturing location at Long Beach, California—was, nevertheless, of overriding importance to two Monsanto gentlemen on the West Coast: Charles L. Fetzner and Edward Schuler. They had served together as Monsanto's pioneer salesmen on the West Coast—an affiliation lasting 28 years, from 1937 until 1965. Known as the "Gold Dust twins," Schuler and Fetzner spent their careers in what they used to call the "foreign mission" of California. Even today, in 1977, the two pals— living a mile apart in retirement in San Mateo—still believe St. Louis was "a little backward" in recognizing the bountiful potential of the West Coast market.

147

They both remember with fondness the day Monsanto "finally woke up" and established a plastics plant at Long Beach. To hear them tell it, they had been yelling and screaming all along for the company to give more recognition to the sun-kissed glories of the West.

Charlie Fetzner was fifteen and a half when he started as a Monsanto Chemical Works office boy in St. Louis, in 1919. He was sixty-five and a half when he retired in 1969, having been allowed to stay on the payroll beyond his sixty-fifth birthday in order to achieve the distinction of being the first—and only—corporate employe ever to receive a 50-year service award pin.

He was sent to San Francisco as a branch manager in 1927. And from then on, he made a crusade of calling the home office's attention to the growing and glowing potential for chemicals on the West Coast.

This is Fetzner's favorite story:

"In the mid-thirties, Spicer Laboratory in Glendale, California, phoned a sales manager in St. Louis and said it needed a barrel of calcium glycero phosphate in a hurry. The sales manager phoned me in San Francisco and asked if I'd be kind enough to drop it by at the customer's plant on my way home from work that evening. I told the sales manager there were only two things wrong with his request. First, the barrel wouldn't fit into my car. Second, Glendale's a suburb of Los Angeles, not San Francisco. Glendale, I reminded him, is about four hundred and twenty-five miles south. His reply was, 'I've got a U.S. map under a piece of glass atop my desk, and the two dots representing Glendale and San Francisco are less than an inch apart.' "

Fetzner giggled a bit as he recalled this "proof" of the provincial attitude of his Midwestern-rooted home office.

In 1941 Fetzner was transferred from San Francisco to Los Angeles, and was beaming when the Long Beach plant opened next to his left elbow in 1950.

Ed Schuler, also a transplant, established his roots with equal firmness in Calfornia soil. He joined the company as a stock clerk in St. Louis in 1926, at age twenty-one, and he stayed on as a "California missionary" until his early retirement at age sixty in 1965. He was dispatched to San Francisco in 1937 to "make a market survey." Schuler recently recalled, "Believe it or not, total Monsanto sales for eleven Western states and Hawaii were only $263,000 in 1937, compared to $200 million today."

That $200 million today proves Monsanto did wake up to the Western market, Schuler declared. On the one hand, Schuler is proud of all that growth and knows he played a part in it. On the other hand, he is still not sure Monsanto has fully realized the potential, even today.

"We"—and all alumni who were interviewed said "we," just as though they were still aboard—"don't even have our sales office in San Francisco, the business capital of the West Coast. We're in Santa Clara—the wrong place," Schuler complained.

Both Fetzner and Schuler grimaced when they were asked, "Did you regard yourselves as salesmen or as marketing experts during your long West Coast careers?" They both insisted, "We were neither; we were peddlers."

Irreverent as both can be, they were quite serious recently when asked, "In balance, didn't you enjoy your Monsanto careers even though the company didn't see the light in the West sufficiently?" Fetzner summed it up as "a simply fantastic experience." Schuler went a bit further: "The best thing about it all was being able to say, 'I'm Ed Schuler from Monsanto.' That's all you had to say. I may be an alumnus, technically, but I'm a part of Monsanto until I die. Sure, I get a pension check from St. Louis every month plus dividends on my Monsanto stock four times a year. But that's not the reason. My heart was in Monsanto for all those years. My heart will be in Monsanto as long as I live."

That little plastics plant at Long Beach, which was so important to Messrs. Fetzner and Schuler in 1950, has an expanded line of products today, and the California market is—whether or not the "Gold Dust twins" would ever admit it—taken very seriously by all of Monsanto in 1977. Herbicides, in particular, find a growing market in the Western states' (and Hawaii's) burgeoning agricultural sectors.

The Long Beach plastics plant was not the only item in the 1950 Annual Report which telegraphed its punch with respect to future growth. There was also a hint of moving ahead in agricultural chemicals, and there was the initial surfacing of a new piece of chemical language, "isocyanates."

In the former area, capital expenditures were authorized for producing sodium trichloracetate and for expanding the capacity for 2,4-D and 2,4,5-T. All three of these are in the herbicide family—an area where the company was destined to become highly profitable and highly proficient in the development of sophisticated, proprietary, patent-protected products necessary for farmers to attain maximum yields.

As regards the latter, the new word—isocyanates—appearing in an Annual Report for the first time indicated the company's interest in a promising field of chemistry which had been developed in Germany immediately after World War II. The responsibility for isocyanate research was initially given to the Phosphate Division at Anniston, Alabama, but the big news was to come a few years later, when Monsanto entered into a joint venture with Farbenfabriken Bayer, A. G., of Leverkusen, Germany, in the formation of Mobay Chemical Company. Purpose: the manufacture of polyurethane foam from isocyanates.

In the basic product lines, the year 1950 saw the completion of a sixth electric furnace at the elemental phosphorus plant at Columbia, Tennessee, as well as ground breaking for a major Texas City installation to manufacture acrylonitrile, the basic raw material for Chemstrand's Acrilan fiber.

Increases in plastics production included but went beyond the little polystyrene plant at Long Beach, California, and beyond the U.S. Up north at Montreal, Monsanto (Canada) Limited got into the vinyl chloride resins business and increased its capacity for polystyrene. Down south, Monsanto Mexicana, S.A., was formed in Mexico City for the specific purpose of making polystyrene molding powders.

Before leaving 1950 there's one other small item meriting comment. The 1950 Annual Report said, somewhat guardedly, "Of particular importance was the production of substantial quantities of a synthetic antibiotic." But that's all it said. Antibiotics were new following World War II, and Monsanto, which had been founded by a man from a drug company, was still very much interested in the drug business—as a supplier—almost half a century later.

The 1951 Annual Report was more explicit. It identified the synthetic antibiotic as chloramphenicol.

The chloramphenicol episode had its ups and downs.

Dr. R. E. Kelly, longtime director of the company's medical department, who retired in 1975, recalled, "Parke Davis came out in the late forties with its own brand of chloramphenicol, Chloromycetin, a broad-range antibiotic which was popularly received. But Parke Davis couldn't keep up with the demand with its fermentation process, so it farmed out to Monsanto the job of making several of the intermediates. Subsequently, Monsanto took over the job of making the entire finished product—and by an improved process. We supplied a substantial part of Parke Davis's requirements."

Sadly, the dread ailment aplastic anemia developed as a side effect in a very tiny percentage of Chloromycetin users, after which the product was prescribed much more selectively, Dr. Kelly recalled.

Dr. Kelly added, "A drug house like Parke Davis could have as many as seventy-five Ph.D.s working on a new antibiotic and could develop son-of-Chloromycetin and son-of-son-of-Chloromycetin. Monsanto had no such resources or experience."

In addition, Parke Davis developed its own synthetic process for manufacturing the drug, and help from Monsanto was no longer required. Yet at one time, in 1951, Monsanto was selling chloramphenicol for up to $450 a pound.

Former President and Board Chairman Charles H. Sommer recently recalled, "Yes, it was a highly profitable product for a short time. But the Organic Division imbalanced its research department by calling on too many chemists to help with chloramphenicol—to the detriment of other research projects which cried for attention. It is normally far preferable to deploy research manpower—or any manpower—on projects which seem to be enduring rather than on 'spot crises,' even though the temporary projects offer a real temptation."

The fiftieth anniversary year, 1951, saw Monsanto form an associate company in Japan to manufacture chemicals and plastics at Yokkaichi and Nagoya, as well as a subsidiary in São Paulo, Brazil, for plastics. A large piece of news on the home front came from John L. Christian, general manager of the Phosphate Division. Psyched by the booming success of the expansive elemental phosphorus complex at Columbia, Tennessee, Christian looked west for more of the same kind of profitable manufacturing, west to Soda Springs, Idaho, where—it was decided in 1951—electric furnace technology from Tennessee could be used to establish a plant in the heart of a smaller yet equally rich field of phosphate ore.

The plant was scheduled to go on stream in 1953 with one electric furnace like the six in Tennessee, yet larger than the largest in Tennessee.

To John Christian, "scheduled to go on stream" meant actually going on stream when promised, if not before. He was impatient with shortfalls and particularly sensitive that his Phosphate Division should break no promises, internal or external surprises notwithstanding.

During 1951 one of his fastest-rising, high-potential proteges was the plant manager at Columbia, Tennessee, Edward J. Bock, who would in 1968 become Monsanto's president and chief executive officer. Bock recently recalled the challenges of the "John Christian era" in the early fifties.

Bock remembers that Christian was quite demanding. Bock said, "He could drive you up the wall. If you didn't stand up to John Christian he'd walk all over you. Quite often all he was doing was testing people in his own hard-boiled way."

Whether or not Christian intended to intimidate people is a moot point, and whether or not everyone knew of the "testing game" is also a moot point, but there seems to be no disagreement that in the early fifties Christian was feeling his oats, no doubt encouraged by the profitability, growth and razzle-dazzle spirit of his operating division. People meeting him for the first time discerned he was no run-of-the-mill executive. The "real" John Christian was a spirited leader who had his own style and his own set of disciplines within his Phosphate group. He could be, and quite often was, a soft-spoken and ultra-polite Southern charmer when business or social formalities so dictated. He could also be a martinet within his own division, spurring people on to accomplishments they might not otherwise have achieved—or driving people "up the wall."

Bock recalls both sides of Christian: the impatient, insistent, harsh, seemingly opinionated ruler of his own divisional roost who could be merciless in his demands; and the softer John Christian, who would go out of his way to make sure those who performed best were rewarded best.

Christian was elected a vice president in 1951 and was gaining rapidly in influence at the time the decision was made to broaden the base of his division by going out to Soda Springs—on schedule.

Politically astute as well as performance-oriented, John Christian made no bones about the need to stay "in cahoots" with Edgar Queeny, who seemed not only to enjoy but also to encourage the audible and visible individualism of this very individualistic general manager. Christian not only had Queeny's respect as an action-oriented "operating man's operating man," but he also had Queeny's ear, particularly when Christian felt anyone in the company was about to "mess around" with the Phosphate Division's big customers, the soapers.

The year 1951 took John L. Gillis to Organic as general manager and Charles H. Sommer to Merrimac, replacing Gillis there. But the biggest news was that which occurred on May 1, when President Bill Rand retired at age sixty-five and was succeeded by Dr. Charles Allen Thomas, who had been executive vice president since 1947.

Here was a man up from the lab. Thomas had often told his friends he was "happiest in a lab coat." If his heart belonged to chemistry, this was understandable. He had by 1951 achieved a worldwide reputation as a scientist. But now he would have no more time for the lab coat. Now he was to be a business leader in a science company, not a scientist in a business organization.

That the transformation period worked well is attributable to several factors, of which Thomas's own tireless spirit must be identified as dominant. In the ensuing years, his leadership was aided by what was referred to as the "triumvirate situation." Freely translated, this meant that Edgar Queeny was always nearby—and his looking-over-the-shoulder presence was felt even when he was in Africa. In addition, there was the ever-present, quiet, astute, thoughtful Vice President Robert R. (Rush) Cole, whose sound judgment and operations experience not only qualified him eminently to be regarded as part of the "triumvirate" but within a few years won him the title of Executive Vice President.

Charlie Thomas was a new kind of president beyond such attributes as personal vitality and scientific stature. He was an extrovert unafraid of the podium and unwilling to accept some of the earlier, "low profile" attitudes within the company. His "let's speak up and speak out" style involved refreshing innovations. He perceived a relationship between spokesmanship and leadership and made no bones about behavior to match.

There were some insiders and outsiders both who thought he spoke up and spoke out too rapidly late in 1951 when Krilium was announced. In most instances, though, the Thomas posture added constructive zest to Monsanto's presence in the fields of science and even marketing. "Charlie Thomas is a born salesman" was a not infrequent commentary. (Yet company finance remained pretty much in the firm hand of Edgar Queeny, who, as chairman, had by this time a fair amount of experience in the matter.)

The bubbling interests of Charlie Thomas knew no bounds. After becoming president he went on a small crusade in behalf of the recruitment of young people into chemistry. It was his feeling that too many young men and women simply didn't consider chemistry or chemical engineering as a career, not so much because they were turned off by these fields but because, in his view, they hadn't been given sufficient information about them.

At the 1952 Annual Meeting he told shareowners, "Industry needs more than fifty thousand new scientists, engineers and other technologists each year for normal replacement and growth. We have a real shortage. Meanwhile, Russia is believed to be training chemical engineers alone at a rate approaching fifty thousand a year."

Thomas implemented his crusade by strongly endorsing a project for Monsanto to produce a high-quality documentary film titled *Decision for Chemistry.* Objective: to show upon the screen the excitement, promise and fulfillment in chemical careers.

The film met a high standard of excellence and had an unusual "soft sell" credibility, largely because the producers found that at every turn the unofficial assistant director was Edgar M. Queeny, who by this time was becoming fairly well versed in the art and science of movie-making, as a hobby.

Two nonchemical projects, involving "methods," were announced in 1952 and, unhappily, were destined to be short-lived.

One was a project in cooperation with National Research Corporation, to make titanium, a metal "as strong as steel but half the weight." Charlie Thomas was recently asked, "How about that titanium thing?" First he sighed. Then he said, "It was announced too soon. Because titanium involved a mining operation, we thought perhaps it could have been handled by the Phosphate Division. But when we looked more deeply into it, we saw we weren't positioned right. It was more for a metals company than a chemical company."

The other "methods" project announced in 1952 involved a joint effort with Union Electric Company of Missouri for studying the feasibility of using atomic reactors for generating power. Allowing that this was almost 20 years before "the energy crisis" became a household phrase, Charlie Thomas commented recently that the announcement was probably premature or perhaps even unnecessary. "Things like that should be shepherded quietly and not exploited prematurely," he observed. "Getting into the nuclear business would have involved the government deeply. It would have involved a massive investment. Nuclear power doesn't involve much chemistry. It involves a lot of good engineering. This project was not Monsanto's 'bag' and I'm sorry we did or said anything about it."

The year 1952 also brought two non-product-related news items: Monsanto announced it had purchased almost 300 acres in suburban Creve Coeur for the purpose of establishing new world headquarters offices there, and President Charlie Thomas was advised he had been selected for the Perkin Medal, the highest honor the American chemical industry can bestow.

A particularly interesting item of 1952 concerned air and water pollution. When Dr. R. E. Kelly, director of the medical department, and his associate, Elmer P. Wheeler, advised the Executive Committee that "more attention to pollution control could add several million dollars to the cost of a plant but that's the way we should go," they expected resistance—but didn't get it. The committee agreed that thereafter any appropriations request going to the board would have to carry a statement indicating that the medical department had analyzed the proposal and had approved the measures for controlling pollution and toxicological effects.

The project of 1953 that undoubtedly commanded the greatest number of executive man-hours was one called simply "the reorganization." This new plan—comprehensive in sweep—reshaped the face of the company. It was announced in November and went into effect at the start of 1954.

As there had been no restructuring since 1939, the new plan involved picking up on some of the general principles of decentralization adopted almost fifteen years earlier, and making some modifications in the light of Monsanto's growth during the interim and its projection of future growth. In 1939 the employe head count stood at 6580; in 1953, the number approached 20,000.

President Thomas commented, "In addition to studying our own company, we looked at many others in order to check our experiences against theirs. The study confirmed our belief in the decentralized line and staff organization. It reaffirmed many of the principles involving personnel practices and policies which Monsanto's management had adopted through the years."

Under the new plan the company was divided into three general domains: the trustee, executive and operating.

The trustee responsibility to the shareowners continued to be lodged in the Board of Directors and its Finance and Executive Committees. Thus there was no change in this category.

Executive responsibility was vested—and this was new—in the Executive Offices of the President (to become known promptly as the EOP) composed of the president, the new position of executive vice president (Rush Cole), and six other executive officers with functional responsibilities in their respective specialized fields: finance, general counsel, manufacturing, marketing, personnel, and research, development and engineering. There was this further explanation: "Although having no line authority, these officers will, within their respective fields, provide advice and guidance to operating officers, evaluate the job that has been done, coordinate activities, and prevent overlap."

In the third domain, operations, divisions were realigned on a product basis, almost without regard to geography and historic chains of command. It was also determined that, for the first time, "two or more divisions can be financially interested in the same plant site."

As is true in all such organizational overhauls, some units won and others lost. The Merrimac Division, Texas Division and Western Division were summarily obliterated.

Least surprising was the elimination of the Western Division, which had sprung from the I. F. Laucks acquisition. It had the very commendable purpose of establishing Monsanto more firmly on the West Coast. But its product line was limited. The elimination of the Texas Division was understandable in that its holdings were mainly at one location, Texas City. The much older Merrimac Division, headquartered at Everett, Massachusetts, and known as the "cradle of presidents" (two: Belknap and Rand) was simply not growing as fast as the rest of the company, and it was suffering from disadvantageous freight rates in commerce beyond New England. It too had a limited product line of industrial chemicals.

One of the winners in the new lineup was the Plastics Division, which heretofore had had a plant only at Springfield, Massachusetts, and newer installations at Addyston, Ohio, and Long Beach, California. As the result of the reorganization it picked up the crown jewel of the Texas Division at Texas City and also the Seattle and Santa Clara, California, locations of the Western Division.

Another winner was the Phosphate Division, which was rechristened the Inorganic Chemicals Division. In addition to its plants at Columbia, Tennessee, Carondelet, Missouri, Soda Springs, Idaho, and Trenton, Michigan, it picked up (from Merrimac) the Everett, Massachusetts, and Camden, New Jersey, locations.

In anticipation of growing multinational markets—even though that word "multinational" was not in general use in 1953—Edward A. O'Neal was brought back from London to head up a new Overseas Division. He had earned his stripes running the British company.

One other divisional unit was established, a Research and Engineering Division; and the ill-fated Consumer Products Division was temporarily continued.

Personnel moves abounded in the wake of the organizational changes.

Starting at the new EOP level, John L. Gillis left the general managership at Organic to make way for upcoming Charlie Sommer and to move into corporate marketing responsibilities—the first such thrust in this direction in the company's history. W. W. Schneider became general counsel; Edgar Queeny, of course, continued to call the shots in finance; Felix Williams took over the functional portfolio for production; Frank Curtis the same for personnel; and Ted Hochwalt for research, development and engineering, with the new Research and Engineering Division reporting to him.

The seven general staff departments remained essentially the same as they had been and were the least affected by the reorganization.

But that wasn't the end of it. A new echelon was established for regional vice presidents. These were later to be nicknamed "Kentucky colonels," since they were not officers elected by the board but, rather, appointive officers. The first two of this species were Edward W. Gamble, Jr., who had been manager of the company's Washington, D.C., offices, and the veteran Victor E. Williams, director of sales in New York, who had joined Monsanto in 1915.

To sum up, the most immediately noticeable "new wrinkles" in the organization were: 1) the end of the line for three divisions; 2) the new layer of management known as EOP; and 3) the new position of regional vice president.

It is easier to assess the latter two innovations from the perspective of 1977's hindsight than it would have been at the time.

The Executive Offices of the President was a concept that didn't work. Period. The new coterie was composed of eight people, five of whom also served on the Executive Committee of the board. One of the stated objectives of the EOP was to "prevent overlap," yet the EOP went into business somewhat in competition with, and with a strong overlap into, the Executive Committee.

The motive was exemplary. With the company expanding at a fast pace both geographically and in product lines, Charlie Thomas wanted to be sure sufficient corporate attention was given to the "vertical" tracks, such as marketing and manufacturing. Yet, the irony was that the operating divisions were consolidated while, at the same time, a new layer of management was added topside.

"Why did you do it?" Charlie Thomas was asked recently. "We knew it would provide a forum for bringing different viewpoints into play," Thomas recalled. "It didn't work mainly, I suspect, because a committee can't run a company. I was the advocate for the EOP. I started it. As soon as I saw it wasn't working I folded it up." The experiment lasted for three years—enough time for an adequate test. To Thomas's credit, he didn't shuffle his feet once he was convinced it was a layer of management that caused more problems than it solved.

The EOP's most lasting contribution was the somewhat permanent establishment of a top corporate slot for marketing and a top corporate slot for technology. In the former, John Gillis went ahead to become the company's "Mr. Marketing," and in the latter Ted Hochwalt became the firm and guiding hand for research, development, engineering and patents.

The concept of the regional vice president, which also surfaced during the reorganization, was new to Monsanto though not new to industry. It had been tested with success by General Electric Company. Upon observing this, Gillis borrowed the idea for Monsanto.

In subsequent years the idea worked well for the Washington, D.C., office but had a rocky road in New York City and in other major marketing areas: Detroit, Atlanta and Santa Clara, California. In such cities the regional vice president wound up with what was largely a staff job —a sort of minister without portfolio. Line authority for marketing rested with the operating people in these offices, people inclined to resist tampering by "superimposed nonofficers."

As in the case of the EOP, the regional vice president concept was exemplary—perhaps even more so because it wound up being somewhat permanently, though somewhat shakily, accepted during the subsequent two decades.

Under the guidelines of the 1954 reorganization it was the job of the regional vice president to establish contact with those customers served by more than one division—an obvious plus. It was also his job to explore areas where a single customer of a single operating division might be persuaded to sample the wares of other Monsanto divisions, where appropriate. It was also his job to advise and coordinate at the local level, without interfering with line responsibilities.

Line marketing people took a dim view of such St. Louis–established ambassadors-at-large. Some said they regarded the whole idea as an intrusion. John Gillis took the view that under cooperative circumstances, regional vice presidents and line marketing people could help each other. But his perception of potential synergism was not always shared by line marketing people reporting to divisional general managers.

Gillis knew there were bound to be some overall advantages if prestigious people at key offices could become "Mr. Monsantos" in regions where the line marketing people, of necessity, were restricted to acting like "Mr. Organic" or "Mr. Inorganic" or "Mr. Plastics."

Looking back on the experience, Gillis later said, "The regional vice president concept hasn't been one of my greatest triumphs, because it was never fully accepted or understood by the operating people who had the bottom-line responsibility. Perhaps if I had been in their shoes I might have felt the same way."

When 1953's curtain came down, amid the hubbub of reorganizational stirrings, the general mood within Monsanto was upbeat, because business conditions so dictated. The only discordant note was sounded by no less than Edgar Monsanto Queeny himself, who pulled his company out of the ranks of the National Association of Manufacturers because the NAM, in his view, wasn't sufficiently active in promoting the cause of protective tariffs for the chemical industry.

Queeny knew the NAM was populated with companies holding different viewpoints on "free trade." Some companies shared Queeny's view, some didn't. The NAM's "compromise position," as Queeny called it, was too wishy-washy for his taste. So, in a bit of a pique, Queeny flashed the red light and Monsanto's long relationship with the NAM came to a sudden end.

Some businessmen said, "Edgar shouldn't have done it that way. If the NAM needed a more enlightened policy he should have stayed in there and tried to bring such a policy about. Once on the outside, there was no longer a chance for him to exert any beneficial influence." Another businessman put it less charitably when he said, "Edgar told the NAM if it didn't play his way, he would simply pick up his marbles and leave." Another, agreeing with Queeny, said, "Why should Monsanto support an organization espousing a position Monsanto doesn't believe in?"

In the following year, 1954, no news was sweeter than the word that Acrilan's technical difficulties had been overcome. Partially for this reason (but owing more to nylon) the Chemstrand Corporation turned the corner into the black shortly thereafter.

For what was now known as "worldwide Monsanto," the skies were getting brighter all the time.

CHAPTER XI

Mobay and Lion

THE acronym "Mobay" is composed of the first two letters of Monsanto and the first three letters of Bayer, the latter name being the shorthand for Farbenfabriken Bayer, A. G., of Leverkusen, Germany.

Mobay Chemical Company was a joint venture which started in 1954 and ended in 1967, when Bayer took over total ownership.

Actually there were three principals in the scenario: Monsanto, Bayer and the United States Department of Justice.

The story is best told by two people who were in the middle of the excitment: J. R. (Rusty) Wilson, Monsanto's former patent department director and a former member of the Mobay board, and Dr. Otto Bayer, who was director of research of the German company. Both have since retired.

Rusty Wilson recently recalled: "Prior to 1954 Monsanto had been experimenting with isocyanate chemistry at the Inorganic Division's Anniston, Alabama, laboratory, but we weren't progressing too well. We hadn't figured out a way of producing isocyanates economically and, in addition, we had problems making urethane foam.

"It was widely known that Bayer had been working on isocyanates in Germany even prior to World War II. After V-E Day the Allies had prohibited the Germans from continuing their development of buna-S synthetic rubber, because this was identified as a war material. Restrictions weren't lifted by the Allies until 1958.

"Yet Bayer was able to resume its research into isocyanates shortly after the end of World War II, and some basic patents had been issued to Bayer by the early fifties.

"In 1953 Monsanto decided urethane foams from isocyanates would have a real potential in the U.S., and we decided the best bet would be to purchase know-how and patent licenses from Bayer, which had had a commanding head start.

"After visiting Germany, I was convinced Bayer would be willing to license Monsanto under the right circumstances, but a month later Bayer

159

changed its mind and decided it would prefer to create an equity interest in the U.S. and not simply license an American company. Late in 1953 Bayer sent a team to interview people at various American chemical companies and to inquire about the possibilities of a joint venture.

"After the Germans visited Monsanto, Edgar Queeny's interest was greater than ever. He suggested we not simply sit and wait for a verdict from Leverkusen. He reasoned, 'The decision will be made in Germany, so let's go to Germany and see if we can influence the decision.'

"Late in 1953, W. W. Schneider, our general counsel, John Christian, Phosphate Division general manager, and I went to Germany to try to work out a deal. And we did."

Monsanto's 1954 Annual Report states: "Mobay . . . is constructing the first full-scale production plant in the United States for the manufacture of isocyanate chemicals. These new chemicals will be combined with polyester resins, which Mobay will produce, in flexible and rigid foamed plastics, wire coatings, paints, synthetic rubber formulations and adhesives."

Before the plant was completed, late in 1955, at New Martinsville, West Virginia, a pilot plant had been established in a converted garage a block away from Monsanto headquarters at 800 South Second Street in St. Louis.

Rusty Wilson recalls how people used to gaze wide-eyed and make comments such as "It's just like Bromo Seltzer" when they saw, for the first time, the fascinating way urethane foam was made in the converted garage, using German chemicals and German machinery. Visitors would see a nozzle squirting a liquid down onto a moving belt; they'd see the liquid turn milky as carbon dioxide was formed within it; and they'd see the liquid mass rather suddenly begin to foam up, increasing in volume many times.

The product could be made in a wide range of densities. It could be hard as a brick or soft as a feather.

Once Mobay had established an office in Pittsburgh and once production was under way at New Martinsville, the new company seemed all set to compete head-on with the rubber industry, then making great quantities of latex foam for automobile seats, furniture, insulation and a wide variety of other applications. So-called "foam rubber" was a major and growing market—and Mobay was now into it with a "newer and better mousetrap."

Well, at least newer.

In automobile seats, particularly—largely because of the warm and humid condition frequently encountered inside automobiles—the urethane foam tended to disintegrate. In technical language, the foam was subject to hydrolysis in warm and humid air. The rubber industry, whose market position in latex foam was threatened, capitalized on the Mobay product's weakness by offering a ten-year warranty, which of course Mobay could not match.

The Texas City styrene plant prior to April 16, 1947.

The Texas City styrene plant in flames.

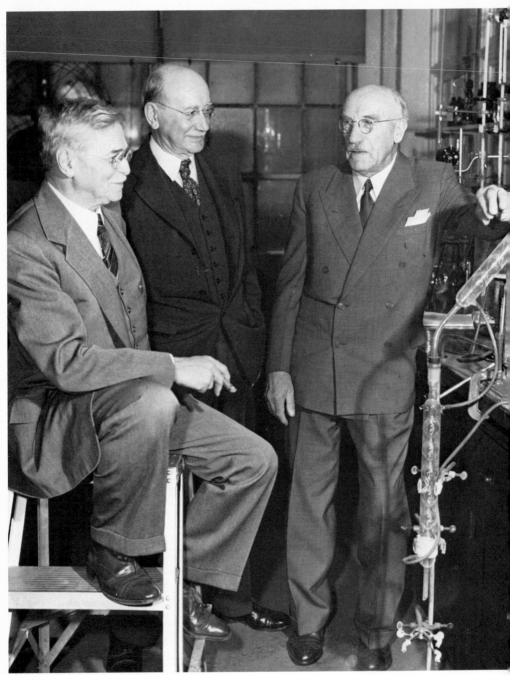

The three "original Swiss," who were hired in the early days of Monsanto, as they appeared at a St. Louis reunion in 1951. From the left, Gaston F. DuBois, Jules Bebie and Louis Veillon.

Technicians in Monsanto-operated, government-owned Mound Laboratory, Miamisburg, Ohio, are shown in 1954 assaying the amount of polonium in air samples through the use of sophisticated measuring equipment. Mound Lab's polonium was used to power generators in the nation's first satellites.

Vice President John L. Gillis stepping into the first Chevrolet Corvette delivered in St. Louis—in 1953. The reinforced plastic body of the car contained Monsanto resins materials.

Two new products in the fifties were "all" low-sudsing detergent, developed by Monsanto, and Acrilan acrylic fiber from the Chemstrand Corporation, a Monsanto associate company. Both products originated at Monsanto's Central Research Department at Dayton, Ohio.

The Monsanto board at El Dorado, Arkansas, following the Lion Oil Company merger in 1955.

Edgar and Ethel Queeny in 1961, in a photo both regarded as their favorite.

THE WORD'S OUT...

Monsanto Company

We've outgrown our middle name

We've dropped the "Chemical" from our formal name for a good reason—growth. We have today eight divisions operating in many diverse areas, ranging from petroleum and fibers to building materials and packaging. (Yes, we are still in the chemical business with both feet and expanding rapidly—already the fourth largest in the world.)

Officially, our full name is now Monsanto Company . . . but our "working" name is still the same as always: Monsanto, St. Louis, Missouri 63166.

The advertisement that announced the company's name change in 1964.

In 1967, three former presidents posed with President Charles H. Sommer (right). The others are, from the left, Edgar M. Queeny, William M. Rand and Charles A. Thomas.

Edward A. O'Neal was Monsanto's board chairman from 1965 to 1968. Earlier he had been president of Chemstrand Corporation. He is shown here at Chemstrand's nylon plant in Pensacola, Florida, in 1963.

Mobay's problem was not the basic isocyanates but the polyester intermediates that were mixed in. Dr. Otto Bayer picks up the story, as follows: "At this point we were most fortunate. Fifteen years after Bayer's unsuccessful experiments with polyesters, coupled with results generated in the interim period, we saw the possibility to react even secondary hydroxyl groups of polypropylene glycol ethers with valuable diisocyanates. Foams prepared in this fashion showed special properties because, in addition to hydrolysis resistance, these foams displayed some of the characteristic properties of latex foam and, furthermore, were cheaper to prepare than polyester foams. From then on, polyurethane chemistry started on a victory procession without comparison."

Once the technical problem was licked, Mobay's urethane foam began its step-by-step battle with latex foam and within a few years had virtually taken over the U.S. market. Not only flexible foams were made. There was a market also for rigid foams and for elastomers and coatings. But the basic strength was in soft and cushiony foams, and the basic profits, for both parents, stemmed from a new and better way to make such foams.

By the early sixties the eminent Dr. Bayer could remark to a U.S. host, "It looks like we've got what you Americans call a home run."

But not for long.

To pick up with Rusty Wilson: "In 1964 the Department of Justice filed a suit against Mobay. Earlier, the U.S. Supreme Court had handed down a decision suggesting that if two companies had joined together, and if both had had the 'potential' for going it alone, that might be the basis for antitrust action.

"It was interesting to speculate on what was meant by the word 'potential.' Is a one-year-old boy a 'potential' father? Monsanto felt the Justice Department was simply using Mobay as a vehicle to test the scope and meaning of the Supreme Court language. Actually, prior to Mobay, Monsanto was simply doing a little research, mostly ineffective. Bayer, with its depth of research and its patents, qualified totally for the use of the word 'potential.' All evidence showed how tremendously far ahead Bayer was. Monsanto's pre-Mobay 'potential' was meager, at best.

"Naturally Monsanto was anxious to fight the suit strenuously. Over a period of several years we prepared our case diligently. As things developed, we got a few blocks from the Court House steps when Bayer came to us at the eleventh hour and said it would prefer not to be involved in litigation in the U.S. and would offer a fair price to take over Monsanto's 50-percent interest in Mobay. Which it did. In total, it was a profitable venture for Monsanto. What we lost was the ability to continue participating in a growing field of plastics. Isocyanates now account for at least five percent of all world plastics. Mobay has since found it necessary to build a second plant."

In its 1967 Annual Report, Monsanto said: ". . . an extraordinary profit [was] realized in 1967's first quarter from the sale of Monsanto's interest in Mobay Chemical Company. This nonrecurring gain amounted to $6,394,000, or 19 cents a share."

Dr. Bayer recalls that the joint venture was based on a "very friendly and fruitful cooperation. . . . We unfortunately could not continue our association."

When Dr. Bayer was awarded the Goodyear Medal by the American Chemical Society in Cleveland in 1975, he looked back on the trying days of early research. And he contributed several bits of philosophy, which apply not only to isocyanate chemistry but to all chemical experimentation worldwide:

"It was imagination which gave us wings. We were helped by clear working hypotheses, although in theory these were not always correct. Unexpected observations, which we tracked down in the best Sherlock Holmes fashion, the fine art of experimentation, and the enthusiasm of my colleagues were all of crucial importance to the end result. Naturally, we also had a good deal of luck.

"Although I call the development of polyurethane chemistry an odyssey, this comparison is not totally correct. Homer does have his hero navigate all cliffs successfully, and tells us that after his return he finds his wife, Penelope, surrounded by suitors who are having a good time at his expense. But here the parallel ends, as Odysseus slays them all with his sword. I, on the other hand, am happy about anyone who continues my work and devotes his efforts to isocyanate chemistry."

Mobay was one of two substantial ventures undertaken by Monsanto in the mid-fifties.

The second involved Lion Oil Company, of El Dorado, Arkansas, which in September of 1955 became a full-fledged—as contrasted with Mobay's 50-50 status—member of the Monsanto family.

The "Lion deal" was not based on a new and exotic technology, as was the "Mobay deal." The Lion venture was instead based on Monsanto's high-noon realization of the growing interdependence of: 1) petroleum raw materials and products therefrom, and 2) the chemical industry. By 1955 the petroleum industry was beginning to "invade" the chemical industry and vice versa.

Monsanto's experience in using petroleum products, rather than coal tar products, for raw materials and intermediates had traced back to the late twenties. Even before Monsanto acquired the Thomas and Hochwalt Laboratories in 1936 Charlie Thomas and Ted Hochwalt had been busily engaged in hydrocarbons chemistry.

The Lion Oil negotiations were also different in other ways from the negotiations with Bayer regarding Mobay. Lion's assets were nonspeculative. They were demonstrable, visible and tangible. No new chemical hypotheses were involved.

The terms of the Monsanto-Lion agreement were approved in July,

1955, when Monsanto Corporate Secretary E. J. Putzell, Jr., handled the formalities at a morning board meeting in St. Louis and then flew down to El Dorado in the afternoon to wrap up the remaining legal paperwork there. Shareowners of both companies gave their approval two months later. The acquisition agreement specified that Monsanto would issue 1½ shares of its stock for each of the 3,090,915 outstanding shares of Lion. This meant a purchase amounting to approximately $210 million.

To appreciate the substance of Lion's entry into the world of Monsanto, some other data merits examination.

Monsanto assets jumped from $481 million in 1954 to $690 million in 1955; net sales went from $410 million to $632 million. The Monsanto shareowner family increased from 24,000 to 43,000, partly because 15,000 Lion shareowners joined the ranks in 1955, but also because a three-for-one stock split in July made the price of Monsanto stock more attractive. The employe head count showed only a modest increase, from 22,000 in 1954 to 27,000 in 1955. Of this 5000 gain, 3000 were from Lion.

Beyond doubt, Lion added more, instantly, to Monsanto's total numbers than any previous acquisition.

Of Monsanto's $200 million-plus gain in assets, Lion brought a dowry accounting for approximately $150 million, including more than 1000 producing wells in 11 states, from the Canadian border to the Gulf of Mexico. Lion's sales were more than $100 million at the time of the merger.

Only 32 years before, when the company was born in the South Arkansas oil boom of 1923, Lion had been a tiny refining unit of 25 employes, extracting gasoline, kerosene and crude oil from about 5000 barrels a day.

The mutual advantage that had been the ruling motive in all previous Monsanto acquisitions was not difficult to perceive in the Lion venture. Much of Lion's growth following World War II stemmed from the fact that petroleum is useful not only for fuel and lubricants but also for chemical raw materials. Lion had moved into chemicals during the war when, in response to the urgent need for nitrogen for explosives, it began to produce anhydrous ammonia at the government's Ozark Ordnance Works at El Dorado. After the war Lion decided to make the nitrogenous fertilizer business a major part of its long-range plan. By 1955 it had become one of the nation's major producers of chemical fertilizers, and about half of its sales and earnings were from the chemical side.

On the oil side, Lion had not only its 1000 wells but also a refinery at El Dorado with a daily processing capacity of 27,500 barrels of crude oil. Covering 257 acres, the plant manufactured more than 70 petroleum products ranging from high-octane gasolines and liquefied petroleum gases to heavy fuels and specialty asphalts. Not far away in El Dorado was the chemical plant, on a 1350-acre site, with a capacity for ammonia and derivatives approximating 450,000 tons annually.

Also, Lion had a well-positioned chemical plant at Luling, Louisiana, near New Orleans, destined ultimately to become the first front-to-back computer-controlled installation in Monsanto.

Fertilizers were not new to the St. Louis company. But Monsanto had never owned an oil company.

Lion was a big move into petroleum compared with Monsanto's previous stake in "liquid gold," although Lion was a midget compared with such major companies as Shell and Texaco. It brought to Monsanto a 150-mile oil pipeline from El Dorado to Helena, Arkansas, a port on the Mississippi River, and several other water terminals. And it brought the Lion network of 1840 service stations and dealers in eight Southern states.

Some observers surmised from this that Monsanto was determined to go retail by pumping its own gasoline into motorists' automobiles. This was in no way a motive for the merger. In fact there was never any serious discussion of changing Lion gasoline to Monsanto gasoline, even though later in the St. Louis area a dozen Lion service stations did indeed add Monsanto's big, bold block M to their signage—principally because Monsanto was almost a household word in its own community.

The Lion merger prompted Edgar Queeny to undertake some special homework, not in the area of oil wells or fertilizers but in shareowner relations. He noticed a marked increase in so-called small shareowners (those owning fewer than 100 shares), and he expressed the view that in future years Monsanto might well continue to have an increasing number of such small shareowners.

His anticipation was correct. Figures show that in 1955 Monsanto had about the same number of small shareowners and large shareowners, and that ten years later 69 percent of Monsanto's shareowners were those holding fewer than 100 shares of common stock.

Queeny commented, "It's common sense to assume most of our small shareowners are not chemists and not accountants. Yet our Annual Reports are written in the foreign languages of chemistry and accountancy."

Queeny concluded, "We have, in fact, two audiences—two quite different audiences, and the small-shareowner audience will continue to grow."

Out of this analysis came Monsanto's decision, in 1956, to have two books—an Annual Report and a pictorial Annual Review—instead of the customary single, illustrated Annual Report, and to distribute both books to all shareowners.

Queeny cautioned, "Let's don't 'talk down' to the little shareowners in the Annual Review and let's don't try to tell the Monsanto story in an oversimplified 'Mother Goose' fashion." The upshot was the introduction of a supplementary book using a generous array of photos, plus narrative and captions written largely in lay terminology. From 1956 until 1975 Monsanto used the two-book system, traceable to Edgar Queeny's insistence that the little shareowner be given a better break in terms of material that would be easy to comprehend.

In 1956, the year following the merger, most of Lion's chemical operations were moved into Monsanto's Inorganic Division, where the production and marketing of fertilizers fit nicely. Monsanto had some rather sophisticated marketing strategies for chemical fertilizers, and it lost little time in extending these to the ammonia-based products of Lion.

Monsanto President Charlie Thomas had said at the time of the merger, "More than one half of our raw materials and products can be or are produced from petroleum fractions or natural gas. It is the belief of both organizations that this union will hasten a long-range program of producing a greater variety of chemical raw materials."

How did the Lion merger work out?

Dillon Anderson, a prominent attorney in Houston, "the Wall Street of the petroleum world," and a longtime Monsanto board member, commented, "The Lion outcome, I think, wasn't exactly what Monsanto had in mind in 1955."

The service stations (most of which were not owned by Lion but had lease arrangements or purchase-of-product arrangements) had their ups and downs, depending on national price trends for gasoline. They were a disappointment more years than not.

Lion wasn't big enough to be a major oil company and wasn't small enough to disregard.

On the oil side, exploration and production were pressed strenuously in the U.S. and as far away as the North Sea and Java Sea, with a view to increasing Monsanto's supply of raw materials. Yet, in the aggregate, the Lion reserves turned out to be a drop in the bucket for a fast-growing company's almost ravenous appetite for petroleum-based products.

In September of 1972 Monsanto sold its Lion refinery and marketing properties, including its service station equities—but not its oil and gas reserves or exploration ventures—to The Oil Shale Corporation (also known as TOSCO) for an after-tax income of $3.4 million.

Monsanto's 1972 Annual Report contained a telling sentence and a telling phrase concerning Lion refining and marketing.

The telling sentence: "As a regional refiner and marketer of petroleum products, Lion Oil would have required large capital expenditures to improve and expand its position in the petroleum industry, particularly to meet the new ecological requirements."

The telling phrase: "While the divestment of marginal businesses must be a continuing program in any viable company . . ."

So at least that part of Lion was marginal.

The fact is the Lion acquisition was somewhat responsible for focusing Monsanto's attention on petroleum resources and on a broader agricultural market.

Looking back recently on this large merger occurring during his tenure as president, Charlie Thomas commented: "Lion forced Monsanto to take a harder look and to develop a firmer plan for the agricultural market. Necessity is the mother of invention and Lion brought us face to face with the need to sharpen our sights. The Lion situation was at least partially responsible for the thinking which ultimately went into the establishing of our petrochemicals plant at Chocolate Bayou in Texas. Don't forget Lion brought us ninety million barrels of oil in reserves. It brought us closer to the petroleum industry. It had had its own, substantial stake in the agricultural market—and this worked out to Monsanto's advantage."

Edgar Queeny called the Lion experience "part of our maturing." On balance, Lion's entry into Monsanto is more often regarded as a plus than a minus. But it was not the "wonder child" initially envisioned by the Monsanto architects who worked out the blueprints in 1955.

CHAPTER XII

New Headquarters,
New Profits, New Problems

D ESPITE zigzags in earnings, with the zags due primarily to weakness in selling prices, Monsanto confronted the last half of the fifties in a strong growth mood, its new reach bringing a faster-than-ever expansion, with additional products and plants as well as a concentrated and aggressive marketing effort. Undistracted by consumer products and other time-consuming side issues, Monsanto entered a period of full-steam-ahead all-out growth on the road to becoming a billion-dollar enterprise. This was the era of worldwide marketing.

Make no bones about that word, "marketing." All one had to do was to listen to personable, tireless Vice President John L. Gillis, whose job was corporate coordination of companywide marketing function. Coordination can be an ineffective and dull knife in a big company, but in Gillis's hands it was a rallying point for a strong corporate effort supplemental to the marketing programs of the operating divisions. In the fifties, the term "sales" was all but gone from Monsanto's lexicon. The new term was "marketing" and the new world was marketing. Gillis so insisted.

In earlier eras Monsanto had stressed technology and production. The new era not only stressed marketing: unless one was cautious one could have been led by Gillis to believe that all other functions—such subsidiary and minor matters as personnel, financial relations, manufacturing, research, public relations, safety, medical and whatever—existed only as satellites to "the sun and the moon of corporate purpose," the end-all and be-all called marketing. Gillis was a persuasive evangelist. Some hapless specialist in something else who was insensitive to the towering power of marketing would find scant hospitality in the Gillis domain.

Yet other areas flowered, too.

The year 1955 brought 15,000 new shareowners from Lion into the Monsanto family. By year's end the shareowner rolls totaled 43,000. This was also the year of a three-for-one split of Monsanto common stock,

167

putting it within a price range that was more attractive to investors. (The pre-split high for the year was $156.50; the post-split high for the year was $52.375.)

With its offices at several downtown locations overcrowded to the point of imperiling efficiency, the company finally decided to make use of the almost 300 acres it had purchased in 1952 in the suburban St. Louis County community of Creve Coeur. By mid-1955, work was under way on four office buildings east of Lindbergh Boulevard and south of Olive Street Road. Simultaneously the construction began on a research laboratory for the Inorganic Division at the same location.

The matter of conditioning employes for the move involved a bit of doing. The "educational campaign" was scripted in 1955 and carried on full force through 1956 and during early 1957.

The strategy was mapped out by Robert H. Gadd of Shaw-Walker Company, New York.

Shaw-Walker, manufacturer of office equipment, had worked closely with the architect, Vincent Kling of Philadelphia, in planning the office arrangement at the county site. Shaw-Walker had provided the overall concept for establishing individual offices and "interior open spaces" at the new location. In addition, Shaw-Walker provided the partitions for the new cubicles at the county headquarters. Cubicles? Yes, cubicles.

At South Second Street, where Monsanto's Topsylike growth had culminated in an eight-story office building, occupied in 1947, and at several leased "overflow" locations downtown, most of the offices had been traditional. Most had had floor-to-ceiling walls. Thus, most were private.

This old way of life was not to continue in suburban Creve Coeur. Depending upon job category, fewer than 10 percent of headquarters employes would be moving into offices with floor-to-ceiling walls in the county. Hundreds would be moving into cubicles with six-foot-high partitions—and less privacy.

This should be added: the largely horizontal (vs. high-rise) layout on the east side of Lindbergh Boulevard was planned to have long, low buildings, not exceeding three floors in height, and it was planned to be "literally surrounded by daylight, sky, trees, birds and shrubbery," to quote the indefatigable Bob Gadd. Each office would be "encompassed by windows, letting nature come in," again to quote Bob Gadd. To make matters even better, all the windows would be tinted by an interlayer of gray Saflex plastic—from Monsanto.

In such an environment, too many floor-to-ceiling walls would defeat the purpose, Gadd reasoned. Things like illumination, air-conditioning and heating would be a common umbrella covering all. The open concept, versus the old one of "each in his own vault," was to be the new mood at the new general offices.

The big trick, of course, was persuading those accustomed to private "vaults" how happy they'd be in less-private cubicles. To be sure, Monsanto had decided to go the new route anyway, without regard to the success or failure of Bob Gadd's campaign to show employes how much they'd like the new open arrangement.

There were apprehensions. There were also inquiries about carpeting, water jugs and parking spaces.

In the end, it all worked out admirably. As hoped, there were virtually no surprises once the move was made. Bob Gadd had done his conditioning job with something less than delicacy, but with success.

Executive Vice President R. R. (Rush) Cole had been particularly sensitive in making preparations for the big move. It was Cole who insisted the conditioning be undertaken seriously. "It's a matter of adapting to change," he observed, "and a matter of explaining to employes the almost inconsequential disadvantages and the tremendous advantages of moving to a location where we'll have room to grow—and a location closer to most of their homes."

The year 1955 also brought a highly communicative "I told you so" from Monsanto. In their Annual Report, Chairman Queeny and President Thomas stated: "Tariff reductions, imports and threats of imports of plastics and organic chemicals from low-wage-rate but efficient European manufacturers compelled several price reductions which were uncompensated by lower costs. Manufacture of four pharmaceuticals was discontinued. In addition, our caffeine operations at Norfolk, Va., have been closed since March because of low-priced theobromine and caffeine imports, their effective tariffs having been reduced 75 percent since 1930."

The most poignant footage in Monsanto's annual motion picture "newsreel" for that year was climaxed by a somewhat emotional scene showing the one-armed plant manager at Norfolk, Karl Ellingson, clicking shut the padlock on the front gate for the last time. The scene not only said "closed." It said "closed permanently—because of low-cost, low-wage-rate foreign imports." No sad background music was needed. The sight spoke eloquently for itself.

A less emotional and more upbeat circumstance of 1955 involved a businesslike blessing bestowed on some formidable hardware known as the IBM 702 computer. Principals in attendance at the inauguration ceremony on South Second Street were Edgar Queeny and Charlie Thomas and their principal Monsanto colleagues, along with IBM President Thomas J. Watson, Jr., and several of his executive colleagues.

Queeny had been a longtime friend of Tom Watson, Jr., and his father, Thomas, Sr., historic principals of IBM. Queeny had hoped Monsanto could be the first corporation in the world to install IBM's new electronic technology in data processing—and it was.

Several years earlier, Queeny had advised the junior Watson, during a meeting of the National Industrial Conference Board (now called simply the Conference Board), that Monsanto would like to be a pioneer in learning the language of computers. Watson had assured Queeny that

Monsanto would be first in line, understandably wait-listed behind such high-priority IBM commitments as government and military installations. In 1953 Watson invited Monsanto to send in several "students" from the accounting department to learn the skills of programming for the first generation of computers. IBM people not only explained. They also asked a lot of questions about the requirements at a major chemical manufacturing corporation.

That IBM 702—23 units installed in a special room on the fifth floor at Monsanto's downtown offices—contained almost 5000 vacuum tubes. The formidable hardware was installed in a room with exacting temperature and humidity controls. The 702, in those days, was dubbed "The Brain." It was the forerunner of more sophisticated equipment to come. It gave Monsanto an early entry. It permitted Edgar Queeny, again, to pioneer.

The press in St. Louis was invited to the ceremonies. Co-hosts Queeny and Watson mumbled a few words. Neither was an extrovert. Neither enjoyed speaking. But each was proud of his company's affiliation with the other. It marked the dawn of a new day in business technology.

The IBM 702 was to serve Monsanto until 1968, when, made obsolete by newer electronic equipment, it was shipped off to the Smithsonian Institution in Washington, D.C., to sit inactive in a spot reserved for historic milestones.

The year 1955 also marked a show-business-type first for Monsanto— its entry into mass media as an exhibitor at Disneyland at Anaheim, California. Queeny had known Walt Disney quite well. In fact the two had exchanged choice morsels of motion picture footage on wildlife subjects. Each was a perfectionist. Each had high regard for the other's standards.

What did Monsanto have to sell to the masses of the general public crowding through the Tomorrowland area of Disneyland in the ensuing years? Very little. Yet Queeny thought this would be an appropriate setting for a Monsanto display. When Charlie Thomas learned of the "amusement park project," as some critical wag called it, his longtime interest in recruiting future scientists resurfaced and he suggested the Monsanto exhibit be a "Hall of Chemistry," simplifying and graphically demonstrating the wonders of chemicals, plastics and man-made fibers. And that's precisely what the initial exhibit was—an introduction to chemistry. Monsanto chemistry, of course.

Subsequently the company's relationship with the Disney organization bore fuller fruit. At Disneyland Monsanto also established an all-plastic "Home of the Future" in 1957 and later replaced the Hall of Chemistry with a psychedelic ride called Adventure Thru Inner Space in 1967. Here again Charlie Thomas was influential, this time in persuading Walt Disney to "explore the center of a molecule." The Inner Space contract ran for ten years.

In 1969, almost two years prior to the opening of Walt Disney World, near Orlando, Florida, some rather adroit negotiations resulted in Monsanto's being offered the opportunity to sponsor the most spectacular visual presentation in the park: the nine-screen Circle-Vision show *America, the Beautiful*. A few timid souls wondered why a chemical company should become involved in such an "unrelated matter" as a show about America, and one Monsanto advertising man commented initially, "That would be a good program for Greyhound." Yet, happily, Monsanto did wind up signing a 1971–1981 contract for *America, the Beautiful* and thus had one of the most appropriate, high-impact presentations in the park for the Bicentennial era. The spectacle turned out to be a resounding success and, like all successes, it now has many fathers within Monsanto.

Ed O'Neal, who in 1953 returned to St. Louis from his managing directorship of Monsanto Chemicals Limited, London, and who headed the Overseas Division for the three ensuing years, was elected president of the Chemstrand Corporation in 1956.

The question upon O'Neal's entry at Chemstrand was, "Will Chemstrand Chemstrand-ize this longtime Monsanto executive or will O'Neal of Monsanto Monsanto-ize Chemstrand?" He faced a demanding task and was determined, he recalled recently, "simply to do what I thought was best for Chemstrand, without regard for any other considerations." In retrospect it seems evident that O'Neal became a staunch Chemstrander, sensitive to Monsanto's "control tendencies," but primarily interested in doing the job at hand. It was O'Neal who brought Chemstrand into peak prominence as Chemstrand, and not particularly as an associate of Monsanto, even going so far as to have his own Chemstrand Annual Reports and to make appearances before security analyst groups, frequently at a time when Chemstrand's earnings were greater than those of Monsanto's partner, American Viscose. He was aware, he recalls now, in retirement, of who his parents were. But he adds, "I didn't let it distract me from the job I was assigned to do."

The year 1956 also brought the introduction of a new division within Monsanto—a different kind of division. It was called the Domestic Subsidiaries and Affiliates Division and was headed by Vice President J. R. Wilson, erstwhile director of the patent department. Strangely, the division had little to do with subsidiaries (in which Monsanto held more than 50-percent equity) or affiliates (in which Monsanto held less than 50-percent equity) but dealt primarily with associate companies, in which Monsanto held a 50-percent interest. The associate companies on board when the new division was formed were Shawinigan Resins, Springfield, Massachusetts; Mobay, Pittsburgh; and Chemstrand, New York. (These associates were to be joined in 1957 by the Plax Corporation, pioneer producer of plastic squeeze bottles, half-owned by Emhart Manufacturing Company.)

Prior to the time the DS&A Division was formed, Monsanto had been represented on the several associate company boards by a variety of executives. General Manager Wilson was asked, in his new position, to represent Monsanto on all associate company boards and to be the principal source of information regarding Monsanto's investments and activities at the associate companies. It was another move to tidy up administratively.

Lest any think Monsanto's research and interest in agricultural chemicals, the profit-making heroes of the seventies, may have been of recent vintage, the 1956 record shows two immensely successful and effective herbicides, Randox and Vegadex, which were marketed nationally that year. Randox was introduced as a product to kill weeds without harming corn and soybeans. The initial announcement on Randox proclaimed application of the product at planting time would result in yields increased by six or more bushels of corn per acre and by three to six bushels of soybeans per acre. Vegadex was recommended for killing weeds infesting beans, beets, salad crops and corn, and it was particularly recommended for light and sandy soils.

The year 1956 also brought a significant event in the expanding realm of Chemstrand, when an Acrilan acrylic plant was dedicated at Coleraine, Northern Ireland. No less than Prince Philip represented the British Empire at the dedication ceremonies. President Ed O'Neal of Chemstrand was the official host.

Royalty was nothing new for the erstwhile managing director of Monsanto Chemicals Limited, London. He recalls with delight how encouraging and attentive Prince Philip was during the rather formal ceremonies. He also remembers that the instant the formalities were concluded Prince Philip inquired if by chance there might be a spot of refreshment on the premises. As it happened, there was—right behind a curtain, in an alcove. Moments later, O'Neal recalls, the freshly refreshed Prince was off in his helicopter, back to London.

The Sputnik project, marking Russia's spectacular streak into the skies of scientific achievement, was so sobering that it prompted President Dwight D. Eisenhower to bring the distinguished James R. Killian, Jr., from Massachusetts Institute of Technology to the White House. This was 1957, the time of a less adventurous move for Monsanto: 15 miles west to the new headquarters site in St. Louis County.

The product groups known as "plastics, synthetic resins and surface coatings" accounted for 30 percent of the parent company's sales in 1957. "Phosphate products and detergents" came next at 17 percent. "Intermediates and plasticizers" followed at 13 percent. "Petroleum products" and "wood preservatives and agricultural chemicals" were tied at roughly 10 percent. Then came "rubber and oil chemicals" at 7 percent and "textile and paper chemicals" at 5 percent. Near the bottom of the list was the product group which had been dominant in the days of Founder John F. Queeny: "pharmaceuticals, flavors and condiments." This last group accounted for only 4 percent of 1957's sales. Son Edgar Queeny's comment: "No wonder. If we had had a little help with tariff protection, more of our synthetic organics would have weathered the storm."

The 1957 acquisition of a 50-percent interest in the Plax Corporation merits another mention. This was the plastic-squeeze-bottle company with headquarters in Hartford, Connecticut, and two plants in the East and one in the Midwest. Plax was a promising organization destined to be totally owned by Monsanto in 1962. From the roots of Plax, Monsanto's Packaging Division sprouted.

On one occasion William H. Kester, financial editor of the *St. Louis Post-Dispatch*, queried Ed O'Neal when the latter was chairman, "Why are you fiddling around with a little thing like Plax?" "It's a bit like Las Vegas," O'Neal responded. "We have to put some of our bets on long shots, though most of our bets are in investments where the odds are strongly in our favor. In some ways Plax is something of a long shot. If it eventually pays off, the gain will make us feel the risk was worth the taking."

If a case has to be made for the thesis that profitable businesses founded on proprietary technology are not built overnight, an example in 1958 was the establishment of an agricultural laboratory on Monsanto's Creve Coeur campus. More than 25,000 square feet were devoted to labs, offices, conference rooms, an ag library and eight greenhouses. The facility was inhabited by biochemists, entomologists, plant physiologists, plant pathologists, microbiologists, agronomists and just plain chemists.

At the time, Monsanto noted that weeds, insects and plant diseases were costing the United States about $13 billion annually in crops which could have been grown and harvested but weren't. The chemicals-for-agriculture business was estimated to be a $300-million industry in 1958—and there was agreement that the sky was the limit. Monsanto knew it would have to work hard to merit a future piece of sky.

MHA, a protein supplement for animal feeds, benefited from a process improvement in 1957 and thus started on a road to success as a companion product for sale in the farm belt.

Whereas the bulk of Monsanto's long-range and corporate research was undertaken in the U.S., the company's reach was extended in 1958, when a modern laboratory "with an important long-range assignment," according to Vice President Ted Hochwalt, was opened in Zurich, Switzerland.

The year 1959 marked Monsanto's first step toward becoming a major supplier of a semiconductor material—ultra-pure silicon—for use in transistors and rectifiers. A plant to produce silicon, a material which contains impurities of less than one part in six billion, was constructed in the little town of St. Peters in St. Charles County, Missouri. Within a short time the company would be establishing an electronics profit center and would become a major manufacturer of light-emitting diodes, those brilliant red—or at least usually red—digits on today's pocket calculators and wristwatches.

The most significant news of the year had to do with a person, not a product. In June of 1959 the board elected Charles H. Sommer to the post of executive vice president. It also elected him to the board and to the Executive Committee. He had spent his entire business career—since 1934—with the company and had been both a vice president and general manager at Merrimac. Prior to that, he had had a broad career in administrative and marketing slots in Organic.

Charlie Sommer was forty-eight years old when he was elected executive vice president. It took no reading of the tea leaves to figure out this was a brief interim step. Edgar Queeny, chairman, was sixty-two years of age. Charlie Thomas, president, was fifty-nine. And the clock was running.

Some executives rather traditionally fuss and fume when their public relations aides insist, "Let's put your birth date in your biographical sketch." Some fail to realize that such information is not a military secret. A *Who's Who* will tell it at a glance.

Within Monsanto there was widespread knowledge of executives' ages and a certain feeling that a new man would be coming upstairs shortly. Several executives other than Sommer were mentioned often in what was known as the "winter book," to borrow a Kentucky Derby phrase.

In the winter book, Charlie Sommer's name was seldom whispered. In those speculative huddles next to the Coke machine employes "in the know" had bet their money on other favorites. At the nearby Schnei-thorst's Restaurant bar and at other convenient watering places, Sommer's name seldom surfaced when forecasts were made concerning the impending new "ruling class" of Monsanto.

Edgar Queeny was later asked point blank, "What's so special about Charlie Sommer, who's a quiet guy and not very dynamic?" Queeny replied with unusual promptness, "His integrity, his analytical ability, his capacity for responsibility—and his potential for outstanding leadership." That was enough.

From 1959 until his retirement (as chairman) late in 1975, Charlie Sommer shouldered executive responsibilities during some of the most exciting and exacting years of Monsanto's first seventy-five. Indeed, he had no way of knowing when he stepped into the "D" Building as executive vice president in 1959 that a torrent of unprecedented adventures would be waiting for him down the road during his term as president, as chairman, as president-chairman, as head of a search committee for a new president, who would come in from the outside, and finally in an encore as chairman.

Before going into the so-called Soaring Sixties it might be appropriate to size up Monsanto at the end of the fifties.

Consolidated sales for 1959 were over $800 million for the first time in history. Earnings of almost $62 million were translated into $2.66 per common share. These numbers represented an all-time high. The number of shareowners was approaching 80,000; employes numbered more than 30,000.

Members of the Executive Committee were Queeny, board chairman; Charlie Thomas, president; Ted Hochwalt, vice president for research, development and engineering; John Gillis, vice president for marketing; Trueman M. Martin, who had come in via Lion Oil, vice president for oil and gas operations; Charlie Sommer, the new executive vice president; Felix N. Williams, vice president for manufacturing; and William W. Schneider, vice president for finance and law.

There were four operating divisions and three support divisions. In the former category, H. Harold Bible, also an import from Lion, was a corporate vice president and general manager of the Lion Oil Company Division; John L. Christian was a corporate vice president and general manager of the Inorganic Chemicals Division; Robert M. Morris, who had come up through the Plastics Division and the Texas Division, was a corporate vice president and general manager of the Organic Chemicals Division, having succeeded Charlie Sommer in that slot; and Robert K. Mueller, who had risen rapidly at Plastics, was a corporate vice president and general manager of the Plastics Division.

In the three support divisions, Howard K. Nason, who had achieved remarkable success in research management at Central Research, Plastics and Organic, was a corporate vice president and general manager of the Research & Engineering Division; Marshall E. Young, who had started in 1934 as an odd-jobs boy in the service department, was a corporate vice president and general manager of the Overseas Division; and J. R. Wilson, of patent department fame, was a corporate vice president and general manager of the Domestic Subsidiaries & Affiliates Division.

In addition, there was an import from the 1944 I. F. Laucks acquisition, Canadian-born Irving C. Smith, who was a corporate vice president in charge of planning and control. Further, there were nine corporate staff departments: Accounting, Law, Marketing Services, Medical, Patent, Personnel & Administrative Services, Public Relations, Purchasing and Traffic, and Treasury. There were also three regional vice presidents—one handling Washington, D.C., affairs, with offices in the nation's capital, and two handling marketing coordination, with offices in New York and Santa Clara, California.

That was the lineup as the clock ran out on the fifties. Even though the old slogan "Serving Industry Which Serves Mankind" had perished during the adventurous days of "all" and Krilium, and even though Monsanto was pumping gas in eight southern states, the spirit of the dead slogan was alive when the hands of the clock met at midnight of December 31 to usher in a decade which would enable Monsanto to show what it was made of, largely through service to industry around the world.

CHAPTER XIII

Queenylessness

THE company had known no period when a Queeny had not been in command—except for six months in 1923 when a New York creditor sent in a "caretaker president."

During the company's 59th year, in 1960, the Queeny phaseout began. One journalist, fond of big words, called the new situation "the beginning of Queenylessness."

Edgar and Ethel Queeny had been childless. This time there was no family heir to Monsanto leadership, unlike in 1928, when son succeeded father.

The future had been largely forecast in 1959 when Charles H. Sommer was elected executive vice president, setting the stage for the big news of 1960.

The big news came in quiet words from soft-spoken, still-shy Edgar Queeny at the March Annual Meeting, when he announced he was stepping down as chairman. He was approaching sixty-three years of age. Granted, he remained chairman of the Finance Committee; granted, he remained on the Executive Committee; granted, he remained a board member. But the phaseout was on.

In 1961 Edgar became chairman of the trustees at Barnes Hospital in St. Louis, assuming a strong leadership role there without delay. In 1962, when he reached sixty-five years of age, he left Monsanto's premises and became the first in a series of top management people (to be followed by Messrs. Thomas, Hochwalt and O'Neal) to occupy office space in the Pierre Laclede Building in Clayton.

To continue the Queeny countdown . . .

In 1967, when he became seventy years of age—that being the limit for outside directors (since reduced to sixty-eight)—he earnestly believed he should get off the board, and said so. This was one time—and there weren't many—when the Queeny viewpoint failed to prevail.

The veteran (1947–1975) outside director Fredrick M. Eaton recently recalled, "Edgar insisted on retiring in 1967. The other outside directors came down with a large sledgehammer and insisted he stay on. Edgar

177

fought it. He kept saying he didn't want to create a precedent. I said, 'You're not going to create a precedent. Your father started the company. You're going to stay on the board for the rest of your life.'"

But the rest of his life was brief. Queeny died the following year—in July of 1968.

But back to that memorable 1960 "changing of the guard" . . .

As announced at the Annual Meeting that year, Charlie Thomas, nearing sixty, moved away from what Queeny had referred to as the "enervating burdens" of the presidency—and moved into the chairmanship. Simultaneously, Charlie Sommer went in as president.

When Queeny walked back to his office after that 1960 Annual Meeting had been adjourned, he was asked, "How about Monsanto now?" He replied, "I've gotten it into enough trouble. The two Charlies can take it from here."

People who were not aboard in the Edgar Queeny era find it difficult to grasp the tenor of those times. He ran the show. He made mistakes. But he "made" Monsanto. His greatest dislike was anything short of total honesty. When he had a hangover, he called it a hangover. He scoffed at pretense. His second-greatest dislike was subservient yes-men. He once remarked, "They'll have limited careers if I have anything to say about it."

He left an indelible mark.

The two Charlies gave the new era a strong forward push.

Charlie Thomas, with backup from an able Executive Committee, had as president guided Monsanto through the fifties and was all set to relish his five-year period as board chairman.

Charlie Sommer, with only a year's experience as executive vice president, took over the presidency without fanfare and without any big predictions of things to come. A "dark horse" during earlier speculations, he moved quietly into the chief executive slot and began to sort things out in an orderly way. Little known on the outside, he was rather well known on the inside, and highly respected by those both out and in who had ever crossed his path.

Sommer wasn't the only "operating man" to move up the ladder in 1960. The operating man destined to succeed him as president in 1968, Edward J. Bock, also emerged a bit higher in the hierarchy in 1960, achieving not only a vice presidency but also the general managership of the Inorganic Chemicals Division, succeeding in this latter position John L. Christian, his longtime champion, who joined the board and went on to the Executive Committee.

Another who became a vice president was Tom K. Smith, Jr. The new division he moved in to run, as general manager, alone qualifies as one of the sixties' milestones: the Agricultural Chemicals Division.

Prior to 1960 two operating divisions had been realizing an important part of their earnings through products aimed at the ag market. Inorganic's ammonium nitrate fertilizer had climbed to a new peak, and urea sales were skyrocketing. Anhydrous ammonia was also selling well. Yet the important, profitable and promising segment of the ag business had been developed within the Organic Division, principally in herbicides and, to a lesser degree, in insecticides and feed supplements.

The broadleaf weed killers and brush-control compounds 2,4-D and 2,4,5-T were popular—but only unsophisticated forerunners of more effective and more selective weed killers to come. Randox and Vegadex, herbicides introduced nationally in 1956, were by 1960 moving in large volume. Avadex, a herbicide which had demonstrated its effectiveness against wild oat infestations in Canadian flax fields, came onto the market in 1960, holding promise for the treatment of 21 million farm acres in the U.S., where wild oat infestation hampered the growth of flax, wheat, sugar beets, peas and barley.

Parathion and methyl parathion were the most popular insecticides sold by Organic. MHA was a successful protein supplement for animal feeds. And Organic also had a product called Santoquin, an antioxidant for preserving the nutritive value of feeds and dehydrated forage.

That, in general, was the lineup of products for the ag market that had emanated from two divisions.

Charlie Sommer recently recalled: "A fortuitous breakfast at the Hotel Pierre in New York in 1958 turned out to be a big advantage for Monsanto with respect to consolidating our strength in ag products. I saw Frederick W. Hatch at a table by himself and asked if I could join him. He had recently retired as head of the ag division for Shell Chemical Company, at Shell's early retirement age of sixty.

"I asked Fred if he'd consider coming to Monsanto as a consultant to examine what would be the most effective way of planning the Organic Division's long-range strategy for ag products, which were buried as only one of seven or eight different product groups within the division.

"Fred Hatch came in and devoted a lot of time and attention to the subject. The idea of grouping appropriate ag products into one new division was his. The report he prepared in 1960 was analytical, detailed and perceptive.

"It simply made common sense to consolidate our approach to the ag market by putting all our ag eggs in one basket. We knew we'd be able to serve ag customers better through one division rather than scattering our shots. Also we were convinced we'd be able to do a more intensive job of research by grouping our entire ag R and D under one divisional authority."

Inorganic privately took a dim view of losing its fertilizers to the new division but was somewhat reserved in its criticism of the front office for commandeering its prize products. The Organic Division went beyond taking a dim view; it cried "robbery!" when its profitable and promising pesticides were "pulled out from right under our noses, grabbed from the laboratories that developed them."

The pesticides were not in fact "grabbed from the laboratories." Those scientists who had developed the pesticides—and who were working on new, patented, proprietary formulations—were simply moved under a new banner reading Agricultural Chemicals Division.

Organic was not about to take the "robbery" lightly. Some of its people grumbled long afterward. For many months Organic brought into the Executive Committee not only its regular monthly income statements but also additional exhibits showing what Organic profits would have been if the pesticides had not been "grabbed" for the new Ag Division.

Considering the blue-ribbon, highly profitable role of Monsanto Agricultural Products Company in 1977, there seems to be no one left who is inclined to question the wisdom of Monsanto putting its "ag eggs in one basket" seventeen years earlier.

ARRANGEMENTS were made in 1960 and completed the following year for consolidating all the divisional offices in St. Louis. Management felt there was no longer a need for divisional headquarters to be adjacent to their manufacturing facilities.

In addition, plans were finalized in 1960 for opening a Research Center, with almost 13 acres of floor space, at the Creve Coeur site the following year. This too meant transferring people into the St. Louis area. About 1200 employes and their families were involved in the various moves.

The largest shifts in population involved the staffs of Lion Oil from El Dorado, Arkansas, and the Plastics Division from Springfield, Massachusetts.

It was felt that efficiency would best be served by having all divisional headquarters personnel on the same suburban "campus" as the corporate personnel—excepting Chemstrand, headquartered "where the textiles action is," in New York.

Chemstrand in 1960 was still co-owned with American Viscose, but it became totally owned by Monsanto January 16, 1961, although its headquarters remained in New York until 1968.

When arrangements for the "migration" were being made in 1960, there was quite a bit of speculation as to how families with roots in New England—or wherever—would adapt to the lifestyle of the St. Louis area. Monsanto facilitated the transfers of employe families by providing a wide variety of services. Things like school-finding, house-hunting and loan-getting were made easier by a staff appointed specifically to take care of the newcomers' requirements. There was even a list of baby-sitters to ease what was known as the "Midwest invasion."

From the time the moves were announced there were such questions as "Where's the closest snow and slope for skiing?" and "Where's the handiest dock for my sailboat?" Granted, St. Louis couldn't boast of handy mountains for skiing or a nearby ocean for saltwater recreation, but its counterbalancing charms, comforts and conveniences soon made a strong and positive impression on the new settlers. Plentiful recreation, strong school systems, an abundance of cultural activity, full schedules of professional sports, and summer weather pretty warm but not as bad as advertised—these and other factors converted most transferees into "natives" in short order. It took little time for the transplants to become actively engaged in civic, charitable, educational and social activities in their new community.

The business advantages to the corporation were obvious. Ease of communication at one headquarters location was an instant advantage. And considering that the company's plants, offices and customers were in all parts of the nation, another strong advantage involved being fairly close to the hub of the nation, with easy access to all points.

A new and wholly owned subsidiary established in 1960 was called Monsanto Research Corporation. It was charged with the responsibility of handling contract research for the U.S. government and for supervising Mound Laboratories at Miamisburg, Ohio, a facility which Monsanto had been operating under contract to the Atomic Energy Commission since 1943. Howard K. Nason was elected president of the new subsidiary. Nason had earned his stripes as director of Central Research in Dayton, as research director for the Organic Division and as general manager of the Research and Engineering Division.

Also, 1960 marked the first full year of front-to-back computer control of the ammonia process at Luling, La. Monsanto production systems had long since been controlled by sophisticated instrumentation and mechanization, but the Luling plant had the distinction of putting the first fully computerized process on stream.

On the international front, the formation of Monsanto Belgium, S.A., in Brussels (1960) and the establishment of temporary European headquarters of Monsanto Overseas, S.A., in Geneva (1961) were interim moves preceding the selection of Brussels, in 1962, as the permanent headquarters of Monsanto Europe, S.A. After some hemming and hawing in the fifties, the company was now on course to achieve rapid expansion in continental Europe and the British Isles.

But there was one pesky slowdown, one lingering deterrent to the kind of unified force needed for a big push: Monsanto people in Europe—and perhaps equally in the states—were divided into two camps: 1) Chemstrand, and 2) chemicals and plastics. The historic provincial loyalties ran deep. A European management consultant commented, "Monsanto's troops are divided; some salute one flag, others salute another." It would be some time before this "civil war" would be resolved. There was a hope that the establishment of an omnibus Monsanto Europe, S.A., would work toward a truce. But it didn't. After all, the St. Louis parent company had its own Overseas Division and Chemstrand had its own International Division. Each had worldwide ambitions. Each was going its own way.

In an attempt to bring about some integration, an uninhibited and free-swinging Englishman from Chemstrand, Ltd., London, was selected to be the first managing director of Monsanto Europe, S.A., in Brussels, where most of the employes had chemicals or plastics roots. His name was Peter Weston-Webb. He was colorful, imaginative and resourceful, but not overly organized. He kept envying the prominent locations of the Cinzano and Martini & Rossi signs and posters throughout Europe and suggested a course of action for Monsanto "which would get our name up there, too." Also there was a book distributing company in Spain he kept eyeing, feeling this could give Monsanto some breadth and diversity.

The slow start for Monsanto Europe, S.A., was not all Weston-Webb's fault. The charter for the European subsidiary was insufficiently defined and the existing units in Europe were inclined to continue going their own routes. The two-camps syndrome persisted. Weston-Webb's comment was "If we can't have peace, I'll settle for an armed truce in the hope we can get on with the bloody show."

The most profitable new production in Europe in the early sixties involved the establishment of a plant in Ghent, Belgium, for the manufacture of Saflex plastic interlayer for automotive safety glass. The Plastics Division had seen Europe as a growing market for laminated glass in automobile "windscreens" and had correctly envisioned market enhancement through the convenience of a nearby source of supply.

In 1964 Weston-Webb was succeeded as Monsanto Europe, S.A., managing director by Irving C. Smith of St. Louis, a serious, methodical, highly organized conservative, who brought some fresh and needed discipline into Brussels administration. In 1965 Smith was succeeded by Vice President Monte C. Throdahl, general manager of what was no longer called the Overseas Division but, rather, the International Division. Throdahl saw Europe as a major challenge, so he and his family packed their bags and moved to Brussels for a year's stay, even though his International Division responsibilities were worldwide.

Throdahl not only injected his own management style into the European operations but, in addition, he developed a "worldwide concept" for all the company's product groups—a concept placing primary responsibility for R&D, production and marketing with the various stateside operating divisions.

"The man in charge of the rubber chemicals profit center will have worldwide accountability for rubber chemicals," was the way Throdahl described his concept. His blueprint—a bit harsh, in the view of some—served to clear the air. It was endorsed by the Executive Committee. It set forth an orderly system for the control and growth of all product groups on a multinational basis, with fixed responsibility given to the product group directors of the operating divisions. All other management assists—including those from the International Division itself—would become stafflike and supplementary.

Prior to 1960 overseas subsidiaries had operated rather autonomously, in coordination with the St. Louis–based Overseas Division. In many principal cities of the world Monsanto products were sold by agents. Under the Throdahl plan, Monsanto would establish its own employes in its own offices in many such cities, on a step-by-step basis.

Back on the home front, the "nomenclature nightmare" inadvertently caused in 1955 by the formation of the Lion Oil Company Division was exacerbated in 1961 when Lion became part of the Hydrocarbons Division—which in turn became the Hydrocarbons and Polymers Division in 1965, to be succeeded by Monsanto Polymers and Petrochemicals Company in the reorganization of 1971. Then in 1976 the name was again changed—to Monsanto Plastics and Resins Company, and the product lineup was slightly changed as well.

Former Senior Vice President John L. Gillis opined, "I have always been convinced that customers couldn't care less about our complicated nomenclature and about the way we divide ourselves up into operating companies, divisions, product groups and departments. Often we have lost sight of the fact that we have apportioned ourselves only for the purpose of internal efficiency, convenience and necessity. Some of the nomenclature has been atrocious—not to mention always changing.

"I have often thought that if we had ever set out with the objective of deliberately confusing our customers we couldn't have found a better way to do it. Actually I doubt if there are many employes within Monsanto today who could pass a written examination on our nomenclature, much less on who's in charge of what across the whole spectrum. We invent our own silly language and we take it seriously, oblivious of the fact others probably don't care or understand."

John Gillis—when he was vice president for marketing—was himself deeply involved in 1961 in the establishment of an incentive and recognition plan under the easy-to-comprehend label the Master Salesman Award Program.

"Prior to 1961," Gillis recalls, "as the result of many meetings with operating marketing executives, we had set up and knocked down a variety of approaches. But then we finally hit on a system of establishing standards for field salesmen, with suitable awards for the winners from the various divisions. The thing that makes the program such a success is the fact that top salesmen have to keep winning every year if they're to remain in the Master Salesman category."

Winners are given cash awards and blazers. And they are showered with attention when they gather in St. Louis for a three-day schedule of events.

Gillis further stated: "The program was a hit from the start. I'll never forget when Larry Richards, who was living in New Jersey, was one of the winners during the first year of the contest. When he returned home with his reward and his jacket, he found a big sign on his lawn saying, 'Welcome home, our hero.' This—plus a brass band. From time to time we worked on refinements. As an example, it took us a while to awaken to the idea of notifying the wife of each winner by telegram. When a victorious but surprised husband would arrive home at the end of the day, he'd find a bottle of Monsanto-sent champagne and a proud lady waiting."

(In February of 1976, thirty-three Master Salesmen were honored for 1975 achievements. They were responsible for an aggregate of $233.8 million in sales. Eleven of the thirty-three were repeat winners.)

The big news on the production front in 1962 involved the dedication and start-up of a chemical refinery to provide Monsanto with its own hydrocarbon raw materials at a substantial cost saving. The location— Chocolate Bayou, at Alvin, Texas, on the Gulf Coast.

The initial investment was more than $100 million. The specific assignment was to convert petroleum into ethylene, propylene, napthalene, benzene and other products to serve as feedstocks for Monsanto plants elsewhere. An illustrated foldout in the previous year's pictorial Annual Review had demonstrated to shareowners how Chocolate Bayou's production would contribute to the manufacture elsewhere of fine chemicals, intermediates, functional fluids, plasticizers, resin materials, styrene copolymers and terpolymers, polystyrene, polyvinyl chloride and polypropylene.

The 1962 Annual Report highlighted the dedication of Chocolate Bayou and said it "signaled the start of a new era of Monsanto self-sufficiency in important raw materials." Start-up costs were high and start-up problems were many at the new 550-acre plant. Operational problems became so severe that a three-week shutdown was required for engineering modifications in February of 1963. Such difficulties were, of course, a drain on earnings.

But, despite Chocolate Bayou's problems, the year 1962 went into the history books as something special. This was the first year Monsanto sales exceeded one billion dollars. Not only were sales of $1,063,195,000 a new record, but so was the $78,368,000 net income posted for the year.

During 1963 a technological breakthrough was announced involving the manufacture of organic compounds electrochemically, thanks to a "scientific hunch" of Vice President C. A. Hochwalt, after reading some technical literature from Russia five years earlier. The most important aspect of the breakthrough involved Monsanto's ability to manufacture adiponitrile, a nylon intermediate, from acrylonitrile starting material. Prior to this time acrylonitrile had been used only for Acrilan acrylic fiber. Now Monsanto would be able to derive nylon as well from its own expanding acrylonitrile production.

Dr. Manuel M. Baizer of the company's Central Research Department at Dayton was the principal hero who, with his colleagues, blazed the trail into the wonders of electrochemical processes, to such an extent that by 1965 ten electrochemical and associated patents were issued in a bloc in Dr. Baizer's name.

Like many discoveries in chemistry, the electrochemical breakthrough was an easy one for the Monsanto technical community to understand, but it wasn't simple to translate for lay audiences. The important facts were: It involved new discoveries; it was proprietary and patentable; and it involved processes particularly efficient and economical for a company with Monsanto's product mix. Board Chairman Charlie Thomas called it "a scientific victory."

Thomas recently remarked: "The improved process which enabled Monsanto to use acrylonitrile as the key raw material for two kinds of fibers instead of one is symbolic of the kind of technological progress that has spurred the company's growth over the years. Yet, unfortunately, many of the most significant breakthroughs in the chemical industry are not always easy to explain to shareowners and financial analysts.

"New processes can be as important as new products. Inventive chemists and chemical engineers can work wonders.

"The electrochemical technology announced in 1963 was typical of the quiet conquest which exemplifies the fruits of research."

On the world scene, Monsanto continued to expand. In Europe Monsanto Cie, S.A., a wholly owned subsidiary, was formed in the little nation of Luxembourg for the specific purpose of establishing a major nylon plant in Echternach. At about the same time, land was purchased at Dundonald, Scotland, also for the production of nylon.

With Chemstrand fully owned by Monsanto, Ed O'Neal had been back on the parent company board since 1961, and was reelected a corporate vice president in 1962, when Chemstrand shifted from subsidiary to division status. In 1964 he went onto the company's Executive Committee in St. Louis, and Tom K. Smith, Jr., went from St. Louis headquarters to New York to succeed O'Neal as president of the Chemstrand Division.

Looking back on the first four years of Queenylessness, with the "two Charlies" (Sommer as president and Thomas as chairman) in control, it is quite obvious that Edgar Queeny's fade-out was not as detrimental to Monsanto as some observers had thought it might be. Sommer recently commented as follows:

"Make no mistake about it. The early sixties did involve a period of transition. Leadership means, among other things, establishing a momentum which will have a substantial amount of staying power. When Edgar Queeny stepped down as chairman in 1960, Monsanto had a powerful sense of momentum.

"The name Queeny had become somewhat synonymous with the name Monsanto. There were those who said 'I wonder what will happen to Monsanto now!' The record will show we not only survived but we grew and prospered. Charlie Thomas and I realized full well that achieving a billion dollars in sales was not the end of the road but only the beginning of a new era. Countless new opportunities arose and we tried to take advantage of each. Edgar Queeny was always available in the event we ever needed his counsel. But, by and large, he became more remote. His interest remained high, of course. Even when he moved his office to Barnes Hospital, no one was more encouraged by Monsanto progress than Edgar. From time to time he'd call and express his pleasure at how well things were going without his on-the-scene guidance. He envisioned Monsanto as a company capable of becoming one of the world's major enterprises. He once remarked to a friend, 'They don't miss me at all. Who needs Queeny?' "

CHAPTER XIV

A New Hat

"W E need a new hat." That was the analysis by Vice President John L. Gillis in 1964.

This was his way of voicing the need of a new name for Monsanto Chemical Company.

The company had been christened in 1901 and rechristened in 1933 prior to being re-rechristened in 1964. No re-re-rechristening in the years ahead seems likely.

The 1901 terminology, Monsanto Chemical Works, was obviously regarded as sufficient and appropriate by John F. Queeny—the first word for his wife's maiden name, the second for his product line, and the third word to connote the capability of manufacturing.

"Works" seemed obsolete to Edgar Queeny in 1933. It suggested a factory. His choice of the word "Company" therefore was simply a move toward more contemporary terminology. He didn't want anyone to think Monsanto was stuck in the mud of old-fashioned anything, and he was particularly sensitive to—and annoyed by—old-fashioned language.

The change from "Works" to "Company" was totally cosmetic. There was no deeper significance. No out-of-town experts were called in to provide extracurricular incantations. The switch was made quietly, without ceremony or pomp.

But the 1964 name change was a major undertaking, involving a large cast of characters and expert outside assistance. It was not just cosmetic. As the saying goes, emotions flared.

Early in 1976 Gillis recalled, "The very direction of the company was involved. We asked ourselves, 'Where are we headed? In what product lines will we be operating twenty-five years from now? Is that word 'Chemical' too restrictive for a growing Monsanto?' "

By 1964 Monsanto was getting more involved in nonchemical products or, as Gillis put it, "products which are related to chemistry but not perceived by others as chemicals."

Before examining 1964's solution—plus another solution to come in

1966—it might be interesting to take a look at some of the nomenclature challenges that had sprung up in the early sixties.

Chemstrand was a problem. After becoming fully owned by Monsanto, it was initially a subsidiary and then became a division. But it
was a "special" division. It had its own market, its own upbeat New
York offices, its own style, its own traditions, and its own internal
loyalties.

It was particularly proud of its name. The word "Chemstrand" not
only appeared prominently in consumer advertising (in behalf of customers' products made from Acrilan and nylon) but it also appeared on
things like paychecks, invoices, tank cars, plant signage and stationery.
In a few isolated instances it might be followed by "a division of Monsanto"—in small print.

The parent company meanwhile was trying in its overall marketing,
merchandising and advertising efforts to focus on the corporation's
total resources. Particularly in its financial communications to shareowners, security analysts and the business press, the parent company
was zeroing in on identifying "Monsanto Chemical Company."

Some insiders at company headquarters were expressing the viewpoint that it was hard enough for a company not primarily in consumer
goods to make a sufficient impact with advertising, even when it was
trying to feature only one name—Monsanto. But the complexities proliferated when the corporation's total effort and dollars were diffused into
two "identity campaigns," one for Monsanto and one for Chemstrand.

There was, of course, ample recognition that Chemstrand had its own
specialized market and that Chemstrand shouldn't have its hands tied
in deciding how best to appeal to its market. Yet the parent company
took a dim view of some of Chemstrand's external overtures, particularly when these were far more costly and extensive than the parent's
and especially when such external communications programs seemed to
be totally unrelated to and uncoordinated with St. Louis desires and
plans.

Plainly, the child seemed to be courting more acclaim than the parent
was achieving. The parent regarded this as precociousness.

Advertising and nomenclature were only surface manifestations of
deeper feelings. Some people at Chemstrand not only insisted on autonomy but threatened to resign if "St. Louis meddling" persisted. There
was even a movement at Chemstrand aimed at calling the entire company Chemstrand and dropping the word Monsanto!

Monsanto's block M—dating back to pre-World War II days—also
was a problem. Chemstrand advertising people and their agency, Doyle
Dane Bernbach Inc., pointed out that a magazine advertisement would
be overloaded with heavy-handed symbols if it were to contain the
Red A (for Acrilan) alongside what the Chemstranders called "that
overpowering, masculine block M."

The corporation's advertising department had come up with a simple logo for Monsanto. The individual letters in the logo were not very distinctive, but it was a nice, inoffensive logo. In retrospect, it was precisely what was needed.

Despite its lack of uniqueness, the new logo did have one powerful plus. It was not as blatant as the block M. It could rather conveniently be fitted in under most graphics circumstances.

There was one more small problem: The company's subsidiaries around the world seemed to have no rhyme nor reason to their nomenclature. Some subsidiaries' names contained the names of the countries in which they operated. Some didn't.

Some Monsanto executives had strong feelings on what subsidiaries around the world should and should not be called, regardless of whether such executives had any experience or knowledge of such things.

Even though the Common Market seemed to be emerging in Europe, there was general agreement that European countries would—Common Market notwithstanding—retain strong nationalistic feelings about the investment, performance and behavior of American guest corporations, nomenclature notwithstanding.

One line of thought at Creve Coeur went like this: "We shouldn't call our new German subsidiary 'Monsanto (Deutschland) GmbH' because this only serves to reinforce the impression we're an American company." An opposite line of thought went like this: "Most major multinational companies have no hesitancy at all in affixing geographic terminology to their foreign subsidiaries. Such a system helps indicate where the subsidiaries operate. After all, the influential 'people who count' in Germany, or wherever, already know Monsanto is a U.S.-based company and there's nothing we can do, or should do, to try to disguise the facts."

With these and other puzzlements crying for solution, the Monsanto Executive Committee decided to do something about it. It called in the prestigious New York corporate identity consulting firm Lippincott & Margulies, Inc.—which had already developed designs, nomenclature, symbols and graphics for many blue-chip corporations, and which, in the seventies, would be involved in Standard of Jersey's switch to Exxon and, more controversially, National Broadcasting Company's changeover from its multicolored peacock symbol to the new and stylized N, which had all along been unobtrusively employed by an educational TV network in Nebraska.

When Lippincott & Margulies in 1963 sent in an account executive named Edward Lefkowith to referee the various Monsanto identification and nomenclature disputes, the poor visitor didn't know the hornet's nest he'd be exploring. He was an unrufflable sort, armed with the convictions of his own experience and with his own jargon. Somewhat aloof and detached at the start, he became involved in the pros and cons of various Monsanto arguments to the point of "feeling a lot less confident about things than when I came in."

The worldwide public relations agency Hill and Knowlton, Inc., was also enlisted to provide recommendations, particularly considering that Hill and Knowlton's European staff was quite sensitive to the nationalistic nuances of European countries where Monsanto had, or was planning, plants and sales offices.

The upshot was a 1964 Lippincott & Margulies report which suggested changing "Monsanto Chemical Company" to "Monsanto Corporation" or "Monsanto, Inc." or "Monsanto Company." This was the most important of all the recommendations. There was general agreement that the word "Chemical" should be dropped.

Board Chairman Charlie Thomas leaned toward "Monsanto Company" because in his view it was warmer and more friendly than "Monsanto Corporation" or "Monsanto, Inc."

When Charlie Thomas was asked, "Won't it be confusing someday if the parent has some other 'companies' and has to live with 'company' meaning both the total and the fractions?" he was not daunted. He liked the sound of "Monsanto Company" and that was that. Lippincott & Margulies wasn't 100 percent sure this was the ideal nomenclature, but Ed Lefkowith settled for it. "The important thing was to get rid of the word, 'Chemical,'" he observed. "Who is there, really, to say 'Company' or 'Corporation' or 'Inc.' is the best? After all, Monsanto has to live with its new nomenclature. There is nothing really wrong with the ultimate solution."

Lippincott & Margulies also suggested downplaying geographic names in foreign countries, but after checking into practices of other major companies, Monsanto gave little heed to this aspect of the consultant's expertise.

Lippincott & Margulies suggested increased use of the logo and a sharply restricted use of the block M. J. R. (Rusty) Wilson of the patent department was skeptical of such a proposal. He realized, perhaps better than anyone, that Monsanto had—over the years—invested millions of dollars in protecting its corporate trademark, the block M. He appreciated the simplicity of the newer and much needed logo. But he predicted, "It'll be curtains down the road for the block M. This has been an important symbol for Monsanto. It's sad to see us walk away from such an asset."

Lippincott & Margulies suggested that the word "Chemstrand" should be retained as a trademark but should no longer be the name of the Chemstrand Division. The Chemstrand Division should become the "Monsanto Textiles Division" or something similar, Lippincott & Margulies said. "Monsanto Fibers" and "Monsanto Textile" (vs. "Textiles") were also considered.

As things turned out, many Chemstranders objected rather vehemently. They didn't like their Chemstrand flag being run down from the top of the mast. They resisted—until 1966, when "Monsanto Textiles" became their official new banner. It was a hard fight. But they lost.

In retrospect perhaps the most memorable outcome of the Lippincott & Margulies study was an extraordinary advertisement which appeared in April, 1964, in *Time, Newsweek, Fortune, Business Week, Forbes* and *U.S. News and World Report.*

Developed by Gardner Advertising Comany of St. Louis, the ad carried the headline "The Word's Out." The ad featured a literal tear-out of the word "Chemical" from the top center position between the words "Monsanto" and "Company."

The text beneath read as follows:

"We've outgrown our middle name.

"We've dropped the 'Chemical' from our formal name for a good reason—growth. We have today eight divisions operating in many diverse areas, ranging from petroleum to fibers to building materials to packaging. (Yes, we're still in the chemical business with both feet and expanding rapidly—already the fourth largest in the world.)

"Officially, our full name is now Monsanto Company . . . but our 'working' name is still the same, as always: Monsanto, St. Louis, Missouri—63166."

This ad was a classic. Occasionally since 1964, when other companies have decided to change their formal and legal corporate names, phone calls have come into Monsanto with this comment: "I hear you had a great ad when you changed your name; can you send along a copy of it, please?"

Yet everybody was not enthusiastic about the name change.

At the 1964 Annual Meeting of shareowners a woman stood up and said a few critical things. She called the new name "uninspiring and dull" and said she would have preferred Monsanto International or Monsanto Incorporated or something with a little more zip.

Charlie Sommer, then president, recently recalled this incident—and added the following tidbit: "After the lady shareowner had expressed her viewpoint in no uncertain terms, Edgar Queeny leaned over to me, upon the dais, and whispered into my ear, 'I think she's right.' "

In actual practice the shift from a three-word name to a two-word name was not made overnight. Corporate stationery and principal business forms were reprinted without delay, but the various imprintings on tank cars and water towers were phased out slowly, over a long period.

In countries beyond U.S. borders most companies affiliated with Monsanto were not directly affected by the parent's shorter name, but there was a push to replace the block M with the new logo. Here again the changeover was gradual.

And Monsanto was becoming quite multinational in 1964. It proudly pointed north and south to subsidiaries in which it had total or major-

ity control—in Canada, Mexico, Argentina, Brazil, Guatemala and
Venezuela.

In Continental Europe and the Middle East there were subsidiaries
in Belgium, France, West Germany, Luxembourg and Israel. In London,
Monsanto Chemicals Limited was a 67-percent-owned subsidiary and
Chemstrand Limited (where a name change would be coming up
shortly) was 100 percent owned.

Even farther away from St. Louis were subsidiaries in India, Australia and Japan.

The little old saccharin company was making worldwide tracks.

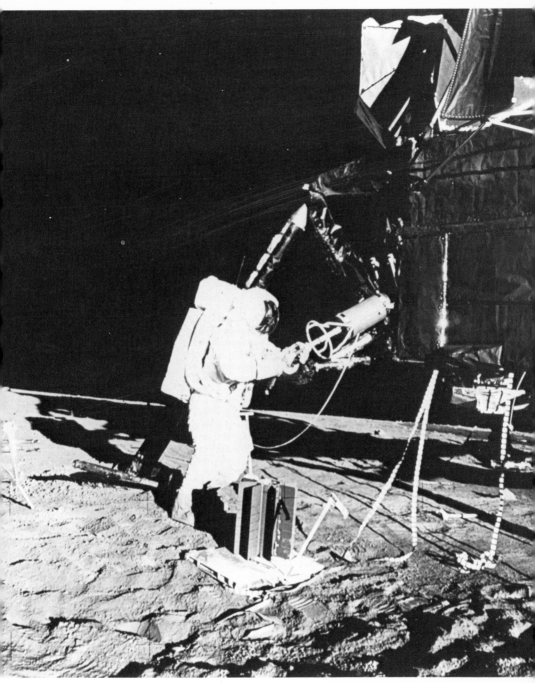

This shot on the moon shows Neil Armstrong, Apollo astronaut, removing a capsule containing plutonium 238 produced at Monsanto-operated Mound Laboratory. The radioactive material provided power for operating various kinds of instruments and equipment on the lunar surface.

President Edward J. Bock and Chairman Charles H. Sommer in the Grand Place, Brussels, in 1969, prior to the company's board meeting in its European headquarters.

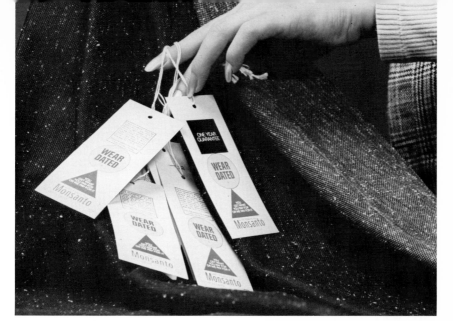

Wear-Dated hang tags, an innovative, consumer-oriented system of marketing introduced by Monsanto. A broad range of apparel containing Monsanto fibers is guaranteed by the Wear-Dated program.

The Mona Lisa in the Louvre, Paris, in 1972, when it became protected by Monsanto's laminated Saflex safety glass.

Monsanto Lustrex plastic molding compound being unloaded in Hong Kong harbor.

John W. Hanley (center), October 26, 1972, at a press conference on the day he was elected president of Monsanto, effective November 1. Chairman Charles H. Sommer is at left.

In 1976 Monsanto revealed plans to construct a $12 million toxicology laboratory in St. Louis adjacent to the Washington University School of Medicine. An architectural drawing of that laboratory is shown to Mrs. Margaret Bush Wilson, a member of Monsanto's Board of Directors, by Chairman and President John W. Hanley.

The company's new acrylonitrile plant, at Seal Sands on the northwest coast of England.

A recent shot of the many buildings comprising the company's headquarters on both sides of Lindbergh Boulevard in St. Louis County. Monsanto moved from its original downtown St. Louis location and consolidated its offices at this suburban setting in 1957.

James S. McDonnell (left), chairman of McDonnell Douglas Corporation, and John W. Hanley, president and chairman of Monsanto Company, with trade representatives of the People's Republic of China at a dinner meeting in St. Louis in 1974.

Monsanto's new European headquarters building on Avenue de Tervuren in Brussels, Belgium. The offices were completed in 1976.

CHAPTER XV

The Era of the Activists

ONSANTO had been a rather "low profile" company long
before the words "low profile" became a popular part of the
lexicon of modern business. Edgar M. Queeny's comment
on corporate spokesmanship took two words: "We're conservative."

Dr. Charles A. Thomas had achieved some prominence in the fifties
as president of the American Chemical Society and as an advocate of
chemistry as a preeminent professional career. Queeny himself had
spoken up on isolated occasions and had been particularly articulate in
the written word in his campaign against what he regarded as government oversteering and against free trade.

In the main, however, up until the sixties Monsanto was not among
the most vocal companies in American industry. Taking a safe and
cautious course, Monsanto was often inclined to avoid controversy, or
at least to avoid provoking controversy, in the press and other public
forums.

But a new day dawned in the sixties, when the era of the activists
arrived. Critics and reformers and antibusiness spokesmen proliferated,
seemingly overnight.

Monsanto—in company with other companies—began to hear new
noises from beyond its walls.

Management Consultant Peter Drucker called it "the era of the great
American debate."

Critics in government, critics on the campus, critics within the newly
flowering consumer movement, critics in journalism—these and others
were shaking their fists, making accusations, hurling charges, issuing
threats and attempting to marshal public opinion in causes aimed at
"protecting the public interest."

The business system—including Monsanto—had not been without its
vocal critics before. Founder John F. Queeny had had to fight accusations about the purity of saccharin during his company's early years. In
the interim, criticism from governmental, academic, labor and other
quarters had been a part of life's struggle.

193

During Edgar Queeny's long period of influence and leadership, he often commented that the business system had brought on some of the hostility it faced. In his book *The Spirit of Enterprise* Queeny specifically declared, "Business did not have clean hands; but its critics and detractors were not fair nor honest toward it, either."

Queeny's mid-sixties estimate was: "Some of the criticism has been brought about by the behavior of the business system, itself. Some has been valid. Some is being voiced by sincere, well-meaning people striving for a better way of life. But some seems to have been mounted for political purposes. Some seems founded on something less than facts. And some seems simply vicious."

If Monsanto officers bridled a bit at the negative implications from the activists in the sixties, this was understandable. Monsanto officers were confident—and perhaps, then, a bit overconfident—that their company's performance and behavior were always in the public interest. Such confidence was reinforced by their knowledge that Monsanto products were serving such essential fields as safety, food, housing, transportation, apparel and health. A few Monsanto people became so upset by the new noises that they resorted to calling activists "eco-nuts"—but fortunately this sort of thing met with scowls from top officers and had a brief life span.

On the U.S. scene in the sixties two best-selling books had a towering influence toward anti-establishmentism and reform. They were *Silent Spring,* by Rachel Carson (Houghton Mifflin, 1962), and *Unsafe At Any Speed,* by Ralph Nader (Grossman, 1965).

Miss Carson was no newcomer to the literary scene. She had already achieved fame as a conservationist, a serious scientist and a prolific author.

Ralph Nader, a young man from Winsted, Connecticut, was virtually unknown. He had decided to write a book "exposing the lethal design of the Corvair" as a method of confrontation with General Motors and as a manifesto to rally others to the already developing cause of consumerism. He was on the threshold of becoming a dominant symbol of the new era.

Monsanto felt only marginally involved in the Nader book's argument, but it felt directly implicated by the earlier work by Rachel Carson. And Monsanto responded in non-Monsanto style—with a rebuttal which burst upon the scene like a skyful of skyrockets.

New Yorker Magazine was the trigger. Without an assist from *The New Yorker,* Monsanto might very well have adopted a safe and cautious course of not making waves.

But it did make waves in the matter of *Silent Spring,* in which Miss Carson issued a frightening warning on the worldwide dangers of chemical pesticides.

In May, 1962, Monsanto learned—quite accidentally—that *New Yorker* Magazine planned to run a major excerpt of the Carson book in advance of the book's scheduled October publishing date—in *New Yorker* issues of June 16, 23 and 30.

Thus Monsanto had an early warning of what was to come. And thus it learned, in three installments, how *Silent Spring* unleashed terrifying criticism of the perils and potential perils of pesticides.

Board Chairman Thomas's reaction was: "The airplane also involves risks but no one wants to eliminate aviation. The challenge is to make aviation even safer. Pesticides involve the matter of tradeoffs. Their benefits far outweigh their perils. We in the pesticides business should continue to keep increasing their benefits and keep minimizing their risks."

"Let's not throw out the baby with the bathwater" had long been a popular expression at Monsanto, and when the three *New Yorker* issues were passed around from office to office, the expression became more popular than ever.

Aware on the one hand that wrongly used or carelessly used pesticides can be harmful to man, birds, fish, livestock, crops and flowers, Monsanto was also aware, on the other hand, that the world could never produce sufficient food without chemicals to combat insects and weeds which, if left uncontrolled, would take a disastrous toll.

In 1962 Monsanto was a major manufacturer of selective weed killers, but it was not a major manufacturer of insecticides, except for parathion. The most controversial insecticide of the period, DDT, had already been discontinued by Monsanto and was no longer in its product catalogue.

Against this background . . .

Chairman Thomas and President Sommer noticed in *The New Yorker*'s excerpts that Miss Carson spent very little time explaining the need for insect control and weed control in order to feed the world.

Sommer commented, "She accentuated the negative. I am sure she felt she could get maximum impact by dramatizing the worst."

Thomas kept reiterating his disappointment that Miss Carson, a respected fellow scientist, had not presented a both-sides-of-the-story analysis.

Two principal options were considered: to ignore the whole thing and let some other company or a trade association speak up, or to fight back.

The vehicle for fighting back was a spirited essay in the October 1, 1962, issue of *Monsanto Magazine*, entitled "The Desolate Year"—a rebuttal which received widespread exposure and acclaim.

Based largely on quotes from eminent agronomists, biologists, entomologists and other scientists unrelated to Monsanto, "The Desolate Year" speculated on what the world would be like if pesticides were nonexistent for a year.

Walter Sullivan of *The New York Times Book Review* commented, "Miss Carson forfeits persuasiveness among those who know she is not telling the whole story. She lays herself open to parody. Some unsung hero of the chemical industry has written . . . 'The Desolate Year.' "

But Edward Weeks in the same book review section wrote, "Yes, but it took Miss Carson to remind us that in our uncoordinated, often selfish, use of chemicals, we have too often thrown nature out of balance."

Recently, when Charlie Sommer was asked for comment on Monsanto's widely quoted 1962 rebuttal, he said, "We felt we had a responsibility to demonstrate the other side of the tradeoff—namely, the perils of abandoning pesticides. I remember that a few years after *Silent Spring* was published a House subcommitee on agriculture in Washington declared the book had created 'an atmosphere of panic.' "

Sommer added, "I've been asked in recent years whether Monsanto didn't overreact. At the time, it didn't seem so. Actually, I'm glad we spoke out. Yet as I look back, perspective suggests Miss Carson's work was surely a lot more enduring in its influence than our rebuttal. Many people today believe her warnings should have been sounded. And her cry for a better and safer world still reverberates.

"I realize a lot of people remember that Monsanto spoke out with force and conviction, dramatizing the importance of pesticides, but the major thing to remember is that the new era forced all companies to take a harder look at the way they and their products were impacting the quality of life.

"I happen to know that all along Monsanto had been doing a diligent job in assuring the safe use of its products, and I also believe we had been doing a diligent job in attempting to control pollution at our plants. However, the record also shows that we had only just begun."

Monsanto's 1963 Annual Report made a one-paragraph reference to the pesticides issue: "A best-selling book which made some disturbing charges against weed and insect killers performed one useful service. It reminded the public that pesticides must be tested thoroughly, marketed responsibly, and applied discriminately. Monsanto has always said so."

The same Annual Report dealt with another kind of environmental issue by announcing the advent of some new technology. It said, "As a major supplier of detergent chemicals, Monsanto has realized for several years that present detergents feed hard-to-remove residues into rivers and streams, where they continue to foam—harmlessly but annoyingly. As detergent use has increased, so has the problem.

"Detergent makers have also been sensitive to this problem and have searched with us and with others for a solution. That solution has come in the form of biodegradables—the so-called 'soft' detergents—that leave residues easily decomposed by microscopic organisms found in water.

"Monsanto will begin producing biodegradables commercially in 1964. Major detergent companies say they will start using them in proprietary formulations immediately thereafter."

But not all new chemical technology for the detergent industry turned out so well. Example: There was that seven-syllable problem product nitrilotriacetate, which had that handy nickname of NTA.

Why NTA?

Here's the background: During the fifties and early sixties, phosphates —and especially phosphate-related detergents—were widely blamed for the degradation of lakes and rivers. (The eutrophication of Lake Erie was perhaps the most dramatic and frequently cited case.) In the course of a search for alternate raw materials for detergents, NTA was judged by the detergent industry and its suppliers as a promising candidate.

In 1968 Monsanto announced that at Chocolate Bayou, near Alvin, Texas, it had completed a production unit for NTA, the then-new chemical wonder destined to be used with sodium phosphate in a new generation of detergents.

Two years later, when Monsanto reported an extraordinary charge against earnings in the amount of $11,343,000, it explained: "The largest of 1970's extraordinary charges resulted when detergent makers accepted a federal government regulation to stop using NTA detergent builder, thus forcing Monsanto to halt manufacture of the product. Detergent makers, although satisfied that NTA is both safe and effective, agreed to discontinue all use of the material. Monsanto had no choice but immediate shutdown."

The 1970 Annual Report also mentioned that "Detergent phosphates were under fire. It was charged that the product caused excessive plant growth in lakes and streams. And proposals were advanced to ban their use.

"Although it is generally recognized that phosphates are plant nutrients, Monsanto does not believe that removal of phosphates from detergents will solve the eutrophication problem. Furthermore, the company takes the position that not only phosphates but other nutrients must be brought under control to combat the problem effectively. Monsanto believes a better solution would be efficient removal of plant nutrients, including phosphates, in sewage-treatment plants. Such plants would extract all sources of nutrients in municipal wastes—an approach Monsanto believes to be far more desirable than a nationwide attack against a single source of just one nutrient."

Few if any chemicals escaped fresh scrutiny in the sixties. And whereas Monsanto experienced no trauma like that of Dow Chemical Company during the latter's participation in the U.S. napalm project, Monsanto nonetheless was occasionally mentioned as a manufacturer of 2,4,5-T weed and brush killers, some of which were identified as defoliants used during the war in Vietnam.

Cyclamates for soft drinks joined the Monsanto product catalogue in 1965 but remained there for only two years, chiefly because of the lack of profitability. In 1969 cyclamates were banned by the U.S. Food and Drug Administration as a possible health hazard, yet, ironically, the FDA subsequently indicated the ban was imposed on the basis of inconclusive evidence.

But the problem of an ubiquitous chemical called PCB became the most persistent of all.

In the company's 1970 Annual Report, it was stated: "Monsanto voluntarily undertook a program to reduce the presence of polychlorinated biphenyl (PCB) in the environment. The company withdrew PCB from the plasticizer market and introduced specially tailored replacements. Sales of PCB to the electrical industry (as a dielectric insulating fluid) were not affected because the product can be safely disposed of."

When the company announced in 1976 its intention to phase out the production of PCB, it explained:

> To fully comprehend the dilemma Monsanto had experienced as the sole producer in North America, it is ncessary to understand the risks and benefits of PCB. The chemical structure of PCB has been known for almost 100 years. But it wasn't until 1929 that commercial production was initiated. This start-up was in response to the needs of the electrical industry for an improved dielectric fluid which would also provide increased fire resistance in transformers and capacitors.
>
> The only known alternative at that time was mineral oil. But it was very hazardous since it is unstable and flammable. The unique properties of PCB answered the special needs of the electrical industry by eliminating the threat of fires, explosions, equipment damage and personal injuries.
>
> For almost 40 years, PCB was used without any apparent problems. It wasn't until the late 1960s that the first signs of hazards began to surface.
>
> In 1968, almost 1,000 people in Japan became ill from eating rice contaminated with PCB as a result of an industrial accident. Symptoms of those eating the rice included dizziness, weakness and nausea. In addition, children born to mothers exposed during pregnancy had darkened skin at birth. In every case, however, the skin condition cleared within three months.
>
> An environmental problem was reported for the first time in the early sixties by a Swedish biologist, who identified PCB in the bodies of fish. Monsanto and others immediately began to study the Swedish work.
>
> When the study confirmed the presence of PCB in the U.S. environment, Monsanto began voluntarily withdrawing its sales of PCB to open application which could result in losses to the environment. This action reduced the company's annual PCB production from about 85 million pounds to less than 40 million. At the same time, Monsanto made the conscientious decision to continue supplying PCB to the electrical power distribution industry where it is used in sealed transformers and capacitors. Withdrawal from these appli-

cations would have halted production of equipment essential to the safe and efficient distribution of electrical energy, since no alternative was available.

In 1972, Monsanto's restricted program was reviewed, supported and endorsed by a federal task force. But despite this endorsement, there were increasing reports that the entry of PCB into the environment had not been curbed.

We were convinced that these reports were not evidence our program was not effective, but rather substantiated our theory that PCB remains in the environment for a long period of time. The findings of yet another task force, initiated in 1975, supported our theory that the majority of present quantities of PCB in the environment were the result of losses in past years.

Monsanto had invested millions of dollars to implement and maintain its restrictive sales program, which we believe had been effective. And we have invested additional millions in our search for replacement dielectric fluids which would be more compatible with the environment.

Yet Monsanto was not content in the mid-seventies simply to stick with a restricted sales program. It had many sessions with the Environmental Protection Agency and, of course, with its industrial customers using PCB. On October 5, 1976, Monsanto announced its intention to withdraw as a PCB supplier effective no later than October 31, 1977.

In 1969, realizing it had some proprietary technology which would help other industries combat pollution, the company formed a subsidiary, Monsanto Enviro-Chem Systems, Inc.

The new subsidiary's strength was more or less assured by its dowry of Monsanto's formidable technology in the design, engineering, construction and catalysts for sulfuric acid plants. More than 600 such plants have been established in 56 nations over the past 50 years. With such a solid and profitable base, Enviro-Chem was initially regarded as a sure winner. President Edward J. Bock in 1969 called it "our white hat."

The most notable success in Enviro-Chem's pollution-control package has been the Brink mist eliminator, named for its Monsanto scientist-inventor, Dr. Joseph A. Brink. This device is designed to remove and collect virtually any liquid mist or soluble solid from any manufacturing gas stream with up to 99.95-percent efficiency on sub-micron particles.

The Brink technology was developed during the mid-fifties and was successfully tested at Monsanto's phosphoric acid plant at Trenton, Michigan, starting in 1959. The first sale outside of Monsanto was accomplished in 1960 to Collier Carbon and Chemical Co., Wilmington, California. Brink elements have since been put into service in approximately 2000 installations in 54 countries.

The rest of Enviro-Chem has not done as well.

A process to remove sulfur dioxide from the stack gas of coal-fired

electric power plants got off to a good start in a small, prototype installation in Pennsylvania, but it encountered difficulties when a full-scale
system was installed by Illinois Power Company at Wood River, Illinois.
Called the Cat-Ox system, it met performance guarantees during its
start-up at Wood River in 1973, but when operating problems were subsequently more than Illinois Power felt it could cope with, the system
was shut down. The Environmental Protection Agency had helped
Illinois Power fund the project.

Another Enviro-Chem venture was a company called Monsanto Biodize Systems, Inc. It had technology for treating waste waters, particularly those of industrial origin. Biodize was dissolved in 1972 with the
terse obituary notice that its "technology was not superior to the state
of the art."

Equally unsuccessful was an Enviro-Chem effort to install systems to
handle sewage disposal for municipalities. Engineering costs far exceeded initial estimates, and the venture wound up as an unfortunate
experiment. Cost overruns for three years (1972, 1973 and 1974) resulted in a $19.5 million reduction of net income. This offspring of
Enviro-Chem was accordingly also short-lived, and was plainly not
superior to the "state of the art."

Enviro-Chem presently boasts of technology for dealing with solid
waste problems. This system is called Landgard. After a laboratory
model of a direct-fire, continuous pyrolysis unit had been built and operated in Dayton, a pilot plant with a capacity of 35 tons a day was
installed and operated in St. Louis, largely to develop scale-up data for
a full-size plant. A full-size plant with an anticipated capacity of 1000
tons a day was started in 1973 in Baltimore, funded by the city of
Baltimore, the state of Maryland and the EPA. When the plant neared
completion, mechanical problems and emission problems developed.
Corrective measures were taken.

(In February, 1977, the program headed toward oblivion when Monsanto Enviro-Chem recommended to the city of Baltimore that the Landgard resource recovery project be terminated because of the "mechanical
unreliability" of the system and the "inability to predict clearcut success.")

Challenging as technical problems can be in the invention and development of pollution control equipment, Monsanto and other manufacturing companies have found another kind of problem which is not only
challenging but annoying, costly, time-consuming and chain-reacting:
the matter of dealing with innumerable federal, state and local regulations.

Sometimes called "the fourth branch of government," the federal
regulatory agencies have multiplied dramatically. Recently compiled
data show that in 1965 there were only twelve major federal regulatory
agencies and that they spent about $860 million, but that now there are
twenty-four major regulatory agencies with a budget of $4 billion. A

later count by the Library of Congress indicates there are actually sixty-seven federal regulatory bodies of all kinds in operation.

During 1974 alone, Congress enacted 404 laws but the federal bureaucrary spewed out 7496 new or amended regulations.

Charles H. Sommer recently observed, "The public is demanding more respect for the environment and the public will get what it demands—but it will pay for it. Naturally, government guidelines are needed, but it's unfortunate that there have been so many changing, overlapping, contradictory and confusing regulations. The paperwork causes a pollution of its own. More seriously, the situation brings about a relentless upward pressure on costs and it fuels the fires of inflation."

Sommer recalls that the countdown of the sixties ended in a nation-wide observance of Earth Day in April, 1970. As president, he was in the driver's seat over the bumpy roads from 1960 to 1968, and he was chairman in 1970 when the company announced it had more than 175 technical and professional people spending full time on antipollution activities. Speaking at the 1970 Annual Meeting of shareowners, Sommer said:

> Paramount among today's and tomorrow's needs are the needs of society. A company operating in the public interest is the only kind of company which will merit progress.
>
> Take pollution. On the front pages, it competes with Vietnam as a major issue of our times. We in Monsanto hope the day has finally dawned when all major elements of our society will work together to find effective measures for environmental control. This task is a necessary part of the new job we face, the job which Norman Cousins described as 'the management of our planet.'
>
> Healthy concern is being shown not only about air pollution and water pollution but also about pollution of our land by solid wastes. In addition, there has been increased attention given lately to a fourth element disturbing our tranquility, namely, pollution by noise.
>
> And it's all due to the fifth element of pollution, people—to a world population due to double by around the year 2000. It is this fifth pollution—overpopulation—that has put the pressure on the other four.
>
> As you know, it took many years for pollution to reach its present critical stage. Perhaps we can all say it's too bad all major elements of our society didn't wake up sooner. But that's in retrospect. And let's face it: Industry has contributed to pollution. Municipalities have surely done their share to worsen the problem. So have public utilities. Yet individuals are the most blameworthy. And as individual citizens we must face the fact that the fault is largely our own.
>
> Some remedies will come rapidly; others will take time and thought and skill and patience and persistence. But in any case, let's make certain our programs are motivated by a genuine desire to control pollution and not by mere political expediency.
>
> It is interesting to see the younger generation take up this fight

with plan and purpose. If the clamor of youth for improvement can
stir a populace into wise courses of action, then we owe the young
a sincere vote of thanks.

The young—idealistic and, above all, compassionate—are precisely
the right people to be concerned about the quality of life tomorrow.
For it is their life and it is their tomorrow.

Students, conservationists, ecologists and others will find Monsanto striving for the same blue sky, the same clear water, the same
uncluttered land. We also strive for equitable and reasonable standards, divorced from political considerations, yet dedicated to public
insistence on action.

Rhetoric about pollution abounds. And if this helps dramatize the
problems and force solutions it is probably helpful. Yet there is a
tremendous gap between rhetoric and commitment. At Monsanto,
our commitment began long ago.

Some observers have said that technology cannot save us from this
sorry mess. I do not share this despair. I ask you not to sell technology short. For technology can cure as well as cause. Technology can
lead us to better and cleaner processes in all industries and will lead
the way to retarding the despoilment of our fragile environment.
The physical sciences, employed in their ultimate role, are indispens-
able in the struggle for a healthful environment, as man seeks to
balance his own needs with nature's irrevocable laws.

Since 1970's Earth Day, many of the concerns voiced by Charlie
Sommer have been similarly recited by a wide variety of executives
within Monsanto. New environmental pressures have since become a
part of daily life, adding not only a new sense of corporate responsibility but a new set of high price tags to the "cost of doing business."

In the three-year period from 1974 to 1976 Monsanto spent approximately $136 million on pollution-abatement equipment alone, a figure
which does not include operating and maintenance costs. The tab for
the ensuing three years, 1977 to 1979, is expected to be at almost the
same level, bringing the six-year total beyond a quarter billion dollars.

CHAPTER XVI

Old Faces in New Places

L
EADERSHIP during the sixties and early seventies came principally
from three executives whose Monsanto roots ran deep.

The year 1965 provides a particularly good vantage point for
views of Charles H. Sommer, Edward A. O'Neal and Edward J. Bock.

Charlie Sommer was in his fifth year as president and was firmly
settled in a position for guiding the orderly operations of a growing
company. Sales approached $1.5 billion in 1965; net income approached
$125 million, and per share earnings were up to $3.89. The shareowner
family totaled almost 95,000 and the payroll numbered over 56,000.

In March of 1965, the much-traveled and versatile Ed O'Neal took
over the chairmanship for a three-year period when Dr. Charles A.
Thomas stepped down. Thomas in turn remained a board member for
the ensuing five years until his retirement at age seventy.

In April of 1965 Vice President Ed Bock, general manager of Inorganic, moved into greater prominence in a new corporate position
called Vice President, Administration. He also became a member of the
board and of the Executive Committee.

Sommer, in particular, was sensitive to the need for adapting Monsanto's organizational concepts to the problems and opportunities of a
fastgrowing multinational company.

Heretofore, principal organizational attention had been given to the
so-called line activity and to the various operating divisions charged
with the responsibility of inventing, developing, making and marketing
products on a worldwide basis. Responding to the pains and glories of
growth, Monsanto had concentrated on the first priority of making sure
its line operations were properly and solidly based, because that's where
the action was.

This had been no small task in itself, particularly considering the
pressing demands for servicing a constantly widening circle of customers with an expanding product line in a larger world market.
Virtually all of the growth was internal. There had been no major
acquisitions since the 1960 decision to purchase American Viscose's 50-

percent ownership of Chemstrand, and there would be no other major acquisitions until 1969.

There were seven operating divisions in 1965 and one service division, International. The former were the Agricultural Division, the Chemstrand Company Division, the Hydrocarbons & Polymers Division, the Inorganic Chemicals Division, the Packaging Division, and the Plastic Products & Resins Division.

But there were also thirteen general staff departments.

Sommer felt something should be done about the organizational structure affecting these staff departments, whose directors reported to a variety of members of the Executive Committee. He disliked the words "controls" and "constraints," but he felt the need for a structure that would assure that the operations of the thirteen staff departments would keep aligned with the corporation's and the operating divisions' major objectives.

The solution was to establish, for the first time, the title of vice president for administration. The staff departments began reporting to this new incumbent administratively. Yet functionally, in policy matters, they continued to report to appropriate members of the Executive Committee.

Sommer's internal General Bulletin of April 30, 1965, expressed the conviction that Monsanto's efficiency would thus be enhanced. And it was.

To a large degree, the company's course for future growth was rather firmly positioned in 1965, under Sommer's quiet, insistent and firm command.

A bit in the mold of Edgar Queeny, who hired him in 1934, Sommer was retiring in nature and not given to public outbursts. A touch of shyness—a Queeny trait—was also part and parcel of his makeup.

More vocal and visible executives were, during the sixties, more identified with plans made for the company's growth. Only those who worked intimately with Sommer were aware of the day-to-day influence he had in preparing Monsanto for new and demanding adventures. Acclaim and trumpets meant little to Sommer. He knew, anyway, that fanfare didn't always mean a forward march.

Just as Queeny had two sides—the granitic pragmatist and the crusading idealist—so did Sommer.

The former side prompted him to suggest tightening the company's organizational structure, including more fixed accountability for staff departments, in 1965.

The latter side showed itself throughout his career and particularly in the mid-sixties and early seventies.

Sommer was in accord with a *Fortune* Magazine author who had commented earlier, "The spirit of Monsanto is not something to be acquired with money, or even by a systematic hiring of likeable people. Its roots are in human freedom—and in this course may be found the ultimate significance of Monsanto."

In Sommer's words, Monsanto represented "a distinctive culture, implanted by its people, nurtured and harvested by its people. It is a company with a spirit, a personality and a strong sense of morality. It stands for something.

"From time to time, we read about the various apprehensions of youth. We see many of them turning their backs on the business system. As they read about the caricatures of business, and the misbehaviors of business, they quite understandably come to the conclusion that all businesses represent the absence of freedoms, the absence of individual opportunities—plus the imposition of uniformity, entrapment and depersonalization."

Sommer resented anyone who placed Monsanto in such light. His perception of Monsanto always identified the company with "opportunity, integrity and an enjoyable place to work." And he felt it was very much a part of his mission to protect this tradition.

Sommer also felt it was part of his mission to make sure the various business functions within the company—line and staff—received due attention, including "the people who make our products in our plants."

A technical man by formal education (a degree in chemical engineering), by 1965 Sommer had had a broad range of functional and administrative experience, for more than 31 years. During his early period in sales, in the thirties and early forties, he had learned at first hand the advantages of staying geared in with manufacturing schedules at the plants. He recently commented:

> Back when I was a product sales manager for intermediates in the old Organic Chemicals Division, we found it helpful to have monthly meetings at the Queeny plant in St. Louis and the Krummrich plant on the other side of the Mississippi. It was important for sales people to share their planning with the manufacturing people, and important for production employes to understand the relationship of their efforts to Monsanto in the marketplace.
>
> I very well remember how in more recent years the manufacturing teams at Queeny and Krummrich were locked into the realities of profits. The workers thus knew the relationship of product yield to the bottom line. The whole spirit of teamwork is always enhanced when everyone knows all the signals.
>
> I think it can be safely said that over the years the role of manufacturing within Monsanto was never taken for granted. Particularly in a capital-intensive industry dealing with great volumes of materials, productivity at the plant level can make or break a corporation. Especially in so-called commodity products, I've always been convinced it's pretty hard to force a company out of any given line of business if that company is the lowest-cost manufacturer in that line and if it keeps its quality standards high.
>
> Monsanto has achieved a remarkable reputation in manufacturing. Our processes have generally been out in front. And through the years we've been in a leadership role in labor relations, dealing

with about 35 local unions in 16 internationals. And we've been near the top—but, let's face it, behind DuPont—in safety. In spite of, or perhaps because of, the potential perils in handling hazardous materials, the chemical industry has been among the safest, and Monsanto has worked very hard to be among the safest of the safest.

High productivity, essential as it is, cannot be engineered into a plant by hardware alone. It results from a human effort which, in the case of the chemical industry, is a twenty-four-hours-a-day, seven-days-a-week effort for most products.

No offense to such functions as research and marketing, but when their advocates remind me of their importance I like to mention the fact that while researchers and salesmen are playing golf or celebrating on New Year's Eve, Monsanto's production people are keeping a vigil on productivity, around the clock and around the world.

Sommer's conception of the central role of manufacturing is not surprising in the light of 1965 events, during which he, as president, stressed the urgency of productivity. Indeed, even in 1965 there were those who said, "Charlie's doing very nicely as president, but he is still somewhat influenced by the habits he picked up as general manager of the Organic Chemicals Division."

Sommer's 1965 organizational changes and the new concept of Vice President, Administration, focused attention on an Inorganic Chemicals Division executive who had also been a champion of the cause of manufacturing. The executive prominently involved in the new Sommer line-up was Ed Bock, who moved from divisional responsibilities to that special Monsanto Shangri-la known as the D Building.

Bock's ascent into higher prominence in 1965 was the result of several factors. He had scored many accomplishments since joining Monsanto in 1941. Tireless and enthusiastic, he had tackled each new job with a special kind of relish. In addition, he had developed intense loyalties, particularly in the Inorganic Division.

Bock was a "people person." He ardently believed in the principle of delegation of authority, and he enjoyed giving subordinates "all the freedom they needed as long as there was an understanding of commensurate accountability."

Assisting Bock's rise was his longtime mentor, Vice President John L. Christian. Being a Christian protégé had its distinct political advantages. Bock was not only a protégé. He was a favorite.

Bock had one special distinction when he moved into the D Building: He was the first high officer in almost 20 years who had had prior experience in only one operating division.

Ed O'Neal also had a special distinction when he moved into the chairmanship, with flair and confidence, that same year: He was the first chairman who had not previously been a president of the company.

Monsanto's technology-related highlights of 1965 were: becoming the world's first large-scale producer of adiponitrile, an intermediate for nylon, by an electrolytic process from acrylonitrile, the latter product being the raw material also for the company's other major fiber, Acrilan; beginning the commercial production of Ramrod weed killer; establishing itself as a producer of polyester fibers at Decatur, Alabama; and greatly increasing the capacity for acrylonitrile and for ammonia.

Chemstrand was still the free-swinging, almost autonomous Chemstrand Company Division in 1965, but during the following year it folded in as a more regular part of the corporation and its name was changed for a few months to the Monsanto Chemstrand Division and then, before 1966 ran out, to the Monsanto Textiles Division. The name Chemstrand, though still a valuable and protected trademark, began to fade away.

One of the most interesting developments of 1966 involved the introduction of a unique and proprietary product called AstroTurf synthetic surface—often referred to as man-made grass. Perhaps no one then appreciated that this trademark would become the most widely used of all Monsanto trademarks, destined to appear worldwide not only on sports pages of newspapers and magazines but equally ubiquitously on radio and television.

There would probably have been no such thing as AstroTurf surface if Chemstrand had not decided in the fifties to dig deeply into the technology of carpets. Its Acrilan acrylic fibers and its nylon both lent themselves ideally to use in carpeting, and Chemstrand lost little time in establishing leadership in this field.

As an outgrowth of this technology, Chemstrand developed a synthetic turf made of heavy-denier ribbon from the Pensacola, Florida, plant. Standard carpet fibers were found to be unsatisfactory for synthetic turf, principally because of their denier but also because they tended to hold rainwater and thwart drainage. The new ribbonlike pile surface could meet exacting requirements as to drainage, color uniformity (to some degree) and durability.

In 1964, with financial support from the Ford Foundation, a test installation was made in the field house of Moses Brown School in Providence, Rhode Island.

But the big event that brought AstroTurf and its trademark into being was the erection of the Astrodome in Houston, billed by its principal owner, Judge Roy M. Hofheinz, as the "eighth wonder of the world."

During the first full season of major league baseball in the Astrodome, in 1965, players had complained they were unable to see fly balls because of the glare of light coming through the transparent roof of the dome. To improve visibility for the players, Judge Hofheinz had the roof painted white, the result being that it was changed from transparent to translucent. A concomitant result was that there wasn't sufficient daylight for growing grass.

Having heard of the synthetic turf at the Moses Brown School, Judge

Hofheinz contacted Monsanto—and the new Monsanto synthetic surface stepped into the big league and promptly was called AstroTurf. By the spring of 1966 the baseball infield at Houston was installed, the nylon surface having been produced on an around-the-clock basis at a Monsanto pilot plant. By midsummer of 1966 enough fabric was available to cover the outfield and also to provide for a football field configuration that fall and winter.

Unlike most subsequent installations, the Astrodome's AstroTurf was installed on a "roll it out and roll it up" basis. An anchoring system was required plus more than three miles of zippers.

Even though this was a first-generation product, manufactured under circumstances of stress, and installed by methods that were primitive compared with today's installation technology, the 1966 AstroTurf at Houston is still actively and satisfactorily in use in 1977, a new underpad being the only improvement in the interim.

In 1967 the first two outdoor football fields were established—at Memorial Stadium in Seattle and at the Indiana State University Stadium at Terre Haute.

Since then AstroTurf surfaces have been installed at hundreds of stadiums and sports fields in 30 nations.

Initially the big advantage seemed to be the readiness of a field, almost regardless of weather. An additional and obvious advantage was what Monsanto phrased "no grow, no mow, no H_2O." But it didn't take long for a third and compelling advantage to become apparent—a substantial economic advantage.

University and college campuses had become more and more crowded. Many an administrator had cast a longing eye at the acreage tied up in a stadium and in practice fields and intramural fields, along with their parking and service areas.

A single AstroTurf stadium can be used day in, day out. It can be used for practice and for the big game. Double-header and triple-header football contests in high school leagues have been made possible by AstroTurf. One stadium with dressing rooms, grandstands and adjacent parking can be kept busy around the clock, if its owner wishes to press for maximum utility. Many colleges share their AstroTurf facilities with high schools and thus apportion the costs. The old days of "don't dare set foot on the stadium grass until Saturday afternoon" are gone.

Thus the ability to utilize land and facilities to the maximum has become the major reason for the installation of AstroTurf fields.

But there are other benefits. There are no longer football players coated with mud, no longer players injured by rough, frozen areas of natural turf. Hard, uneven, icy mud can be a cruel surface to fall on.

Football and soccer are naturals for AstroTurf. For baseball, a big advantage is the consistency of the surface and the resultant consistency of a ball's bounce. It is also used for tennis. Yet the stadium is the major market, mainly the football stadium in the U.S. and the soccer stadium in countries where soccer is king.

In spite of the advantages of AstroTurf, not all the early publicity was favorable. For a while some in Monsanto were apprehensive about Monsanto and AstroTurf being too closely identified. Certain baseball players complained that the center field in the summer sun was unbearably hot on AstroTurf. The product does hold heat. Some football players and coaches attributed an increasing rate of injuries to Astro-Turf; though when reliable data came in, it became evident that Astro-Turf resulted in fewer injuries, not more.

The only big advantage that was slow in coming was profitability for the inventor, Monsanto. It took seven years for the product to get into the black.

A strong assist in achieving profitability came not from baseball or football but from the lowly doormat. Starting in 1969, millions of Astro-Turf doormats were sold, bringing not only profits to Monsanto but also a new, yet relatively risk-free, adventure into the often-troublesome realm of consumer merchandise.

In retrospect the 1966 introduction of AstroTurf holds significance beyond "bottom line" considerations. For those who were looking for an obviously dramatic and easy-to-comprehend legitimate invention, AstroTurf filled the bill. Its impact on corporate earnings was meager compared with something like the electrolytic process for making adiponitrile from acrylonitrile, but it was the kind of invention that was immensely newsworthy.

When 1967 got under way, the traditional Executive Committee— once referred to by Executive Vice President R. R. Cole as "Monsanto's ruling class"—was given a newer and lesser role, and a Corporate Development Committee was set up. Its assignment was to be "concerned with all elements of establishing corporate objectives, defining key issues facing the corporation, and developing a broad, alternate long-term course of action to resolve and define business policies for growth."

That word "development" meant different things to different people. Traditionally it had been used within Monsanto to define an activity somewhere between research and marketing. Actually at one time the company had had a corporate staff department known as the Development Department, which was technically oriented.

"Development" was intended to have a broader connotation in the new circumstance. But the word was never comfortably received nor precisely understood. As a result, within three years the committee was renamed the Corporate Management Committee, without any change in its assignment.

Another nomenclature dilemma came up for review in 1967 and was forthrightly resolved when Monsanto, Illinois—a small industrial town near East St. Louis, incorporated in 1926 and the location of a major Monsanto manufacturing plant—was renamed Sauget, Illinois, in honor of the town's first mayor.

There had in fact been a Monsanto, Tennessee, and a Monsanto, Idaho —since renamed Columbia, Tennessee, and Soda Springs, Idaho. In the early forties when James W. Irwin was assistant to the president he had voiced the opinion that the company was gaining extra identity by having certain manufacturing locations named after itself.

The company learned that in practice the idea had drawbacks as well as benefits. It caused confusion.

When a newspaper headline read, "Monsanto Man Held in Robbery," this became a bit of a problem. The simplest solution was to forget the so-called Irwin system. Thus, when Monsanto, Illinois, became Sauget, Illinois, the company's quite distinctive name reverted to its initial and principal function: to identify the company. Period.

Perhaps the most colorful and precedent-setting organizational change of 1967 involved the establishment of a New Enterprise Division for the purpose of "searching for and creating new business ideas inside and outside the company, for testing and evaluating them, and bringing them to predetermined profitability levels."

The announcement concerning the new division also said the new unit would have as its objective "the spawning of new businesses which can become new divisions in themselves or independent operating departments of existing divisions."

Initially the New Enterprise Division had the following groups assigned to it: 1) electronic semiconductor materials, displays, instruments and systems; 2) recreational surfaces, including AstroTurf; 3) engineered composite systems; 4) protein food enterprises; and 5) graphic systems. Subsequently it moved into such unrelated fields as educational toys for schools and playgrounds, and a high-protein, soybean-based soft drink called "Puma," both of which made brief appearances on the Monsanto horizon.

Dr. Richard S. Gordon, who had had a broad range of experience as head of research for the Ag Division and for Central Research, was named general manager of the New Enterprise Division.

As might be expected from a free-swinging experimental division commissioned to press ahead in new technology and in occasional high-risk product groups, some of its enterprises succeeded, some failed—and a few succeeded and were transferred to regular operating divisions. At no time did anyone believe every enterprise would triumph.

The concept of providing an environment for speeding along new enterprises was readily understood. Vice President Monte C. Throdahl, with corporate responsibilities for technology in the wake of Dr. C. A. Hochwalt's retirement in 1964, had his fingers crossed, but he expressed the belief that a spirit of inventiveness could be engendered in such an environment.

Perhaps the most creative and colorful element of the new division was its general manager, Dick Gordon, a spirited, imaginative entrepreneur not always given to customary, orthodox tendencies. Some of his associates called him a genius. And it was generally conceded that he was, above all, uninhibited and inventive.

Affiliated with Monsanto since 1951, Dick Gordon had from time to time run up against certain traditional practices of business and had demonstrated scant respect for "establishment constraints" when he felt they were obstacles to reaching a difficult goal.

On one occasion, while being interviewed by an editor from *Business Week,* he engaged in two rather theatrical exercises to punctuate his remarks. To begin with, he broke a wooden yardstick by slamming it on his desk, to provide an exclamation mark for some conclusion he was making. Also, he rushed into a nearby lab and grabbed a chicken by the neck and shook the chicken under the editor's chin to emphasize another point.

Monsanto, according to many of its alumni and current employes, has a special place in human hearts because it encourages individuals to act as individuals. However, the alumni and employes also add "within the normal bounds of business practice."

Dick Gordon, some felt, went a bit beyond the normal bounds of Monsanto rules of the road.

Undoubtedly the height of his creativity occurred when he had his office redecorated in the New Enterprise Division wing on the third floor of the C Building shortly after the division was formed.

The principal piece of furniture ordered and installed by Dr. Gordon was a four-poster bed!

Several of his colleagues thought this was going a little too far, even considering the entrepreneurial freedoms granted to the new and experimental division. Reluctantly, once the shock waves subsided, Dick Gordon contacted the local furniture store that had furnished the elaborate bed and mattress; reluctantly he traded it all in on more orthodox office furniture, with the comment, "I guess we all have to try to conform to the corporate mold." Serta or Beautyrest or whatever had had a brief, shining hour in the halls of commerce but was returned unceremoniously to the bedroom department in a suburban furniture store. The traditional desk-and-chair era of business had unwittingly been challenged, but had won out, its commonplaceness notwithstanding.

During 1968 the man known as "Mr. Salesman," John L. Gillis, joined John Christian in the high echelon of senior vice presidents, but the big executive news involved the election of Monsanto's tenth president, Edward J. Bock.

The high-level change was triggered when Chairman O'Neal retired at age sixty-three, at the March Annual Meeting, to be succeeded as chairman by Sommer—thus opening the way for a new president and chief executive officer.

The chain of events bringing about the need for a new president had actually been precipitated in 1967, when O'Neal, in less than perfect health, had advised Sommer of his wish to leave the chairman's post, bringing a sense of urgency to the questions, "Who'll be the next chairman?" and "Who'll be president?"

The first question was easy to deal with considering the availability of Sommer to move into O'Neal's chair and also considering the distinction he'd bring to it. The second matter was not quite as cut-and-dried. Behind-closed-doors huddles at headquarters, plus a few in Edgar Queeny's in-town offices, had a bit of a "we'd better wrap all this up" intensity. Fred Eaton and several other outside board members were important contributors to the deliberations.

At no time was any consideration given to going outside for a new president. The inside candidates seemed to constitute an adequate pool from which to choose.

Ed Bock had a lot of points in his favor. He was the "right" age—fifty-one. Other obvious qualities that influenced the board were these: Bock was tireless, loaded with energy and popular at all echelons. In addition, he had a successful track record as an operating man. He had shown ability and enthusiasm in his role as vice president for administration—a position described by a colleague as "in the wings of the presidential stage." He would be, the board members reasoned, a not-too-surprising choice.

And when Ed Bock ultimately walked down the Acrilan-carpeted aisle to the "big office" 50 feet away, expectations regarding his attitude and style were realized in that he brought a strong sense of determination and an action-oriented mood for getting things done.

At the outset his presidential door was open more often than it was closed. He was aware of the perils of "the loneliness of the high command" and determined to stay a bit gregarious. He even brought, for the first time, a flavor of football fame into the slightly conservative trappings of the presidential suite. In 1938 Bock had been chosen an All-American lineman when he starred as guard and co-captain at Iowa State University.

Bock was a "roll up the sleeves and get to work" executive, determined from the start to place fresh emphasis on employe relations, and determined also to use all his physical, mental and spiritual stamina in behalf of the company. His attitude and intention were capsulized in his own two words: "total involvement."

An unfortunate combination of circumstances—some controllable, some uncontrollable—were, unknown to Bock, not far beyond the horizon when he took over as president. His term lasted a month less than four years.

There was more shock than surprise when, on July 7, 1968, Edgar Queeny died. The impact within Monsanto was heavy, expectedness notwithstanding. The man who "made Monsanto" was forever gone.

CHAPTER XVII

A Downturn and
Its Consequences

PRESIDENT Edward J. Bock's first full year in office, 1969, was a bittersweet experience. In a sluggish national economy, Monsanto's operating income was down 5 percent even though sales were up 4 percent.

Closer scrutiny revealed that earnings were decreased 57 cents a share (on a year-to-year, 1969 vs. 1968 basis) by high nonmanufacturing overhead—in sales, administrative, research and development activities.

Rising costs and declining selling prices were identified by management as the primary villains. However, declining selling prices cost only 26 cents a share compared with a thumping 57 cents for internal nonmanufacturing expenses. In five words: Overhead got out of control.

The idea that Monsanto could not keep its expenses under control was a bitter pill for Ed Bock. He pointed out that high costs for research into new fields and for aggressive marketing programs would have long-range benefits but, alas, that much of the cost burden for these hoped-for advances was lumped into an otherwise depressing and downbeat period.

But the year also had an array of bright spots and elements of growth and diversity.

Perhaps the biggest news was Monsanto's issuing 2,299,710 shares of its $2.75 preferred stock for the common stock of Fisher Governor Company of Marshalltown, Iowa. This was not only Monsanto's first acquisition since 1960 but was also another large step in diversification, considering that Fisher Governor was in the business of making valves, regulators and control systems for process industries.

With its name changed to Fisher Controls Company, Inc., it came into the Monsanto fold as part of a freshly established Electronic Products & Controls Division. Over the years Monsanto had accumulated a storehouse of knowledge in instrumentation for chemical processes, and in addition, during the mid-sixties, Monsanto had developed sophisticated electronic systems which were marriageable to the Fisher hardware.

Whereas Fisher was the principal component of the Electronic Products & Controls Division, there was another segment meriting attention, making silicon wafers for semiconductor devices and also making chemical materials for the light-emitting diode (LED) industry, then still in its infancy.

Another 1969 Monsanto acquisition was the so-called "public share," or the remaining one third ownership, of Monsanto Chemicals Limited, London. A final and smaller acquisition involved the purchase of Farmers Hybrid Companies, Inc., of Hampton, Iowa, a producer of hybrid seed corn and hybrid breeding swine.

Crop-protection chemicals continued their growth through increased volume of existing products and the introduction of Lasso herbicide for weed control in corn and soybeans and a packaged mix of Ramrod herbicide and atrazine for weed control in corn and sorghum.

Two prominent product lines were sold: the company's U.S. operations involving low-density polyethylene (although high-density polyethylene remained a major Monsanto product), and petroleum additives operations in the U.S. and the United Kingdom.

One of the most dramatic contributions came not from the parent company but from the subsidiary known as Monsanto Research Corporation, whose Mound Laboratories at Miamisburg, Ohio, developed a highly newsworthy item. MRC scientists designed and constructed a nuclear heating system to protect data-recording instruments and transmitting devices from lunar cold during the Apollo 11 moon flight mission.

Subsequently a Monsanto Research Corporation plutonium capsule was the energy source for the first atomic-fueled electrical power generator, which was left on the moon's surface by Apollo 12 astronauts.

To symbolize its multinational status and its heavy investment in Europe, the parent company created its own launching pad in 1969 by scheduling its first overseas board meeting in history—at European headquarters in Brussels. Following the meeting, six groups of several board members each visited the various offices, plants and laboratories in the European area. The entire event was so successful that it was essentially duplicated in September of 1976.

The highlight of the 1969 Brussels gathering was a formal dinner for customers, financial leaders and government dignitaries from all over Europe. Charles H. Sommer was understandably a bit proud when, at dinner's end, he announced that each guest would be given a souvenir book containing extremely high quality photos of the Apollo 11 moon mission and featuring, in the first photo in the book, the Monsanto Research Corporation nuclear heater protecting recording and transmitting instruments installed by the American astronauts. Monsanto had not only gone to Europe. It had gone to the moon.

The following year, 1970, brought some stringent controls over non-manufacturing expenses, but it brought no overall joy to Monsanto. Sales were up 2 percent over those for 1969 but earnings were down a shattering 29 percent.

Monsanto's Annual Report blamed "the economic slowdown, which the government correctly induced to combat severe inflationary trends, and the reduced demand for man-made fibers." The net income from Textiles dropped from $55 million in 1969 to $23 million in 1970.

President Bock commented, "When it rains, it really rains." Sunshine was intermittent, at best, throughout the year.

There were strikes in the tire, automobile and appliance industries, closing off major sales outlets for prolonged periods. Wages and utility and transportation charges increased substantially. Imports of man-made fibers and products made from them flooded U.S. markets in unprecedented volume. Start-up costs at new manufacturing installations increased. And more money and manpower were needed for "matters of ecological concern."

The profit-making hero of the year was, unsurprisingly, the Agricultural Chemicals Division, well on its way to the glory of supplanting once-proud Textiles as the corporation's blue-ribbon division.

The 1970 Annual Report mentioned that nonmanufacturing costs were cut $5.6 million and that "an additional $17 million reduction for 1971 has been implemented."

Those cuts were not made easily.

Many were made on what since has been termed "Black Friday." Many employes around the world didn't hear Friday's sad news until after the weekend was over, and they called it "Black Monday." Friday or Monday or whenever, there was unanimity it was black.

When the Corporate Management Committee met at 9 A.M. Friday, December 11, 1970, the objective was as clear as it was grim—to pare nonmanufacturing costs. No favorite or "pet" projects were spared. Ed Bock called it "major surgery."

A news release appearing December 11 told the story as follows:

> Monsanto Company has announced nonmanufacturing costs will be curtailed in 1971 by more than $20 million [later reduced to $17 million] through a year-long process of reducing or eliminating projects and programs not compatible with future growth and by reductions in personnel. The announcement was made by Edward J. Bock, president.
>
> "These actions will bring the company's costs for sales, administration, research and engineering well below the figure expended for such activities in 1969," Bock said.
>
> In the years 1969 and 1970, the company has invested one-half billion dollars in capital investments, including a substantial amount designed to reduce costs and to replace old and obsolete equipment with new, low-cost processes and facilities, Bock explained.

Elimination or scaling down of programs and projects, along with personnel reductions worldwide, has taken place throughout 1970. A number of businesses have been phased out or sold and others will be dropped, Bock said.

Reductions in personnel on a worldwide basis have amounted to 1300 employes since the first of 1970, and when additional cutbacks already in progress are made, this number will be increased to over 2000, Bock said. Present worldwide personnel count is approximately 60,000.

"Based on results of the last two months, it is now apparent that earnings for the fourth quarter will be below those reported for the third quarter and substantially lower than results for the comparable period of last year," Bock said.

Understandably, employe morale sagged a bit in the wake of Black Friday.

Ed Bock, serving in 1977 as president of the Cupples Company, Clayton, Missouri, recently reminisced:

In 1969 and 1970 we had done a comprehensive analysis of all product groups, concentrating on those which were providing less than four percent return on investment. We called in the divisions and asked what they were going to do about the poor-performing products.

Among the products identified in 1970 as having poor profitability and poor potential was the company's first product, saccharin. Granted, everyone had a sentimental attachment to it. But I am sure if Edgar Queeny had been alive, he would have gone right down the line with our decision to question saccharin. He didn't like any products that didn't carry their own weight. Our saccharin process was an old process. The Japanese were bringing saccharin to the U.S. cheaper than we could make it, and Sherwin-Williams was giving us some low-cost competition. The employes of the old Organic Division who had lived with saccharin were understandably reluctant, not just for traditional reasons but also because other product streams were involved with the making of saccharin. By 1972, the operating people decided to discontinue the product.

We also had an outdated process for low-density polyethylene. So we got out of it and put our chips on an efficient high-density polyethylene process, selling the former to Northern Natural Gas, which had an appropriate product mix for getting into the low-density business.

Perhaps our largest decision in 1971 was to sell the Lion refinery and service stations, a matter that had long been under consideration. We had to ask ourselves, "Are we going to be a major factor in petroleum or just continue to piddle along with a marginal operation?" To become a major petroleum company, the numbers were horrendous—in the billions.

We decided to keep the chemical side of Lion, of course, and to continue exploration. But the refinery and service stations were sold in 1972.

We concentrated on modernizing some of our older chemical processes. In 1970 alone we spent over $300 million to get ourselves better positioned. A lot of people in the chemical industry were caught by surprise, including myself, when the economic downturn came. Our expenses got too high. We programmed a massive reduction to get lined up with the stringencies of the downturn. But we knew the upturn would be coming along and we wanted to be ready for it.

That 29-percent drop in earnings in 1970 remains an unhappy cloud in Bock's memory, as does Black Friday of 1970.

When a colleague approached Bock late in the afternoon of Black Friday and inquired, "It wasn't as much fun as eating ice cream, was it?" Bock managed a small smile and replied, "It was more like strong medicine." And when the same colleague pointed out that much of Monsanto's 1970 travail was attributable to uncontrollable external forces, Bock found little comfort in being reminded of facts he already knew. "We've got to be strong internally regardless of what's going on on the outside," was his observation. If he felt sorry for himself, he didn't let it show.

One of the brightest spots of 1970 was the arrival of a different stripe of board member, an intellectual from Harvard University and a self-styled spokesman for the public interest: Dr. Jean Mayer, professor of nutrition, Harvard, and the man who in 1969 had been appointed special consultant to the President of the United States to organize, and then to serve as chairman of, the White House Conference on Food, Nutrition and Health. (Dr. Mayer was elected president of Tufts University in 1976.)

A 1976 interview with Dr. Mayer resulted in the following:

> *Interviewer:* Once you joined the Monsanto board and had an opportunity to look around and to visit major locations, what was your perception of the company?
>
> *Dr. Mayer:* My first impression had to do with the absolute central position of Monsanto—not unlike two or three, but no more than that, large chemical companies—the absolutely central role of Monsanto in the economy of the country and increasingly in the economies of other countries. The chemical industry serves, in effect, every other manufacturing industry, and is quite basic to them all. As an observation point on the economic scene of the country and the world, there is probably no better point, or no better place, than on the board of a major chemical corporation.
>
> My second impression was that Monsanto is not involved with superficial frills that irritate consumers; not interested in the gimmick, the sales trick, the short-term product with no long-run significance. Monsanto is too big to follow transient fashions with

the idea it can grab onto something and make some money and get out before the market collapses. There is nothing frivolous. Instead, there are people who are serious in terms of what the real problems are and how they can best be solved.

Thirdly, I saw no indication of anyone not taking seriously both the legal and social scene. Scrupulous attention is given to the law and its interpretation. Also, there is a desire never to do anything which would in any way, shape or manner be against national policy.

It is not just a matter of integrity. It is integrity translated in terms of positive action.

Interviewer: Who contacted you and asked you to consider membership on the Monsanto board?

Dr. Mayer: Charlie Sommer and Monte Throdahl came to see me. I was immensely flattered and pleased because I had great respect for Monsanto. I had been a consultant for Monsanto for many years and had developed an affection for many of its people. I immediately pointed out to Charlie and Monte the nature of my position—a professor at a major university, and a man who was chairman of a White House conference and consultant to the President, had to be concerned in many aspects of national policy involving, for instance, feeding the poor, involving consumer problems.

I observed that a great deal would be expected of me in upholding certain moral tenets, and that I had a very special interest in not only the letter but also the spirit of environmental protection and of fair employment—and that as a director I would be very insistent on these points—and that they ought to be prepared for the fact I would, perhaps, be more demanding than someone brought up in industry. And I must say Charlie and Monte were extraordinarily ready to assure they would not only tolerate but welcome these concerns. I want to say I have had no occasion since then to feel I ever was in any way, shape or manner violating my principles by sitting on the board and taking a very active part in its deliberations.

Interviewer: Isn't bringing such an outside view really part of the role of an outside director?

Dr. Mayer: I think this is one of the major roles. The major roles I see as an outside director are three. The first is to contribute a more general vision on the future of the country and the world than that which can be seen by people who are immersed in day-to-day operations. Or at least a different viewpoint.

The second role has to do with helping explore the major options. In what area should the company expand? In what area should it contract? As part of this second role I also see the need for examination of the basic needs of the society or societies in which the company operates, along with the examination of whatever political and economic climate might be predictable.

The third role concerns the constant evaluation of management. The outside directors have a very special responsibility to see that the company is in good hands, and they should have absolutely no hesitation to change management if they feel the company could do better with a different management. They are, in a sense, the last resort in terms of judging how well a company is operating in regard to its possibilities.

Interviewer: But don't you also have a special role as a scientist serving as an outside director for a science company?

Dr. Mayer: That's right. I think I have a definite responsibility to the scientists within Monsanto. I constantly find I ought to remind the other board members of the fact that science is the key to Monsanto's success and the key to Monsanto's role in society. One of the first things I asked for when I joined the board was that the amount of money spent on research and development should be broken out and looked at separately, instead of being lumped with other nonmanufacturing expense items, tending to disguise, in a sense, how much or how little we were actually spending for research and development and patents and the like. I feel I am constantly responsible, as a scientist, to make sure the quality of research now, and the building of research for the long term, is as it should be.

Interviewer: What are your thoughts on pollution control and product safety?

Dr. Mayer: In terms of pollution, I think the chemical industry has a special responsibility and a special role to play. It obviously has a responsibility of not itself polluting the environment. And I think, by now, Monsanto is being extremely conscientious. The chemical industry is one which deals with matter as a group of substances. The industry has the analytical methods and capabilities of detecting trace amounts of material in the environment. Also, it has the intellectual capacity of trying to seek alternatives, as well as trying to find new methods of filtering, oxidizing or generally destroying polluting substances.

The chemical industry, therefore, not only has a responsibility to be a particularly good citizen—because it's more competent than other industries in preventing pollution—but it also has the special challenge of constantly finding ways and means whereby other industries will be helped to be less pollutant. The chemical industry, consequently, may have to abide by more stringent limitations because greater knowledge brings about greater responsibility.

As far as product safety is concerned, it's a weird situation because many parts of the chemical industry are not directly in contact with the consuming public except, perhaps, in a few cases such as direct contact with farmers, who are in a position of being sort of consumer producers themselves.

Here again, in product safety, the industry bears a big responsibility, borne of great knowledge of what is needed to assure safe use.

The agricultural market for chemicals will become more complicated by the fact that as Monsanto expands in less-developed countries and as it deals with farmers who are less educated and less able to follow directions, it will have to make its products safer, in a sense, than they are in America, where we have extensive educational services and more competent and technically oriented farm customers.

Interviewer: How about the tradeoffs? Is there sufficient understanding of the short-term and long-term advantages and disadvantages of most chemical products?

Dr. Mayer: I think the applications to social concerns of the general input-output theory are something our young people, in particular, are becoming more educated to. They are understanding more and more the requirement to look at what is needed to obtain a certain result and what are apt to be the distant consequences of obtaining that certain result.

Interviewer: Aren't you in the middle when you hear businessmen complain about Washington regulations and complain about the activists, and when you hear regulators and activists complain about the business system?

Dr. Mayer: I have tried to develop a balanced view although I sometimes feel I am, indeed, in the middle of two paranoias. On the one hand, some industry leaders think that anything a critic mentions is proof that the critic is against American society, wants to destroy our livelihood, wants to destroy our place among the nations, and is no better than a wild-eyed Bolshevik. On the other hand, some activists seem to have the idea that American industrial managers stay up nights trying to find ways of poisoning their customers and that these managers have no interest in the survival of society and that they will do anything for profit.

The fact of the matter is, I think, in many cases both sides are actuated by the best intentions, and by great patriotism, but they have entirely different viewpoints, sometimes quite uninformed and sometimes partially informed. The need is to listen to both sides and try to sift out what is legitimate and then come to a solution in the national interest, which may mean that sometimes one side or the other has to sacrifice something so that the common good can best be served.

Such stimulating ideas are small but revealing glimpses into the mind and heart of Jean Mayer.

Moving to 1971, there was one event so overpowering in its internal, if not external, significance that it overshadowed everything else. It was called simply The Reorganization—the first full overhaul since January, 1954.

The details were announced September 21, 1971, but they had been worked on by Ed Bock and a few of his principal associates for more than a year, with the help of Richard M. Paget of the New York management consultant firm Cresap, McCormick and Paget.

When news of the new plan was circulated by announcements rushed to all world locations as simultaneously as possible, the initial reaction was, in a word, "Wow!" Because it affected or potentially affected so many people, it caused a stir. Despite its impact, it was not an instant magic wand or an all-new remedy. Some of its features were revolutionary. Others were the result of executive discussions tracing back five or more years. To be sure, the total package was more new than old— but not 100 percent new.

In 1976 Ed Bock spoke of the episode as though it had occurred yesterday. He recalled: "Prior to the 1971 reorganization there were nine divisions and thirteen staff departments. It was obvious that Monsanto was about to enter an era of great, worldwide growth. I felt it was my responsibility as president to have the company organized in the most efficient way. I also felt it was prudent to bring in one of the world's most competent management consultants to aid in our planning.

"The problems within the old organization were numerous. There were conflicts between some line organizations and staff departments. We had too many individual units. We had many important customers being served by more than one division, customers who merited a more professional approach from the corporation. There were also problems relating to interdivisional pricing.

"The big question was, 'How can we group ourselves to minimize problems now and in the future?' "

During the early months of his study, Ed Bock had rather freely discussed his objectives with his executive associates. This led to some internal speculation as to which managers would be selected to be in charge in the reorganized company and which managers would lose out.

In an attempt to curb such speculation, Bock decided in the final months to "keep my plans within my head." His only confidante, besides Chairman Sommer, was H. Harold Bible, the new vice president for administration, who established "working headquarters" behind a locked door in a small office in the D Building. During the entire study period Bible had a strong influence on both the concepts and details of the new master plan.

Armed with a supply of Magic Marker pens and sheets of cardboard, Bible became Bock's draftsman for new organization charts in an environment of stringent security. Only a few people knew where his secret workroom was located.

Bock wasn't trying to foreclose helpful suggestions but to prevent leaks, he explained. Principal executives in the operating divisions and principal corporate officers had been interviewed at length by consultant Paget. Yet the corporate staff departments were not on the Paget interview program.

In order to stay on schedule and get the announcement out by September, President Bock had deliberately decided to concentrate on the line operations of the company, feeling that these were of primary importance and that the key to any constructive reorganization would have to be the most efficient alignment of the units of the company that research, develop, manufacture and market products. The "profit center" philosophy was, understandably, the central point of all strategy.

As a consequence, corporate staff considerations were minimal. "Insufficient attention was paid to certain staff and corporate matters," Charlie Sommer recently observed.

When President Bock's announcement was released September 21, it said in part:

> The new format features the establishment of four worldwide operating companies within Monsanto, each headed by a managing director, a new and important position in Monsanto.
>
> Monsanto Polymers & Petrochemicals Company ... includes all product groups of the Hydrocarbons & Polymers Division and several segments of the Plastic Products & Resins Division.
>
> Monsanto Industrial Chemicals Company ... includes most of the product groups of the Organic Chemicals Division and the Inorganic Chemicals Division.
>
> Monsanto Textiles Company ... is, essentially, the Textiles Division as it is presently structured.
>
> Monsanto Commercial Products Company ... includes the Agricultural Division, the Packaging Division, the Electronic Products Division, Monsanto Enviro-Chem Systems, Inc., and Fisher Controls Company, Inc., together with several other product groups of an appropriate nature, such as plastic products produced at our Kenilworth, New Jersey, and Anaheim, California, plants. The bulk of the products manufactured and marketed by this newly assembled company are those which retain their identity in the marketplace and do not, in general, require reprocessing by our customers.
>
> Charters for our two other divisions, International and New Enterpise, will stress development and growth.... The Corporate Management Committee has been dissolved and I will use three corporate advisory groups: the Corporate Operations Group, the Corporate Budget and Control Group and the Corporate Plans Group.

The evening of the September 21 announcement President Ed Bock took his four new managing directors to the nearby Bogey Club to drink a toast to the new adventure. As it happened, Bock and his quartet of new managing directors—John R. Eck, C. P. Cunningham, Louis Fernandez and Tom K. Smith, Jr.—were all alumni of the Inorganic Chemicals Division! Each had, at one time or another, held one or more responsible positions in John Christian's "sand and gravel" group.

There were obvious employe cries of "cronyism!" Bock knew such a reaction would be inevitable. He recently observed, "I also know there was concern that insufficient attention had been paid to corporate staff departments. Actually, I had a 'phase two' program in mind, and it was my plan within the next year to devote fresh attention to balancing corporate staff activities. It was necessary, however, to do first things first.

"I was not trying to run a popularity contest. I was motivated solely by what was best for Monsanto. The fact that all four managing directors had spent time in Inorganic was somewhat a coincidence but also somewhat of an indication of how earnestly Inorganic had always developed people. We picked the four people who would be best to get the job done. There was no other consideration."

The year 1971 was not only marked by the repercussions of a massive reorganization. It was also by a highly satisfactory year insofar as performance was concerned. Sales were up 6 percent and net income was up a rousing 20 percent before extraordinary (unusual and nonrecurring) charges and 41 percent after extraordinary charges.

For President Bock it was an active and profitable year.

To quote a downtown broker: "But the honeymoon was short-lived."

In February, 1972, President Ed Bock resigned at age fifty-five, under duress, because of some serious differences with several outside board members. Chairman Sommer's acceptance of the resignation had the unanimous backing of the outside board members and mixed reactions from the inside board members. Yet, in total, the acceptance met with board approval.

The resignation was, to put it mildly, an unprecedented shock.

Almost equally dramatic was the fact that Bock was not immediately replaced in the president's chair, giving rise to the feeling that, despite a wave of management development programs over the years, Monsanto had not developed a No. 2 man to step into the departing president's shoes.

Newspapers' speculation as to the reason for Bock's sudden exit was encouraged by a brief Monsanto news release which gave no sufficient explanation or details and thus spurred editors—as well as employes—to dig for their own second- and third-hand details. "Explanations"—in the absence of real reasons provided by the company—were many, diverse, often contradictory and frequently inaccurate. It was an uncomfortable period for all concerned.

Some split-second timing was required because prior to Bock's February 23 resignation the Annual Meeting notice and proxy statement had been sent to the printer—with Bock's name and photo among the group of directors standing for reelection at the scheduled March 23 Annual Meeting. It took some fast footwork to remove Bock from the proxy statement insofar as his board candidacy was concerned.

As of February 24, Chairman Charles H. Sommer wore two hats—that of chairman and that of president. In addition, the board appointed him chairman of a search committee to find "absolutely the best candidate anywhere" for the presidency, regardless of whether such a candidate would come from inside or outside.

The proxy statement did not, of course, overlook the Bock departure.

On page 8 it listed Bock's remuneration for 1971 as $152,000. It added: "Mr. Bock recently announced that he had accomplished the implementation of a major reorganization of the company and its activities, which he felt an obligation to complete before requesting retirement as an officer and director. Accordingly, he added that he would not stand for reelection as a director and officer. Pursuant to an agreement with the company, Mr. Bock will remain a full-time employee at his present annual salary until March 1, 1973, after which date he will serve the company and its subsidiaries as a consultant until October 1, 1981, when he shall have reached 65 years of age, or until his death or permanent and total disability, whichever occurs first, and with appropriate noncompetition and confidentiality commitments. For such consulting services, the company has agreed to pay Mr. Bock $50,000 per year."

The circumstances surrounding the resignation received liberal attention externally—in the nation's press and particularly in the St. Louis press. But within Monsanto's walls around the world, the resignation caused a liberal hubbub, liberal confusion, liberal rumors and a liberal state of shock, ameliorated little by the "bare bones" explanations from headquarters. The prevailing questions were "why?" and "what happened?" If Monsanto's global telephone bill peaked for the month of February, 1972, one can safely surmise that a chunk of the tab was traceable to dumbfounded employes trying to learn from some colleagues at other locations the reasons for a president's hasty exit.

A people-oriented person, Ed Bock had made innumerable friends within the company and within the industry. A big and energetic man physically, he seemed to have been conspicuously present immediately prior to February 23, 1972, which all the more made him seem conspicuously absent after he had cleaned out his desk and departed from the Creve Coeur headquarters campus.

Charlie Sommer and his board associates reasoned it would have been inappropriate and inconsiderate to go into a lot of detailed explanations. They knew their silence would be misconstrued; yet they also believed their participation in providing a lot of details would have been more seriously misconstrued and would have added fuel to the fire. They were principally influenced by an agreement they had with Ed Bock not to go beyond the information in a very brief news release and proxy statement. In addition, they had immense respect for Ed Bock the executive and Ed Bock the friend and were determined not to do or say the slightest thing which would seem to violate that respect.

No matter what they did or didn't do, it was bound to be a negative experience. This they knew. The sudden departure of the president and chief executive officer, at age fifty-five, was bound to have high visibility. It was bound to "make waves."

Two outside directors, Fredrick M. Eaton of New York and Dillon Anderson of Houston, both eminent attorneys, were asked by the board to serve with Sommer on the search committee.

Looking back on 1972, Sommer recently commented, "I don't think I ever worked so hard in all my life." He not only had his duties as board chairman and as interim president. In addition, he devoted a great amount of time to the task of searching for a new president.

Knowledgeable editors and other outsiders had speculated while the search was in progress that if Monsanto had had a suitable inside candidate such a man would have been installed in a hurry, or at least shortly after Ed Bock's exit. Consequently, they reasoned, the search was for an outside man.

This was not precisely true. Inside candidates were thoughtfully considered and reconsidered by the search committee. A company that had often pridefully declared, "We specialize in promoting from within," was not about to be frivolous in considering the qualifications, capabilities and credentials of inside executives during such a crisis.

In the local brokerage community the word went around that "Charlie Sommer is searching for a man who can walk on water." Sommer smiled, weakly, when he heard this. And while the brokers' remark was a bit of an exaggeration, Sommer found himself liking the comment more than he disliked it. Plainly the impression had been made that Monsanto was looking for a president with extraordinary qualifications—a mere mortal, of course, but an exceptional mere mortal. "The very strongest candidate is what Monsanto merits," Sommer said.

On November 1, 1972, "the very strongest candidate" became president of Monsanto: John W. Hanley, erstwhile executive of Procter & Gamble, Cincinnati. A new era and a new style of leadership were about to begin for Monsanto.

CHAPTER XVIII

The New Monsanto

URIOSITY reverberated within the multinational walls of Monsanto when the announcement was made on Thursday, October 26, 1972, that the board of directors had elected outsider John W. Hanley of Procter & Gamble as president and chief executive officer of Monsanto.

The instant investigations by curious employes would have been a credit to the FBI. Some of the more inquisitive among them phoned friends in Cincinnati—home of P&G headquarters—and elsewhere for a fast fill-in and for an answer to the inevitable question, "What's he like?" Other employes set out on a search for copies of Procter & Gamble Annual Reports and proxy statements.

Scraps of information picked up through this hasty research were in turn passed along to other Monsanto employes in St. Louis, New York, Brussels or wherever, mostly on a person-to-person basis but also in phone calls ostensibly made for routine business purposes. It was the good old corporate tom-tom system in action—a system more famous for its speed than for its accuracy.

"He means business" and "he doesn't fiddle around" and "he's a superconfident sort" and "he's the tireless type with no energy shortage" and "he's a bit detached and chilly but fair and maybe even brilliant" were among the informal advisories plucked from the grapevine.

Less colorful but fully accurate were the two paragraphs in the formal Monsanto news release:

"A native of Parkersburg, West Virginia, Mr. Hanley is 50 years of age. He graduated from Penn State University with a B.S. degree in metallurgical engineering in 1942. After an affiliation with Allegheny Ludlum Steel Corporation, and following naval service in World War II, he received an M.B.A. degree in 1947 from Harvard University Graduate School of Business Administration. Joining Procter & Gamble shortly after leaving Harvard, he has spent the rest of his career there, primarily in marketing management responsibilities.

"After having served in sales capacities in Los Angeles, Seattle,

Minneapolis and Chicago, he became regional division manager in 1954. He was named manager of the Household Soap Products Division in 1961 and was elected a corporate vice president in 1963. He moved to the Packaged Soap and Detergent Division in 1966, became group executive in 1967, and was elected to the board in 1969. His election as executive vice president occurred in 1970."

The interval between October 26, when Hanley was elected by the Monsanto board, and November 1, when he stepped into office, was short. But it was long enough for both formal and informal communications to penetrate all corners of worldwide Monsanto.

On November 1, the following conversation took place:

> *Assistant director, corporate staff department:* I hear you were with him in his office. What's he like?
> *Director, corporate staff department:* He took notes! He scribbled things in a notebook!
> *Assistant director:* My God! I guess he really means business. What did you tell him?
> *Director:* I'm not 100 percent sure of what I said. But he's 100 percent sure. It's on the record—in his notebook.

On the same day, Chairman Sommer found it possible to relax a bit after a nine-month period serving as head of the board's search committee. One of the roughest nine months of his life was behind him.

Sommer had insisted that all internal and external communications contain the following: "Our search was comprehensive. Our objective from the start was to find the very best man for the job, regardless of where he might be. All along, our board has agreed that we want and need an outstanding executive under whose leadership Monsanto will achieve a new dimension of growth and profitability. Mr. Hanley fits this requirement admirably."

Over the prior 71 years Monsanto's presidents had been, by and large, familiar faces. They had worked their way up from lower echelons, step by step, to the accompaniment of cheers from the internal troops. But when Jack Hanley became the tenth president he was a stranger to 98 or 99 percent of the company's 59,000 employes. The old scenario of familiarity was now scrapped in favor of what Hanley himself described as "a new boy in the neighborhood."

Granted, he had been known to various degrees by many of Monsanto's top corporate executives and by those Monsanto Industrial Chemicals Company people who had had continuing contacts with Procter & Gamble. He had visited Monsanto headquarters on several occasions, wearing the invisible but unmistakable shoulder stripes of a very formidable customer. He had visited the office of President Ed Bock for the purpose of stressing, in person, a few firm demands in behalf of the Cincinnati enterprise.

However, the overwhelming majority of Monsanto employes had not only never seen Jack Hanley but, in all likelihood, had never heard of him. Translating the potentially uncomfortable situation into Navy terms, it was a case of piping an unfamiliar captain to the bridge to bark new orders to a crew of strangers.

Credentials of both captain and crew suggested an element of mutual respect. After all, a man couldn't have reached the executive vice presidency of P&G while still in his forties without a certain extraordinary something. After all, Monsanto couldn't have gotten to No. 45 on *Fortune* Magazine's list of major industrial companies without a certain extraordinary something. Significantly, both P&G and Monsanto had won more than their share of recognition and awards for management and industrial expertise.

But internal apprehensions abounded. The fact that Monsanto had to import an outsider was a jolt in itself, and it pointed up the obvious need for greater emphasis on management development efforts in the future.

It was all in sharp contrast to earlier executive-selection choreography: Veterans remembered that in 1943 longtime Monsanto friends had poured into the executive suite on South Second Street in downtown St. Louis when Charles Belknap took over the presidency from Edgar Queeny. The same thing occurred when William M. Rand succeeded Belknap in 1945; when Charles A. Thomas succeeded Rand in 1951; when Charles H. Sommer succeeded Thomas in 1960; and when Edward J. Bock succeeded Sommer in 1968. In all these instances there had been an "our fellow made it!" cause for celebration when the baton was passed as a symbol of orderly, planned, internal succession.

Charlie Sommer agrees it would have been preferable to have such widespread internal exuberance for a Monsanto-bred winner in 1972. For morale reasons alone, Sommer says, this would have been ideal. Such a customary upbringing within Monsanto could also have aided the so-called "outside image"—or the way the company's managerial evolution process was perceived by shareowners, analysts, bankers, customers, suppliers, journalists.

If short-term internal and external considerations had been the prevailing criteria, the Monsanto board would have chosen an insider, Sommer says. Indeed, the four managing directors of the operating companies, concerned at least in part with such short-term impressions, had implored search committee chairman Sommer in mid-1972 to "choose any one of us and let's get on with the show."

In Sommer's view and in the view of the majority of the board the problem and the opportunity went far above and beyond short-term popularity. The other two members of the search committee, Fredrick M. Eaton and Dillon Anderson, agreed early in the game that Monsanto merited nothing short of the best. And by "the best" they meant the best anywhere and not simply the best in-house. Thus the "job specs" were extremely demanding.

As any IBM card sorting machine will confirm, precious few punched cards fall out when demanding specifications are fed in.

Jack Hanley was quite a special candidate. He didn't knock on Monsanto's door. It was vice versa.

In Sommer's words, "He was without question the top man on our list."

Early in March, 1972, shortly after Bock's departure, a coincidence occurred which had brought Jack Hanley forcefully and positively to Charlie Sommer's attention. The occasion involved Monsanto hosting sixteen industrial leaders and their wives at Walt Disney World near Orlando, Florida, for the unveiling of a program at the new Monsanto pavilion. On hand to represent P&G were Jack and Mary Jane Hanley of Cincinnati.

The top-level visitors had been given red-carpet treatment. They saw the spectacular, nine-screen program *America the Beautiful* in the Monsanto pavilion. Their comfort and convenience had been suitably arranged with respect to tours of the park, living accommodations, social get-togethers and periods permitting discussions of broad business issues.

At the final dinner at the Polynesian Village Hotel it had seemed appropriate that someone should stand up and express gratitude on behalf of all the guests. The articulate Jack Hanley was the man who rose and thanked the Monsanto executives for a well-handled and informative program.

Charlie Sommer recently looked back to that event and recalled, "I was most favorably impressed by Jack Hanley. But at that point I didn't have the slightest idea that about six months later I would be talking to him about coming to Monsanto."

With the expert assistance of Haley Associates, Inc., of New York, a management-recruitment organization, Sommer embarked upon his search.

There was little he could do to throttle back on his chairmanship duties. Board procedures, as spelled out in the bylaws and in corporate policies, play second fiddle to nothing. Some slippage in day-to-day attention was possible in the area of presidential responsibilities with no harm for the short pull, largely because of Sommer's confidence in his executive row colleagues, in his four operating company managing directors (now gung-ho pursuing the fresh autonomy chartered by the reorganization the prior autumn) and in his corporate staff department directors.

But not a bit of slippage was tolerable in Sommer's perception of his "real No. 1 job"—finding a new president. He regarded this as the most urgent and compelling of his tasks.

When he learned of Jack Hanley's possible availability he became quite encouraged. Other interviews had been arranged by Haley Associates, Inc., with prestigious candidates, but, Sommer says, "It was difficult to look in any other direction when Jack Hanley's availability became known. Naturally, we had to be cautiously concerned with P&G's reaction to approaching one of its most valued executives. But my search committee colleagues agreed that we'd best be discharging our Monsanto responsibilities by making a beeline for this man, Hanley."

Why was Jack Hanley possibly available?

During the prior year, 1971, P&G Executive Vice President Hanley had remained in place while a P&G associate of the same rank, Edward G. Harness, moved up to the P&G presidency. Was Hanley sulking because of this? Had his career potential at P&G lost any of its sheen?

Hanley recently responded, "My options ahead at P&G had not at all been foreclosed. As a matter of fact, in my 1971 discussions with the top management at P&G, we examined a number of alternatives, each of which would have positioned me in areas of greater responsibility—but at some point in the future and in a framework which was, of necessity, indefinite. Quite frankly, I became available for Monsanto's consideration because of the challenge of being the head man in one of the great science-based companies of the world."

Charlie Sommer's first formal encounter with candidate Hanley was neither in St. Louis nor Cincinnati. It was at Highlands, North Carolina, where Jack and Mary Jane Hanley were on a mid-September holiday. Hanley recently recalled, "The phone rang. It was Charlie Sommer. He suggested it might be productive if we had a chat. I said, 'My God, I'm way down in North Carolina, reading and playing golf.' But the remoteness of my location didn't seem to faze him at all. Charlie is an ingenious and energetic fellow. He said if it was okay with me he'd come down the next day."

Search committee member Eaton, once described by Edgar Queeny as Monsanto's "eternal board member," had a schedule conflict the following day. Consequently Sommer's North Carolina expedition was composed of himself, Dillon Anderson and Senior Vice President John L. Gillis.

Hanley recently reminisced:

> I knew pretty much what the visiting trio would be talking about. I had been so advised by Bob Gette of Haley Associates. I had told Gette earlier that I'd not entertain any career opportunities competitive to P&G. But when he mentioned Monsanto, my interest peaked because I had long had admiration for its operations, its integrity and its people—or at least for those Monsanto people I had met and who, I presumed, were typical.
>
> At P&G I had been successful in persuading the policymakers to try out some of my management concepts but I had not been persuasive with all of my ideas, some of which I thought then— and think now—merited testing and possible implementation. The Monsanto visit to North Carolina therefore seemed to have the chance of presenting the very kind of challenge I had been looking for.
>
> The discussions with the Monsanto visitors turned out to be

friendly and frank. There was no hemming, no hawing. All three
visitors asked perceptive questions. Charlie Sommer kept emphasiz-
ing the fact that "there is no crisis—but there are opportunities
waiting for someone to grab."

From there on, the negotiations were smooth. A compensation
package in the range of $400,000 was determined. I know some
people think I took the Monsanto job for money. The fact is my
Cincinnati lawyer told me I'd wind up making no more money
in St. Louis than in Cincinnati. That analysis in the long run may
turn out to be right or wrong, but at that point money was of
absolutely no major consequence. The motivation for the move was
the chance to be the boss of one of the world's outstanding institutions and to provide for Monsanto, if possible, a rallying point and a
sense of direction for the years ahead.

The countdown to October 26 was methodical, deliberate—and under
careful wraps. Sommer's principal concern was security. His awareness
of the inherent risks of a leak was matched only by his determination
that no leak would occur. To keep his odds favorable, he chose to inform
the fewest possible people. "Need to know" was his only yardstick.

By the time October 26 dawned, a formidable array of internal and
external preparedness material was ready for release, closely coordinated
at the eleventh hour with plans at P&G. As a result the surprise was
total. The security arrangements had worked.

At a news conference at Monsanto headquarters Sommer exuded pride
and Hanley radiated enthusiasm. The new president adroitly fielded the
sticky and sensitive newspaper, TV and radio questions about his new
job and about water pollution and consumerism—even questions regarding overproduction within the chemical industry and price weaknesses.

In a story appearing in the *St. Louis Post-Dispatch*, Hanley endorsed
the basic organizational structure of Monsanto and called it "logically
sound." He said he expected to be a part of an era of changes but added
that the changes would not be precipitous.

In an internal message to all Monsanto employes, Hanley stressed his
high regard for "the strong management team which Monsanto has on
board—at the top corporate level, in the operating companies and
divisions and in the corporate staff groups. You should know it is
definitely not my intention to start bringing in executives from elsewhere."

If anyone in Monsanto had had any contrary ideas about the new man
importing his own clique of outsiders, discretion kept such ideas sub-
merged. If anyone sighed a sigh and wished an insider had been chosen,
such a sigh remained in low volume. The general feeling seemed to be
that acquiring a man of Hanley's stature was a major accomplishment
and a new badge of honor for Monsanto.

Summing things up in a *New York Times* story was Vice President
James J. Kerley, who said, "I was one of the strongest proponents to get
an outsider. Jack Hanley has more of an opportunity to explore the

rationalization of why we are doing things the way we are doing them. In the long run, it should also be helpful that a lot of people at Monsanto will have to prove themselves to the new man."

From the outset Hanley set a strong example by his behavior as well as his words. He started work early and ended late, often around midnight. He stirred himself to visit the offices of others rather than summoning subordinates to his chambers in that holy-of-holies, the D Building.

He declined well-meaning social invitations and engaged in concentrated homework over weekends.

In meetings with his new associates he asked questions, asked questions, asked questions. His only constant companion on his rounds was his trusty notebook.

Those who may initially have been skeptical about Hanley's commitment to avoid "bringing in executives from elsewhere" soon learned this was no empty promise. Even though it is rather common practice in industry for a new, outside chief executive officer to bring in a favorite secretary or perhaps a few favorite key men—much like a visiting orchestra leader bringing his tried-and-true pianist, drummer and trumpet player—Hanley stuck to his commitment.

In the more than four years that have passed since late 1972, several staff specialists have been brought in from the outside to accommodate the requirements of a growing organization, but there has been no import trend. Today, in 1977, all the operating company managing directors and division managers are Monsanto executives who were aboard when Jack Hanley came in. Hanley explains, "Upon my arrival, I found we had an abundance of extraordinary talent and it has been my job to provide the best possible environment to enable this talent to develop and flourish."

From November 1, 1972, onward, Hanley's closest ally was Charlie Sommer, his next-door neighbor in the D Building until October, 1975, when Sommer retired as chairman and Hanley became both chairman and president. Hanley recalls, 'No one short of the good Lord Himself could have helped me more, especially during the first year of heavy homework. Charlie Sommer injected himself in a subject or initiated discussions with me only when he thought my lack of knowledge or experience in a particular area would handicap me in making the right decision, or when he disagreed with the direction in which I was heading or seemed to be heading. He was remarkable in the sense of not being an inhibitor but a supporter. He was, and is, a continuing and valuable member of our board, a magnificent person by any and all measurements."

Hanley's early influence was almost subliminal, but he didn't overlook many details. Example: He took a dim view of the decor and dishes in the Hillside Room, the traditional executive dining room. It looked a bit too institutional to suit his tastes. He suggested that small improvements in the appointments of this room might merit consideration (and it became, and is today, an exceptionally attractive dining room).

When he asked, "Who speaks for Monsanto?" the response was less than he had wished for. He was told, "People have the authority to speak within the limits of their portfolios but are encouraged to be prudent if corporate considerations are involved." Even though Hanley was assured this formula had worked rather successfully in the past, the new president suggested it was too loose, too imprecise, too general, too prone to risks, too lacking in fixed responsibility. Subsequently he ordered the preparation of detailed guidelines spelling out precisely who could, under what circumstances, speak and/or not speak on what precise subject. "The day of the old ad lib has gone," was his sum-up of the situation.

He was a "new broom" defying forecasts. Those who thought he'd automatically sweep away all old policies were wrong. And those who thought he'd let old policies remain, and simply build upon them, were also wrong.

Almost from the outset he became a dominant advocate of a very serious and very deliberate program for management development, not just for business betterment and upgrading skills but also "to guarantee that Monsanto would never have to go outside again for a president."

His early 1973 inquiries into the workings of Monsanto's various corporate organizational systems were persistent. He was in search of a special kind of forum to serve as an advisory group to the president, a group that would be able to represent every important operation, discipline and staff function in the organization so that total companywide attention and resources could be brought sharply into focus on matters of corporate policy and planning on a continuing basis.

On March 13, 1973, an internal general bulletin signed by John W. Hanley announced the formation of a new administrative arm known as the Corporate Administrative Committee. Without delay, it became known as the CAC.

Short of JWH, no other three letters within Monsanto have since carried more clout.

Hanley's announcement said, "As chief executive officer, I am establishing this group to assist me in the general control and management of the overall operations of Monsanto."

The announcement continued: "Illustrative of the range of matters to be considered by the Corporate Administrative Committee are the following: appropriations requests in excess of $500,000; sales of corporate property and assets in excess of $500,000; major purchase contracts in excess of $300,000; new management positions; changes in personnel at prescribed organizational levels; modifications in accounting practices and procedures. . . ."

There were initially thirteen members of the CAC, including senior corporate officers and the managing directors of the four operating companies. In the four years since the CAC was formed, the membership has been somewhat expanded and is what Hanley calls "subject to change" depending on the complement of executives required to "cover all the bases and to make sure every function is adequately represented."

Also early in 1973, Hanley established a larger, secondary corporate echelon known as the Senior Management Group, numbering forty people. Its purpose is to provide an environment of two-way, face-to-face communications "without," Hanley explained, "letting organizational and ceremonial complications get in the way. Meetings of this group are intended to provide an opportunity for asking questions on anything under the sun. Also it was decided from the start that the people in the Senior Management Group would be invited to regular on-campus luncheons to hear appropriate outside guest speakers."

The "Hanley style" was beginning to show. There was a certain chop-chop to it. Heretofore, internal announcements from top officers had been written in narrative form, businesslike but somewhat relaxed. Hanley's announcements were crisp and frequently in telegraphic style. They conveyed a sense of urgency, finality and "official business." While the old and new styles were quite different, each was inspired by an equal amount of management fervor.

The new president became, step by step, the apostle of spelled-out disciplines and a foe of whatever he perceived as permissiveness. His seeming abruptness prompted some employes to react with "Scoutmaster!" and other such words—from a safe distance, to be sure—at the start, but as the new style became more familiar and more predictable, the sharp and clearcut directives became less of a shock and more of a new way of life, a new set of signals, and a new drum to beat out a new cadence in the halls of a 72-year-old company.

Hanley became a gypsylike itinerant, visiting all possible locations and asking all possible questions. He took nothing for granted. The only thing he always took was his notebook.

He went out of his way to avoid picking, or seeming to pick, "favorites." If there was to be a palace guard, the guard would have to earn its way during business hours. Personable as Jack Hanley was, he also knew how to be sufficiently impersonal during those important early telltale months. Though far from being anti-golf or anti-gin rummy, he scrupulously avoided mixing too much pleasure with business during his settling-in period. A division manager said it all when he commented, "You may hear me call him Jack but on the inside I am calling him Mr. Hanley."

When a colleague asked Hanley, "Is an existing policy threatened with death as the reward for its long and healthy survival?" Hanley replied, "Existing policies are right until they prove themselves wrong, not wrong until they prove themselves right. But I want a thorough evaluation of them before I cast my vote finally on their side. What may have been an excellent policy for a smaller company five years ago may or may not be the best policy for a larger company tomorrow. External forces bearing upon Monsanto are changing with mind-boggling speed and our policies have to be as contemporary as the outside world. Policies merit longevity only to the degree they're aligned with Monsanto's requirements and with our basic objectives. The age of policies, young or old, has nothing to do with it. Effectiveness is the sole consideration."

By the summer of 1973 people in Monsanto were beginning to know their new president pretty well. Every now and then he would disarmingly relate how his three children called him "fossy," a description concocted from the words "fussy" and "bossy." His Monsanto associates were beginning to see the wisdom of the children's appellation.

Looking back, he says he tried very hard to avoid nit-picking but didn't always succeed. Perhaps the first indication that all was not peaches and cream in the new Monsanto regime came on June 11, 1973, when President Hanley called his Senior Management Group together in the board room and unveiled the rules and regulations of what was euphemistically known as Project Equity. After all, who could be against a word like equity?

In retrospect Hanley says, "It was a disaster. It was formulated during meetings of the CAC, but I take full responsibility. It was a real bomb!"

This is what occurred: In an effort to "tighten up" and control costs and bring about greater consistency in practices among Monsanto's various operating units, at home and abroad, the CAC promulgated an edict which set forth some rules of the road for company-paid entertainment, attendance at business meetings, Christmas parties, parking privileges, country clubs, expense account systems, use of tourist-class air travel, vacations, and other such nonchemical matters.

When the seven-page manuscript of constraints and restrictions was given to the assembled group, the grim faces of the senior management audience were matched in grimness only by the stern faces of those CAC people who presented portions of the disciplinary guidelines.

Hanley remembers, "Project Equity was well-intentioned and there was general agreement as to its objectives. We gave copies of the guidelines to the people in attendance and asked them to communicate the new regulations to their groups in any way they saw fit. In most cases the material was passed down orally, but in some cases it was passed down fractionally and in writing. Some groups had explanatory meetings promptly and some waited. It was a good idea which was poorly handled up and down the line. It struck some people as dehumanizing. Later on we regrouped and found a better way to achieve the same aims, and had great cooperation from employes, who realized the spirit of the effort was constructive."

The summer of 1973 also brought a more popular innovation—the announcement of plans for an annual year-end Management Conference for the company's top 500 people from around the world. The two-day meeting culminated with a dinner in the ballroom of a downtown hotel December 14. There Hanley outlined some major objectives to guide the company's growth.

He stated, "We will plan and manage our capital investment program on a consistent, year-to-year basis. . . . We will clearly identify and then exploit those product lines where we intend to remain a principal factor. . . . We are determined to improve our margins by adding value through our proprietary technology. . . . Where we have the skills, we are going to shift the balance of our product mix toward less cyclical markets. . . . We are going to divest ourselves of unacceptable businesses and product lines unworthy of rebuilding or retention."

Perhaps the most popular sentence of Hanley's speech that night was the following: "To the degree that nagging and nit-picking have existed, to the same degree I declare that era is ended—tonight!"

To be sure, this was no apology for the rationale of Project Equity. Yet to some degree it was Jack Hanley's candid and open admission of a bit of human failure in front of an audience quite aware that Project Equity had not been Monsanto's finest hour.

Hanley recalls, "My lowering the boom on nit-picking included but went beyond Project Equity. I wanted to go on the record against *all* nit-picking—by me or anyone else. Nit-picking is debilitating. I'll never forget how one Monsanto man who took early retirement put it. He happened to be a fraternity brother whom I had known quite well twenty-five years earlier, and he had no reason not to level. He told me, 'The main reason I took early retirement was all that nagging and nit-picking. The enjoyment was gone.' "

It was all part of Hanley's settling-in period. Bit by bit, step by step, he exerted more and more influence on policies, behavior and performance. Realizing the chemical industry's traditional time lag between appropriations granted and profits rolling in, he was reluctant for the first few years to accept any direct compliments on Monsanto's resurgence. But in 1977 he can see his systems at work and is not at all bashful in allowing "My skin and bones are now a part of the new momentum."

The pre-Hanley and current numbers are interesting. In the full year prior to Hanley's arrival, 1971, Monsanto sales were $2.087 billion; income was $93.7 million; earnings per share were $2.65. In 1972, the year in which Hanley arrived, November 1, sales were $2.225 billion; income was $122 million; earnings per share were $3.49. In 1976, sales were $4.27 billion; income was $366.4 million; earnings per share were $10.05. These quantum leaps in sales and profitability, even in a period of high inflation, are dramatic enough in themselves.

Monsanto progress since Jack Hanley's arrival is analyzed differently by different people. Hanley himself begins by mentioning the buoyant economy which followed his Monsanto entry. "I came in during a recession year," he observes. But there are many internal causes for the company's new successes. Hanley specifically credits all that had gone on within Monsanto before his arrival; he credits the management people before, during and after his break-in period; he credits a great amount of technology developed by Monsanto scientists and engineers prior to his arrival; he credits the since-expanded storehouse of proprietary science as a crucial wellspring; he credits the employes who have made all the recent advances possible—and recently, only recently, he has begun to accept some credit himself for the broad array of new management practices that have been effected companywide.

Hanley and his executive colleagues have rallied around an assortment of high-priority business systems intended to nurture future growth, but no single element seems more vital than that known as R&D.

"Research and development provide the lifeblood of a science company, of course," Hanley comments. "Without ignoring the tremendous earlier advances in Monsanto R and D, I'd say that today we take a back seat to no one in the planning and management of our technological resources on a worldwide basis. Importantly, we are establishing an environment which is conducive to innovation, encouraging of proper risks and responsive to creativity."

The tab for the company's technical effort in 1976 was $165 million. More than 6000 employes are directly involved on a day-to-day basis with the planning and implementation of technology. Their job: to improve existing products and processes; to search for and establish new products and processes and to design facilities for them.

How does a company divide its technical dollars and manpower between long shots and short shots?

"That's a key question," responds Group Vice President Monte C. Throdahl, who heads the company's technical staff and who began to introduce new concepts ten years ago, after succeeding Dr. C. A. Hochwalt in the leadership of Monsanto's massive technological apparatus. He goes on:

> Keeping our technology up-to-date is a major challenge in itself but we have to go beyond that and make sure, as best we can, that in the years ahead Monsanto has tomorrow's products and tomorrow's processes to meet tomorrow's requirements. It's no task for a faint heart but it's essential, especially in a competitive industry like ours. Indeed, you can be sure our competitors are trying to out-think and out-plan us at every turn.
>
> But don't forget, Monsanto of today has a pretty firm technological base in many important areas of chemistry. The so-called "nitrochlorobenzene tree" has served us very well over the years and has helped give us a leadership position in such areas as rubber chemicals, agricultural pesticides and precursers for pharmaceuticals. The so-called "phenol tree" has positioned us solidly in such areas as aspirin, plasticizers and functional fluids.
>
> Such strengths are quite basic. I'd say we know as much about

rubber chemistry as any company in the world. Plasticizers, which impart qualities of flexibility and durability to polyvinyl chloride, are a longtime Monsanto specialty. We're not only the world's largest in aspirin but we're Number One in elemental phosphorus and in the whole spectrum of phosphorus-related and phosphate-related chemistry. Our petrochemicals operation is as sophisticated as you'll find anywhere, providing many of our own raw-material and intermediate building blocks worldwide.

Just for fun, let me tick off some of the new products and processes since 1965: Roundup herbicide; Lasso herbicide; Ramrod herbicide; Machete herbicide; a new acetic acid process; our Brink mist eliminator; AstroTurf synthetic surfaces; Monvelle stretch nylon; Cadon nylon for carpeting; our electronic process control systems.

No company anywhere has done as much intensive application work on herbicides as Monsanto. And, as you know, there's a direct relationship between herbicides and the world food supply.

I mention these rather recent advances in technology—and that's what they are—to suggest we must be doing something right.

Now as to long shots and short shots for the future. It has to be understood they can't be measured by the same yardstick. But I do think we're becoming more comfortable all the time in learning how to understand and how to handle the concept of uncertainty. In planning for the future we deal of necessity with some commercial uncertainties and some technological uncertainties. Yet, because uncertainties exist, we can't close our eyes to the need for invention—and the need for narrowing, if not closing, some of the knowledge gaps.

I think it's generally conceded that the management of an R and D effort in a worldwide company today is much more complex than it was in bygone days. As we perceive it, innovation involves not only the skills of R and D but it also involves explorations into tomorrow's market pathway and into likely circumstances of manufacturing. Granted, a concept like this requires some pretty ardent championing but it also requires a tremendous sense of teamwork among R and D people themselves and with other groups locked into the R and D planning.

The big trick is sense of direction—and I feel we have just that within Monsanto. In addition we have some of the finest investigative minds and some of the most sophisticated skills in the industry.

Too often it is easy to be discouraged when some new threshold of technology is finally reached and when the threshold seems a little shakier than initially anticipated. Too often there is a tendency to panic, or to pull back, or to lower the expectations. It takes resolve, believe me, to get in there and put the wheels back on the wagon and press ahead. Many, and I mean many, of Monsanto's successes were achieved after overcoming unanticipated shortfalls.

Today R and D efforts are locked in pretty tightly with business strategies. This is another way of saying they're not scattered all over the lot. Also, they're not something apart from the company's basic planning. They're not dreamed up in some remote ivory-tower lab.

Granted, the largest part of our effort will always be in application research, in product and process improvement, in finding new uses for existing products, in developing alternative raw materials, and in the design and building of our facilities, which our engineers handle superbly and creatively.

The company's future depends on such activity, of course, but it also depends on exploring new fields—such as biology of plants at the cellular level. Beyond this, we will be learning how to understand the mechanisms of proteins and other complex materials which serve unusual "messenger functions" in the bodies of animals and humans.

And don't forget, Monsanto has an avowed goal to have more and more proprietary products and fewer commodity and cyclical products. This puts the heat on R and D. In Jack Hanley's view the pursuit of this mission will accomplish enduring strengths for the company. This particular piece of strategy may well be the very thing to provide the thrust for our new growth tomorrow.

The "new growth tomorrow" envisioned by Monte Throdahl will likely occur in many parts of the world, including some areas where the company has only modest operations—or none—today.

In 1976 about one third of the company's total sales were classified as ex-U.S., meaning beyond U.S. borders.

"Our international growth has not been a recent development at Monsanto," notes James E. Crawford Jr., group vice president and managing director of the International Division. "It has been an evolution which began in 1920 with our acquisition of fifty-percent interest in a British firm.

"Today Monsanto's international operations encompass the globe. To manage our ex-U.S. businesses and to coordinate and plan for future growth, we have divided our international operations into four world areas: Europe–Africa, Canada, Latin America, and Asia–Pacific. Each world area director is responsible for coordinating our business activities with the six operating companies and staff departments.

"International growth has followed a pattern. First the company works through sales agents in a particular country. As markets for Monsanto products are identified and sales increase, a Monsanto sales office is established.

"The next step is an initial investment for manufacturing—'a seed investment.' This investment is usually the outgrowth needed to support the initial commercial activity. It then becomes our base for further market development and more capital investment.

"In some world areas, such as Europe, we are well established. We have learned from many years' experience how to do business there. In other world areas our seed investment gives us the local infrastructure we need to identify future opportunities for Monsanto as well as giving us the identity and reputation in the marketplace any company must have to succeed."

Crawford believes that the company's growth outside the U.S. may be accelerated in the next ten years. He says, "Reliable data indicate that eighty percent of the world's growth will occur outside the U.S. in this period. And we have a plan to be where the growth is in order to be part of it.

"But we can't be all things to all people. So we had to analyze where the most growth would occur, then zero in on only certain countries.

"After identifying thirty-two priority countries where the company will concentrate its maximum efforts, the International Division narrowed the company's vast product line down to only priority products which would fit those countries' markets.

"Now we have all the key elements in place to expand internationally in the future—priority countries, priority products and an international organization capable of managing a projected multibillion-dollar business."

An important part of that business will involve exports from the U.S. About one third of Monsanto's international business involves the export of products from U.S. plants to customers or to Monsanto plants overseas. While dollar sales of exports are important to Monsanto's profitability, equally important is the creation of U.S. jobs. Monsanto can point to approximately 5300 jobs related to its U.S. export business.

Crawford adds, "Being a multinational company, as Monsanto is, is not all reflected just in plants, products and profits. It's learning local customs and how different governments work, and it's also learning about the economic and social goals and aspirations of the people. It's speaking different languages and conducting business in different currencies. For example, Monsanto people use twenty-six different languages and use forty-two different currencies."

Crawford philosophizes, "By and large, it's much easier to make and sell a product in the U.S. And, of course, this is where the company's major market is. But people beyond our borders have very real needs and we think Monsanto can contribute in a major way to filling their requirements."

Prospects for faster growth notwithstanding, it would be a mistake to assume that recent years have presented a no-growth situation. Two four-year (1971–1975) examples: U.S. export sales grew from $130 million to $356 million during this period and total ex-U.S. sales grew from $504 million to $1.068 billion.

When Jack Hanley became president late in 1972 his initial plans for a crash course to acquaint himself with Monsanto included a very healthy allotment of time for the "foreign outposts" and for an eyewitness appreciation of the people and plants of far-flung Monsanto. Almost from the start he began planning itineraries. Whether in Northern Ireland or Brazil, his most constant companion was, of course, his little notebook.

The tenor of his research (and the role of the notebook) are best captured by responses in a recent interview:

> *Interviewer:* That notebook! How long have you had that habit?
> *Hanley:* I've had the habit all my adult life. I haven't the world's greatest memory, believe me. I can remember who played the mother in *The Grapes of Wrath* in 1940, but I can't remember the details of some things that occurred yesterday. Once I write down a few notes, several purposes are served. First of all, I have learned to condense and summarize—in cryptic notes which usually only I can decipher. Also, when I write something down it sticks pretty well. In addition, I use those notes as a follow-up. My suspense file is an active one. When someone tells me he'll have something ready on the eighteenth, I write it down and I look for it on the eighteenth—and begin asking questions if the commitment isn't met.
>
> *Interviewer:* What were most of your notes about during your early period at Monsanto?
> *Hanley:* I am sure they'd reflect the fact I entered into many discussions directed to establishing a system for objectives, for results, and for rewarding people in relationship to their ability to pull through certain pre-planned results.
>
> Too often in a large corporation there is a temptation to equate activity, per se, with accomplishment, whereas the principal thing that counts is the result, the box score. I think it was Peter Drucker who said, "There is nothing so useless as doing with great efficiency that which shouldn't be done at all."
>
> *Interviewer:* Did you have a strategy or plan in mind?
> *Hanley:* Yes, I did—and the CAC helped me define it and refine it. So did Ed Schleh, a consultant from Palo Alto, California. We developed a program called Results Management, which I think may be somewhat unique in industry. It is now in its third year of implementation, and by the time we get it fully cranked up it will directly affect the jobs, the productivity, the compensation and the career development of 15,000 of our people—from the foreman on up to the next president of Monsanto.
>
> It's been a monster to get started. But we've been willing to live with all the uphill tradeoffs—the mistakes, the communications problems, the massive training effort.
>
> *Interviewer:* Is it sort of a management-by-objectives drill?
> *Hanley:* It's that but infinitely more than that. Management-by-objectives programs have been around for years. Monsanto had added important ingredients which we think will assure substance and continuity.
>
> To begin with, it is now recognized within Monsanto that Results Management is not a frivolous temporary experiment. It's on the front burner and that's where it's going to stay. Anyone who

doesn't perceive this to be a top priority matter hasn't been paying attention. It's not a fad program. It's not a short-term hypo. It's the core of the improvement we know we can realize in marketing, in production, in technology and in our general grasp of management challenges worldwide.

Furthermore, we've accorded it the status of a line program, not just a supplementary staff program. When we announced the plan in 1974 we took eight high-potential people and made them Directors of Results Management—DRMs, as we call them. These people were the initial installers of Monsanto's new management style. There was an implied promise: Do a good job and we'll put you back into a challenging line operation within two years. These eight DRMs became disciples of the program. Today they're all back in important operating assignments, handling increased responsibilities and remaining the best evangelists we've got.

Interviewer: How does it work?

Hanley: We quantify goals for all participants. The program provides a regular mechanism for a supervisor and his subordinate to agree on reasonable, expected results on a one-year and five-year basis. Once an employe knows exactly what's expected, and agrees with that expectation, that's a major step in itself. Also, we have a formula which directly ties an employe's compensation elements to the way in which expected results are attained.

Interviewer: But how about the poor man or woman who's leashed to some dog of a product group going downhill?

Hanley: Expected results don't always mean a percentage gain in some index. Expected results are reasonable. A person who does an outstanding job in a problem-ridden responsibility can achieve the same kind of high marks as one who is riding the crest of the most popular product group in the catalogue.

Now that the program is getting under way, people are demonstrating a sense of enthusiasm about it. They realize it's going to help them build a record of accomplishment that's going to manifest itself in greater job satisfaction and in new career opportunities.

But we're far from touchdown. On a scale of 0 to 100—100 being my aspiration for full implementation—we're at about point 80 with the first 500 people and at about point 70 with the top 2000. There's a lot of work still to be done in communicating and reviewing goals. But we've got momentum.

I'd call this program the leading edge of the new management style. I see it as the catalyst needed to unleash the capability of Monsanto. And it's also a key to a very serious management development effort.

Interviewer: A program featuring rotation of employes from one specialty to another?

Hanley: No, that's not right. I have no allegiance to the rotation concept, per se. Our program involves the development of both generalists and specialists, and it definitely does widen the opportunity for more managers to be subjected to multiple disciplines. But it does not aim to turn out a lot of Jacks-of-all-trades-and-masters-of-none.

As in all things, there has to be a basic purpose. Our purpose is the maximum development of the individual by whatever means will serve him or her, and Monsanto, best. This might involve the intermixture of specialties or the broadening within the confines of a vertical specialty or discipline.

Interviewer: Is such a program centralized within decentralized Monsanto?

Hanley: It's got to be. I've been told that in the old days you'd find one management style in the Organic Division, another style in Inorganic, still another management approach in Textiles. The old-style divisions were evidently encouraged to develop their own individual personalities, much as though they were unrelated organizations. If and when a man or woman was transferred from one division to the other, he or she frequently would have to spend some time learning the moods and methods of the new host division. Believe me, we can't afford the time for all that interdivisional familiarization. We're going to have a common personality and a common style—a Monsanto personality and a Monsanto style. And let me underline, I am *not* talking about conformity. I *am* talking about *consistency*.

Interviewer: Doesn't all this suggest Monsanto today is more of a structured company, more tightly disciplined?

Hanley: Right.

Interviewer: During your earlier period, wasn't there even a requirement to get presidential approval before an item could be scheduled for the CAC agenda?

Hanley: Yes. Perhaps there was too much agenda-control but my purpose was not just control but setting standards and systems for orderly meetings, for thorough and exhaustive discussions on a planned basis, and for an opportunity for all CAC members to be able to do comprehensive homework prior to meetings.

Sure, during those first six months after the CAC was formed, my colleagues were thinking, and even saying, "It's all just another rubber stamp." It doesn't work that way any more. The CAC knows how to run its own business whether I'm in town or out.

Interviewer: What is this thing called strategic planning that's so often referred to?

Hanley: Strategic planning is the setting of a direction for the corporation. It is the determination of the businesses which we intend to pursue aggressively and, similarly, those which we intend to withdraw from systematically. It is the determination of the way in which we deploy the company's financial and human resources in keeping with a planned direction. We owe our shareowners no less. By its very nature, strategic planning must be a centralized or corporate function. It requires the exercise of the kind of discretionary discipline which only corporate responsibility can fulfill.

Strategic planning is also part of the new management style, resting in the office of the president and delegated for study and analysis by the CAC.

Interviewer: The record shows that in December, 1974, the Agriculture Division ceased being a unit of Monsanto Commercial Products Company and became instead a full-fledged fifth operating company called Monsanto Agricultural Products Company. And in October, 1976, Monsanto Chemical Intermediates Company became your sixth operating group. What will be Monsanto's seventh and eighth operating companies?

Hanley: There will be new companies, of course. When? Making what? These are futuristic questions for which the right answers will come through some of the planning processes and disciplines we are putting in place. I'm not sure I'd tell you the answers today even if I knew them, and I'm not saying that I know them. But I will say we will have the capability of bringing total Monsanto resources into the very crucial role of determining the right answers, within human limitations and economic uncertainties, of course.

Interviewer: A slightly personal question, please. How about the so-called "loneliness of the high command"? Isn't it an occupational hazard of the presidency?

Hanley: I'm sure it can be an occupational hazard if one allows himself to be entrapped and isolated. On my first day at Monsanto I said to my new associates, "Look, I make mistakes every day so you folks are going to have to help me and support me or otherwise we'll all be in trouble."

Edgar Queeny must have been some kind of genius to have played such a major role in developing an organization like this, but even he couldn't have done it without a lot of help and without some exceptional successors in leadership roles.

Today I see my job as one which provides a sense of purpose, which establishes organizational concepts, which enables Monsanto to grow its own managers. I perceive the need for an environment which will not only enable but encourage our people to reach even beyond their own high expectations. Over and over, I hear Monsanto people say there's a new sense of infectious excitement about it all. People may disagree about whether we're going too fast or too slow, but there's little disagreement about our direction.

Considering we're in so many different businesses in so many different parts of the world, I guess a case could be made that variety is the spice of Monsanto's life. Our product usage ranges from the upper-story lofts of Seventh Avenue to the rice fields of Indochina. And our production and marketing activities are wherever the action is, around the globe.

Interviewer: How about marketing? What capabilities are being developed by this function?

Hanley: Before I answer that question, I'll answer a question you didn't ask—about the manufacturing function.

Production proficiency is too often taken for granted. But not within Monsanto, believe me. To begin with, we are absolute fiends on productivity—successful fiends, I might add. The people who literally make Monsanto products simply make Monsanto. Period. They know it. I know it. And they're not about to be unsung heroes as long as I'm aboard.

We give our production people the encouragement they merit. We also give them the tools they need—sophisticated engineering, modern processes and fabulous technology. In turn they give us quality products we're proud to sell.

Marketing? I guess some of my blood cells will always have a marketing tag on them. Particularly in a company like Monsanto I am tempted to put my head out the window and yell toward Lindbergh Boulevard, "You ought to try some of this!"

It takes a superior staff of marketing people to properly represent our broad array of products, selling to almost every industry in the world. We are making things and marketing things in more than forty countries, without even counting the important activities of our subsidiaries and our widely scattered sales agents in all corners of the world.

If I had to select one ingredient which characterizes Monsanto, I'd call enthusiasm—overall enthusiasm—an important denominator. And I think we've got it, or at least are getting it, just about everywhere. Anyway, we're surely working at it, realizing it's a quality that has to be merited. Enthusiasm cannot be legislated or ordained.

My most earnest determination of all is for the creation of an environment in which every employe has the opportunity to use productively—and fully—his and her God-given talents, skills and abilities. We all want to be able to say we're about God's work in the best way we know how to do it.

And don't forget, we don't just make chemicals. We're in the food business, the health business, the transportation business, the housing business, the apparel business—all of which provide opportunities for serving public needs. We're an extroverted, not introverted, company. If we don't serve the public interest we don't deserve to win.

But we'll win—and we'll keep on winning, just as the founder, John F. Queeny, won because he was determined to win. I'm sure that he and his early associates and, yes, his son, Edgar, would have been proud of Monsanto at its seventy-five-year mark. You know, there's a song in the musical, *Sweet Charity*, beginning with the line, "If they could see me now." Sometimes I think of it when I think of the people who started and developed Monsanto. They should see now what they started!

I've come full face with the realities of the so-called Monsanto legend and have found the legend is in fact no less than an adventure which thrives on a compelling sense of involvement. And the key, I believe, is allowing the freedom for individuals to participate as individuals. I hope this environment will continue to attract the best men and women to want to work for us.

When we observed Monsanto's seventy-fifth birthday last November, we were quite aware the milestone was, in fact, only the beginning.

The best is yet to come.

Senior Management

1951-1976

The following brief biographical notations include the initial responsibilities of the persons listed as well as their recent and/or current responsibilities.

ABBIATI, F. A. (1904–1952)—1929, acquisition of Merrimac Chemical Company. General Manager, Plastics Division, 1950. Elected Vice President, 1951.

ANAGNOSTOPOULOS, CONSTANTINE E., DR. (1922–   )—1952, research chemist, Merrimac Division. General Manager, Rubber Chemicals Division, Monsanto Industrial Chemicals Company, 1975.

ANDERSON, DILLON (1906–1974)—To board, 1960. Senior partner in law firm of Baker and Botts, Houston, Texas.

ANDREWS, ALFRED W. (1919–   )—1941, control chemist at Plastics Division's Springfield, Massachusetts, plant. Director of Corporate Engineering Department, 1975.

BARTON, THOMAS H. (1881–1960)—1955, acquisition of Lion Oil Refining Company. To board, 1955; retired from board, 1959.

BAUER, EDMOND S. (1918–   )—1942, member Research Department, Plastics Division, Springfield, Massachusetts. Executive Vice President and board member, 1975.

BERRA, ROBERT L. (1924–   )—1951, Assistant Training Manager, Plastics Division, Springfield, Massachusetts, plant. Vice President, Personnel, 1974.

BIBLE, H. HAROLD (1919–   )—1955, Lion Oil Refining Company acquisition. To board, 1969. Executive Vice President, 1975.

BOCK, EDWARD J. (1916–   )—1941, engineer at Anniston, Alabama, plant. To board, 1965. President, 1968. Resigned, 1972.

BRANDENBURGER, ROY L. (1910–   )—1952, General Manager of Merchandising Division. Retired as Regional Vice President (West Coast), 1975.

BRASFIELD, EARL N. (1934–   )—1957, technical assistant, Plastics Division, Texas City. General Manager, Manufacturing Division, Monsanto Chemical Intermediates Company, 1976.

BRATSCH, GERALD L. (1929–   )—1952, design engineer, Organic Chemicals Division. Director of Manufacturing Coordination, 1975.

BROMLEY, WILLIAM H. (1919–   )—1943, chemist, Shawinigan Resins. Vice President, General Manager, Plastic Products & Resins Division, 1965. Retired, 1976.

BRYAN, ANTHONY J. A. (1923–   )—1947, in the Foreign Department. General Manager, International Division, 1968. Vice President, 1969. To board, 1971. Resigned, 1973.

BURKE, ROBERT E. (1928–   )—1953, sales trainee, Merrimac Division, Everett, Massachusetts. Vice President and Managing Director, Monsanto Textiles Company, 1976.

CALHOUN, DAVID R. (1902–1974)—Board member, 1963–1972. Chairman of board, St. Louis Union Trust Company.

CARROLL, DONALD C. (1930–   )—Board member, 1975. Dean of Wharton School and Professor of Management, University of Pennsylvania.

CHAMBERLIN, JOHN M. (1921–   )—1942, Engineering Group, Springfield, Massachusetts, plant. General Manager, Technology, Monsanto Textiles Company, 1973–1976.

CHESTON, CHARLES S. (1893–1960)—Board member, 1945–1959. Senior partner, Smith Barney & Company of Philadelphia.

CHRISTIAN, JOHN L. (1910–1968)—1935, acquisition of Swann Corporation. To board, 1960. Senior Vice President, 1966.

CLARK, JOHN B. (1924–   )—1968, Director of Corporate Patent Department.

CLARK, RICHARD T. (1917–   )—1939, sales trainee, Merrimac Division, Everett, Massachusetts. Regional Vice President (New York), 1967.

CLEGG, GEORGE F. (1930–   )—1954, technical operating assistant, Plastics Division. Director, Monsanto Plastics & Resins Company—Europe, 1976.

COHN, LEONARD A. (1929–   )—1951, Assistant Supervisor, Queeny plant. General Manager, Plastics Division, Monsanto Plastics & Resins Company, 1975.

COLE, ROBERT R. (1890–1970)—1935, acquisition of Swann Corporation. To board, 1944. Executive Vice President, 1954. Retired, 1956.

CORBETT, HAROLD J. (1927–   )—1950, assistant engineer, Springfield, Massachusetts, plant. General Manager, Resin Products Division, Monsanto Plastics & Resins Company, 1975.

COREY, WINTHROP R. (1915–   )—1945, Sales Department, Phosphate Division. Director, Administration, Monsanto Industrial Chemicals Company, 1975.

CORNWELL, FRANKLIN J. (1919–   )—1953, Director of Sales, Consumer Products Division. Director and chairman of board, Monsanto Chemicals Limited and Monsanto Textiles Limited, 1971. Retired, 1975.

COVERT, MARLETTE C. (1905–1964)—1947, statistician, Accounting Department. Controller and director of accounting department, 1963.

CRAWFORD, JAMES E., JR. (1923–   )—1946, chemist, Phosphate Division's Research Department, Anniston, Alabama. Group Vice President and managing director, International, 1975.

CUNNINGHAM, CECIL P. (1924–   )—1946, research chemist. Board member, 1971–1975. Chairman, Monsanto Europe, S.A., 1975.

CUNNINGHAM, EDWIN J. (1898–   )—1929, Accounting Department. Controller and Director of Accounting Department, 1958. Retired, 1963.

CURTIS, FRANCIS J. (1894–1960)—1929, acquisition of Merrimac Chemical Company. Vice President, 1943. To board, 1949. Retired, 1959.

DANIELS, STEWART D. (1927–   )—1949, salesman, Organic Chemicals Division. General Manager, Fabricated Products Division, Monsanto Commercial Products Company, 1976.

DAUME, WILLIAM B. (1917–   )—1939, hourly employe, Krummrich plant. Director of Corporate Personnel Department, 1965. Retired, 1976.

DAYTON, FRANK H. (1933–   )—1962, sales representative, Inorganic Chemicals Division. General Manager, Apparel and Nonwovens Division, Monsanto Textiles Company, 1976.

DEPP, JOHN M. (1917–   )—1946, maintenance engineer, Columbia, Tennessee, plant. President, Monsanto Enviro-Chem Systems, Inc., Monsanto Commercial Products Company, 1975.

DMYTRYSZYN, MYRON (1926–   )—1947, research chemical engineer, Organic Chemicals Division. General Manager, Technology Division, Monsanto Chemical Intermediates Company, 1976.

DOWD, PATRICK J. (1912–1973)—1941, Director, Payrolls and Pensions. Treasurer, 1958. Vice president, 1964.

DOWNING, COLE (1924–   )—1949, pilot plant engineer, Dayton, Ohio. General Manager, Industrial Fibers & Intermediates Division, Monsanto Textiles Company, 1975–1976.

DUNLOP, RICHARD D. (1908–   )—1933, operating chemist, Plant A. Director of Business Systems Department, 1963. Retired, 1968.

DURLAND, JOHN R., DR. (1914–   )—1939, research chemist, Queeny plant. Area Director, Japan, 1969.

DWYER, E. WATT (1908–   )—1945, Personnel Director, Plastics Division. Director, Personnel and Administrative Services Department, 1959. Retired, 1968.

EATON, FREDRICK M. (1905–   )—Board member, 1947–1960; 1961–1975. Senior partner in New York law firm Shearman & Sterling.

ECK, JOHN R. (1914–   )—1936, research chemist, Dayton, Ohio. To board, 1969. Group Vice President and Managing Director, Monsanto Chemical Intermediates Company, 1976.

ECKERT, H. K. (1899–   )—1929, acquisition of Rubber Service Laboratories Company. General Manager, Chocolate Bayou Project, 1961. Retired, 1965.

ENGLISH, H. BRUCE (1934–   )—1957, Manufacturing Foreman, Pensacola. General Manager, Carpet and Industrial Division, Monsanto Textiles Company, 1975.

ERICSON, HERBERT A. (1920–   )—1968, Director, Market Communications, Textiles Division. Director of Corporate Advertising and Promotion Department, 1971.

EVANS, R. CARL (1906–   )—1940, salesman in Chicago office. Director of Corporate Purchasing Department, 1962. Retired, 1970.

FARRELL, WILLIAM R. (1907–1977)—1954, Manager of Advertising, Advertising and Public Relations Department. Director of Marketing Services Department, 1959. Retired, 1967.

FERNANDEZ, LOUIS, DR. (1924–   )—1949, research chemist, Anniston, Alabama. Vice President, 1969. To board, 1971. Executive Vice President, 1976.

FISCHER, DONALD R. (1926–   )—1956, Product Supervisor, Technical Service Marketing, Inorganic Chemicals Division. General Manager, Animal and Plant Products Division, Monsanto Agricultural Products Company, 1975.

FISHER, J. WILLIAM (1913–   )—Chairman of board (1965–1974), Fisher Controls Co., Inc., Marshalltown, Iowa, a subsidiary of Monsanto. To board, 1971.

FITZGERALD, FRANCIS J. (1927–   )—1951, systems and procedures analyst, Accounting Department. Group Vice President and Managing Director, Monsanto Industrial Chemicals Company, 1976.

FLITCRAFT, RICHARD K. (1920–   )—1942, control chemist, Krummrich plant. President, Monsanto Research Corporation, 1976.

FORRESTAL, DAN J. (1912–   )—1947, Assistant Director, Industrial and Public Relations Department. Director of Public Relations, 1958. Retired, 1974.

FRICKE, RICHARD I. (1922–   )—1975, board member. Vice chairman, National Life Insurance Co., Montpelier, Vermont.

FULLERTON, CHARLES P. (1927–   )—1951, Production Supervisor, Texas City. General Manager, Product Planning & Coordination Division, Monsanto Chemical Intermediates Company, 1976.

GILLIS, JOHN L. (1911–1976)—1933, Assistant Export Manager. Vice President, 1950. To board, 1955. Senior Vice President, 1968. Retired, 1974.

GORDON, RICHARD S., DR. (1925–   )—1951, research chemist, Merrimac Division. General Manager, New Enterprise Division, 1967. Vice President, 1969. Resigned, 1971.

HANLEY, JOHN W. (1922–   )—1972, President and board member. Chairman and President, 1975.

HARBISON, EARLE H., JR. (1928–   )—1967, Director of Management & Information Systems Department. General Manager, Plasticizers Division, Monsanto Industrial Chemicals Company, 1976.

HARRIS, RODNEY (1918–   )—1959, Law Department. Associate General Counsel, 1973.

HAYES, JOHN S. (1909–   )—1939, assistant plant engineer, Shawinigan. Director of Engineering Department, 1963. Retired, 1967.

HEFFERNAN, HOWARD J. (1897–1975)—1929, acquisition of Merrimac Chemical Company. Director of Purchasing & Traffic Department, 1953. Retired, 1962.

HEININGER, S. ALLEN, DR. (1925–   )—1952, research chemist, Central Research Laboratories, Dayton. Director, Corporate Research and Development, 1976.

HOCHWALT, CARROLL A., DR. (1899–)—1936, acquisition of Thomas and Hochwalt Laboratories. To board, 1949. Vice President, Research, Development & Engineering, 1948. Retired, 1964.

HOGEMAN, WYLIE B. (1931–)—1956, chemical engineer, Pensacola. General Manager, Manufacturing Division, Monsanto Textiles Company, 1975.

HOOVER, HERBERT, JR. (1903–1969)—To board, 1958. Consulting engineer, Los Angeles.

HUFF, HARRY R. (1926–)—1955, member of Pensacola accounting group. Director, Planning and Administration, Monsanto Textiles Company, 1975.

KELLY, R. EMMET, DR. (1914–)—1936, Plant A physician (part time). Director, Medical Department, 1946. Retired, 1974.

KERLEY, JAMES J. (1922–)—1970, Vice President, Finance. To board, 1970. Executive Vice President, 1976.

KERMES, KENNETH N. (1935–)—1971, Treasurer. General Manager, Detergents & Phosphates Division, Monsanto Industrial Chemicals Company, 1975. Resigned, 1977.

KLINGSPORN, PAUL A. (1922–)—1943, Plastics Division, Springfield, Massachusetts, plant. Area Director, Latin America, International, 1967.

LAPTHORNE, ATHOL D. (1927–)—1948, research chemist, Australia. Area Director, Australia—Asia/Pacific, 1970.

LAWLER, H. JAMES (1918–)—1946, marketing. Director of Corporate Plans Department, 1975.

LAWRENCE, ERNEST O., DR. (1901–1958)—To board, 1957. Professor of physics and director of the University of California Radiation Laboratory.

LUCAS, ARTHUR W. (1915–)—1951, Assistant Treasurer, Chemstrand. Vice President, 1961. Director, Central Planning, Evaluation and New Ventures, 1966. Resigned, 1967.

MACDONALD, BARTON (1927–)—1951, sales correspondent, New York, Phosphate Division. Director of Corporate Marketing Coordination, 1976.

MACDONALD, DALE A. (1932–)—1969, Regional Sales Manager, Blasting Products. General Manager, Crop Chemicals Division, Monsanto Agricultural Products Company, 1976.

MACLEOD, GEORGE M. (1921–)—1961, Senior Sales Specialist, Silicon, Inorganic Chemicals Division, Santa Clara, California. General Manager, Electronics Division, Monsanto Commercial Products Company, 1974.

MAHONEY, JAMES D. (1918–)—1940, research chemist, Merrimac Division. Group Vice President, General Manager, Textiles Division, 1968. Resigned, 1971.

MAHONEY, RICHARD J. (1934–)—1962, Product Development Specialist, Springfield, Massachusetts. Group Vice President and Managing Director, Monsanto Plastics & Resins Company, 1976.

MARES, JOSEPH R. (1903–1976)—1929, first patent attorney. General Manager, Texas Division, 1947. Elected Vice President, 1949. Resigned, 1954.

MARPLE, HOWARD A. (1899–1970)—1929, acquisition of Merrimac Chemical Company. Director of Public Relations, 1955. Retired, 1958.

MARTIN, TRUEMAN M. (1895–1971)—1955, acquisition of Lion Oil Refinery Company. Board member, 1955–1960.

MASON, JOHN (1924–   )—1949, research chemist, Ruabon, North Wales. Director, Europe, Monsanto Industrial Chemicals Company, 1971.

MAYER, JEAN, DR. (1920–   )—Board member, 1970. President of Tufts University, Medford, Massachusetts.

McKEE, JAMES E., JR. (1916–   )—1946, member of Industrial & Public Relations Department. Director of Public Relations Department, 1974.

MENKE, W. KENNETH (1911–   )—1935, analyst at Monsanto, Illinois, plant. Director of General Development Department, 1946. Resigned, 1952.

MICKEL, BUCK (1925–   )—Board member, 1975. Chairman of board of Daniel International Corporation.

MILLER, LEE A., DR. (1931–   )—1955, research chemist, Dayton. General Manager, Specialty Chemicals Division, Monsanto Industrial Chemicals Company, 1976.

MINCKLER, HOWARD L. (1917–   )—1941, chemist, Queeny plant. General Manager, Organic Chemicals Division, 1968. Vice President, 1969. Retired, 1972.

MORGAN, FINIS (1922–   )—1954, accountant, Chemstrand, Pensacola. Vice President, Finance, 1967. Resigned, 1971.

MORRIS, ROBERT M. (1913–   )—1936, maintenance engineer, Queeny plant. Vice President, General Manager, Organic Chemicals Division, 1959. Resigned, 1965.

MUELLER, ROBERT K. (1913–   )—1935, control chemist, Queeny plant. Vice President, 1954. To board, 1961. Retired, 1968.

NASON, B. ROSS (1918–   )—1941, control lab, Plastics Division, Springfield, Massachusetts. President, Mobay Chemical Company, 1965.

NASON, HOWARD K. (1913–   )—1936, research chemist, Queeny plant. President, Monsanto Research Corporation, 1960. Retired, 1976.

NICHOLS, WILLIAM T. (1901–   )—1949, Director of General Engineering Department. Resigned, 1954.

NOLAN, JOSEPH T., DR. (1920–   )—1976, Vice President, Public Affairs.

OBEL, ARNE (1926–   )—1965, Marketing Manager, Rubber Chemicals, International Division. General Manager, Rubber Chemicals Division, Monsanto Industrial Chemicals Company, 1974. Resigned, 1975.

O'NEAL, EDWARD A., JR. (1905–   )—1935, acquisition of Swann Corporation. Board member, 1955–1956, 1961–1975. Chairman of board, 1965–1968.

O'SULLIVAN, RICHARD C. (1927–   )—1971, Corporate Controller. Vice President-Treasurer, 1976.

PALMER, EDWARD L. (1917–   )—Board member, 1972. Chairman of the Executive Committee, and member of board of Citicorp, N.Y., and its principal subsidiary, Citibank, N.A., N.Y.

PICKARD, SAM (1921–   )—1955, acquisition of Lion Oil Refining Company. Regional Vice President (Washington, D.C.), Governmental and Civic Affairs, 1968.

PLUMB, DAVID S. (1918–   )—1939, chemical engineer, Research Department, Springfield, Massachusetts. Director of Building Products Department, 1961. Retired, 1973.

PUTZELL, EDWIN J., JR. (1913–   )—1945, Assistant Treasurer. Vice President, Secretary and General Counsel, 1963. Retired, 1977.

QUEENY, EDGAR M. (1897–1968)—1919, Advertising and Sales Promotion. To board, 1919. Chairman, 1943–1960.

RAND, WILLIAM M. (1886–   )—1929, acquisition of Merrimac Chemical Company. To board, 1931. President, 1945–1951. Retired from board, 1953.

RASMUSSEN, THOMAS M. (1924–   )—1960, Assistant Director of Treasury Department and Director of Taxes. Director of Tax and Insurance, 1975.

REDING, NICHOLAS L. (1934–   )—1956, technical service representative, Inorganic Chemicals Division, St. Louis. Vice President and Managing Director, Monsanto Agricultural Products Company, 1976.

REESE, FRANCIS E. (1919–   )—1941, research chemist, Plastics Division, Springfield. To board, 1973. Group Vice President, Facilities and Planning, 1975.

RICHARDSON, FRANK (1914–   )—1955, acquisition of Lion Oil Refining Company. Director, Production & Exploration, Monsanto Plastics & Resins Company, 1964.

ROBSON, ERNEST S. (1920–   )—1941, sales trainee, St. Louis. Vice President, Energy & Materials Management, 1974.

ROCKEFELLER, JAMES S. (1902–   )—Board member, 1966–1972. Chairman of the board, First National City Bank.

ROOS, C. WILLIAM, DR. (1927–   )—1951, chemical engineer, Research Department, Organic Chemicals Division. General Manager, New Enterprise Division, 1975.

ROUSH, GEORGE, JR., M.D. (1921–   )—1973, Associate Medical Director. Director, Department of Medicine & Environmental Health, 1974.

RUMER, ROBERT R. (1922–   )—1942, Anniston plant. General Manager, Agricultural Division, 1964. Vice President, 1965. Resigned, 1969.

RUNGE, PAUL W. (1918–   )—1947, research chemist. President, Olympia Industries Inc., 1975.

SAYERS, J. RICHARD (1924–   )—1947, chemical engineer, Norfolk, Virginia. Director of Corporate Distribution Department, 1962.

SCHNEIDER, WILLIAM W. (1897–1969)—1921, assistant, Legal Department. Vice President, 1947. To board, 1951. Vice President of Finance and Law, and General Counsel, 1954. Retired, 1962.

SENGER, JAMES H. (1926–   )—1951, Assistant Supervisor of Phenol Manufacturing Unit, Krummrich plant. General Manager, Technical Division, Monsanto Agricultural Products Company, 1975.

SHEEHAN, DANIEL M. (1902–   )—1936, Controller. Vice President, 1947. Resigned, 1955.

SHIVE, THOMAS M. (1924–   )—President of Fisher Controls Company, Inc., 1969, a subsidiary of Monsanto.

SINGLETON, PHILIP A. (1914–   )—1940, Development Department, Merrimac Division. Managing Director, Monsanto Canada Limited, 1952. Resigned, 1956.

SKATOFF, LAWRENCE B. (1939–   )—1972, Director, Financial Planning and Control, Corporate Finance Department; elected Assistant Corporate Controller. Area General Manager, Asia-Pacific, 1976.

SMITH, IRVING C. (1910–   )—1944, acquisition of I. F. Laucks, Inc. Managing Director, Monsanto Europe S.A., 1964. Resigned, 1967.

SMITH, TOM K., JR. (1918–   )—1939, salesman, Phosphate Division. To board, 1971. Group Vice President, Operations Staff, 1975.

SODEN, ROBERT E. (1917–   )—1939, assistant chemist, Akron Sales Office. Director of Corporate Purchasing Department, 1971.

SOMMER, CHARLES H., JR. (1910–   )—1934, Assistant Manager, Sales. To board, 1959. Chairman of board, 1968–1975.

SOMOGYI, ERWIN G. (1912–   )—1935, analytical chemist, Queeny plant. Vice President, General Manager, Research & Engineering Division, 1960. Resigned, 1963.

SPRINGGATE, JAMES E. (1927–   )—1950, technical trainee, Queeny plant. General Manager, Electronics Division, Monsanto Commercial Products Company, 1975.

STEINBACH, LEWIS (1924–   )—1968, Controller and Director of Accounting Department. Resigned, 1971.

STROBLE, FRANCIS A. (1930–   )—1956, accountant, Queeny plant. Controller, 1975.

TEMPLE, ALAN H. (1896–   )—Board member, 1959–1966. Vice Chairman, Director, The First National City Bank, New York.

THOMAS, CHARLES ALLEN, DR. (1900–   )—1936, acquisition of Thomas and Hochwalt Laboratories. Board member, 1942–1970. Chairman of board, 1960–1965.

THRODAHL, MONTE C. (1919–   )—1941, research chemist, Nitro, West Virginia. To board, 1966. Group Vice President, Technical Staff, 1974.

TOLAND, EDWARD D., JR. (1908–1967)—1951, Assistant to the Treasurer. Treasurer and Director of Treasury Department, 1956. Resigned, 1958.

TULEY, JOHN L. (1933–   )—1955, chemical engineer, Springfield, Massachusetts, plant. Director, Textiles Europe, 1976.

TUYGIL, ONNIK S. (1920–   )—1955, Sales Department, Overseas Division. Vice Chairman of the board, Monsanto Europe, S.A., 1975.

ULMER, FRED A. (1892–1958)—1931, Controller. Treasurer, 1932. Retired, 1953.

WAGGONER, J. VIRGIL (1927–   )—1950, chemist, Research Department, Texas City. General Manager, Cycle-Safe Division, Monsanto Commercial Products Company, 1976.

WEAVER, LEO J. (1924–   )1950, research chemist. President, Enviro-Chem Systems, Inc., 1969. Resigned, 1972.

WESTON-WEBB, PETER (1907–   )—1959, Managing Director of Chemstrand Ltd. Managing Director, Monsanto Europe, S.A., 1962. Retired, 1967.

WHEELER, EARL G., GEN. (1908–1975)—Board member, 1970–1975. U.S. Army, retired.

WILLIAMS, BYRON L., DR. (1920–   )—1954, research chemist, Texas City. General Manager, Technology Division, Monsanto Textiles Company, 1976.

WILLIAMS, FELIX N. (1901–   )—1935, acquisition of Swann Corporation. Vice President, General Manager, Plastics Division, 1944. Board member, 1947–1964.

WILSON, J. RUSSELL (1904–   )—1938, member of Patent Department. Director of Patent Department, 1946. Vice President, 1954. Retired, 1969.

WILSON, MARGARET B. (1919–   )—To Board, 1977. Chairman of NAACP National Board of Directors and a partner with the firm of Wilson, Smith, Wunderlich & Smith in St. Louis.

WIPFLER, EARL J. (1906–   )—1936, Supervisor, Sales Accounting & Budgets. Controller and Director of Accounting Department, 1964. Retired, 1971.

WOLFE, CLAYTON A. (1893–1953)—1929, Supervisor, Queeny plant. Director of Purchasing and Traffic Department, 1939. Vice President, 1947.

WRIGHT, J. HANDLY (1906–   )—1943, Director of Public Relations. Resigned, 1951.

YOUNG, MARSHALL E. (1912–   )—1934, member Export Department. Vice President, General Manager, Overseas Division, 1955. Retired, 1967.

Products Over the Years

1900

0 1 2 3 4 5 6 7 8 9

    saccharin
      caffeine
        vanillin
        iron by hydrogen
          bismuth mining
          acid
          thymol
          phenacetin
            quinidine
              chloral hydrate
                phenolphthalein

1910

0 1 2 3 4 5 6 7 8 9
　　　glycerophosphates
　　　　coumarin
　　　　　nitrochlorobenzene
　　　　　acetanilid
　　　　　　phenol
　　　　　　　chlorobenzol
　　　　　　　aspirin
　　　　　　　salicylic acid
　　　　　　　salol
　　　　　　　methyl salicylate
　　　　　　　　phthalic anhydride
　　　　　　　　chloramine-T
　　　　　　　　sulfuric acid
　　　　　　　　nitric acid
　　　　　　　　hydrochloric acid
　　　　　　　　salt cake
　　　　　　　　zinc chloride
　　　　　　　　chlorosulfonic acid
　　　　　　　　sodium sulfate
　　　　　　　　　dichloramine-T
　　　　　　　　　chlortoluolsulfonate

1920

0 1 2 3 4 5 6 7 8 9

    anthranilic acid
        theobromine
        monochloracetic acid
        vanadium catalyst
          vanadium catalyst type 210
            guaicol
            orthonitraniline
            orthophenetidin
              Santicizer* 1-3-8 plasticizers
                rubber chemicals
                phenolphthalein
                H-acid
                alum
                butyl acetate
                carbonic acid
                chloride of alumina
                acetate of soda
                ethyl acetate
                hypochloride of soda
                benzoic acid
                ammonium benzoate
                sodium benzoate, benzyl alcohol
                benzoyl chloride
                benzaldehyde
                creosol
                oil
                pitch
                napthalene
                benzene
                toluene
                zylene
                puridines
                refined tar
                green oil
                aqua ammonia
                Contact sulfuric acid plant designed, sold
                bisulfate of soda

1930

0 1 2 3 4 5 6 7 8 9

pharmaceuticals
  pyrocatechol
  phthalyl chloride
  ethyl vanillin
    aniline
     tricresyl phosphate
       Santicizer* 9 plasticizer
       glycollate plasticizer
       diethyl phthalate
       acetophentidin
       ethyl alcohol
      Santolube* oil additive
      tetra wax phenol
      triphenyl phosphite
      p-anisidine
      p-nitroanisole
      Santopour* oil additive
      phosphorous compounds
      phosphoric acid
      calcium carbide
      lamp black
      monocalcium phosphate
      Santophen* germicide
      Areskap,* Aresket,* Aresklene* emulsifiers
      dicalcium phosphate
       refined theobromine
        sulfanilamides
         phenol formaldehyde casting resins
         Fibestos* cellulose acetate plastics
         Vue-Pak* transparent acetate
         Formvar* polyvinyl acetal
         Butvar* polyvinyl butyral
         vinyl acetate resins
         tetrasodium pyrophosphate
          butyl laurate
          tri wax phenol
         Santolube* 31-36 oil additive
         Sopanox* amino compound
         Santophen* 20 pentachlorophenol
         Santobrite* sodium pentachlorophenate
         Saflex* polyvinyl butyral film

1940

0 1 2 3 4 5 6 7 8 9

diphenyl phthalate
Santopoid* oil additive
Santolube* 261 oil additive
Resinox* resin/molding compounds
    benzene sulfonyl chloride
    2,3-hydroxy methoxy benzaldehyde
        paratoluene sulfonamide
        Santowax* M-O-P wax substitute
        D. P. Solution* dibutylamine pyrophosphate
            styrene monomer
                Santolube* 394-C oil additive
                d-aminobiphenyl
                p-aminobiphenyl
                DDT (government use only)
                wood sealers, finishes
                Cerex* high-heat styrene resin
                Resloom* melamine resins
                Syton* colloidal silica
                    benzyl benzoate
                    Skylac* aircraft lacquer
                    Santobane* DDT
                    Lytron* plasticized polystyrene latexes
                    Santolube* 203 oil additive
                    Thalid* series hot-melt resins
                    Styramic* HT styrene-based polymer
                    mercaptobenzothiazole
                    Resinox* 470 resin
                        synthetic caffeine
                        radio isotopes
                        tanning agents
                        hexaethyl tetraphosphate
                        polystyrene
                        Sterox* surfacant
                        Santomerse* surfacant
                            maleic anhydride
                            Santomask* odor-masking agent
                            Lustran* TI resin
                            Santodex* oil additive
                            Mertone* WB-2 silica aquasol
                            polyvinyl chloride
                            Lustrex* polystyrene
                            Lustron* PI resin
                            Santocel* refrigerator, freezer insulation
                            Nifos*-T 40% tetraethyl pyrophosphate
                            Sterox* AW surfacant

1940 (*continued*)

0 1 2 3 4 5 6 7 8 9

Skydrol* hydraulic fluid
Ultrasol* vinyl resin coating
Santolube* 222 additive
Ultrasol* vinyl resin dispersion
Santicizer* 141 vinyl plasticizer
HB-40* plasticizer
Ultron* vinyl chloride plastic
Santophen* 1 germicide
  Santicizer* 107 plasticizer
  aminoplasts
  Lytron* 680 acrylic latex
  Lustrex* polystyrene
  Sterox* CD detergent
  Rezgard* A flame-retardant finish
  catalyst AC
  Aroclor* 1248 hydraulic fluid
  2,4,5-T weed killer
  para amino salicylic acid
  Resinox* 10231 black phenolic molding powder
  synthetic resin sealer
  Resimene* 820 powdered melamine resin
  Resinox* 10900 resin
  AE-1 high molecular weight alcohol
  Biolite* sodium pentachlorophenate
  Eskimo* antifreeze
  Santolene* C rust inhibitor

1950

0 1 2 3 4 5 6 7 8 9

Santicizer* 140 plasticizer
Resimene* U-901 urea coating
Santochlor* paradichlorobenzene
OS-16 industrial hydraulic fluid
Lauxite* UF77A cold-setting urea resin glue
Koch acid
Alkophos* bonding agents
   Krilium* soil conditioner
   salicylamide
   inhibitor 038
   high-impact polystyrene
      isopropyl N-phenyl carbamate weed killer
      benthal
      Acrilan* acrylic fibers
      Resinox* Gp-1000 resin
      orthoethylnitrobenzene
      Opalon* resin
      polymer C-3
      methionine analogue poultry feed supplement
      pentachlorophenol
      MCP-90 herbicide
      acrylonitrile
      Merloam* soil conditioning agent
      methanol
         fumaric acid
         nylon
         Santolene* H fuel addition
         Folium* fertilizer
         methyl toluenesulfonate
         Lytron* 886 latexes
         Stymer* LF resins
         Bondite* soil conditioner
         Lustrex* latex 601-50
         Py-ran* coated anhydrous monocalcium phosphate
         Lauxite* UF-101A-UF112 resins
         HB-20 partially hydrogenated alkyl-aryl hydrocarbon
         Resinox* 3700 thermosetting molding material
         Stymer* R warp size
         Resloom* E-50 modified urea resin
         Lytron* X-886 resinous polyelectrolyte
         DPA plasticizer
         DNODP Di-n-octyl, n-decyl phthalate plasticizer
            Santocel* 54 flatting agent
            succinonitrile
            Resinox* 3001 resin

1950 (*continued*)

0 1 2 3 4 5 6 7 8 9

       Ultron* R-117 resin
       Lauxite* 301 polyvinyl acetate
       Santicizer* 601 plasticizer
       Ultron* R-309 vinyl sheets
       PC-1244* defoamer
       NR fabric finish
       Santicizer* 603 plasticizer
       oil drilling mud
       Santolene* J fuel additive
       alpha-chloro-N, N-diallylacetamide pre-emergence herbicide
       alpha-chloro-N, N-diethylacetamide pre-emergence herbicide
       D-Leet* toxicants
       DIDP di-isodecyl phthalate
       Lustrex* HT-88 rubber modified polystyrene resins
          bisphenol A
          Santopoid* 44 oil additive
          adipic acid
          CEDC pre-emergence herbicide
          alkylaniline C-5
          polyethylene
          dibutyl fumarate
          methyl parathion
          Lytron* 886 flocculant
          Lustrex* 710-770 resin
          Lustrex* Hi-Heat 99 resin
          Vyram* vinyl chloride
          Scriptite* 33 wet-strength resin
          Opalon* 75219-1038-72254-72217
          Pydraul* 150–600 hydraulic fluid
          phosphorus pentasulfide
          Scriptite* 50-52-54 resin
          tertiary-butylamine
          dishwasher detergent
          dry bleach
             Lustrex* Hi-Flow 66-77 resin
             Randox* herbicide
             Vegadex* herbicide
             Resinox* RI-4041-5064-5063-5043 resins
             Lytron* 680 resin
             Santopoid* 22 oil additive
             Pydraul* AC hydraulic fluid
             Elastopar* rubber modifier
                glycol monosalicylate
                ACL*-85 sanitizer and bleaching compound
                Fome-Cor* board

1950 (*continued*)

0 1 2 3 4 5 6 7 8 9

isopropylbiphenyl
polymerized ethyl silicate
Santonox* antioxidant
Lustrex* hi-test 89 resin
Opalon* 71344 resin
Lustrex* perma-tone resin
AN as blasting agent
    Santicizer* 165 plasticizer
    Mod-Epox* epoxy resin modifier
    Lustrex* lo-stat 29-22 resin
    Santolube* Q oil additive
    Santicizer* 409 plasticizer
    ammonium nitrate fertilizer
    Santoflex* GP antioxidant
      Randox* T herbicide
      Brink* mist eliminator
      Santocure* vulcanization accelerator
      Santocure* NS vulcanization accelerator
      Pydraul* A-200 hydraulic fluid
      Lytron* 822 resin
      Resloom* E-63 melamine resin
      Resinox* SC-1013 resin
      Micria* AD and AL aluminas
      Micria* TIS titania
      Micria* ZR zirconia
      Santoquin* antioxidant
      Cumuloft* nylon fibers

1960

0 1 2 3 4 5 6 7 8 9

Opalon* 1040 resin
Merlon* polycarbonate resin
Santicizer* 216 plasticizer
Ultron* R-501 resin
single crystal gallium arsenide
Bondite* asphalt adhesive
Stop Scald* fruit preservative
Santofome* resin
Resinox* 495 phenolic varnish
Lytron* 6A styrene copolymer latex
Binstat* sodium metabisulfite
Avadex* pre-emergence herbicide
Lustran* I terpolymers of styrene, acrylonitrile and butadiene
Lustran* A styrene-acrylonitrile copolymers
silicon
   nonyl phenol
   dodecyl phenol
   Coolanol* 35 dielectric coolants
   Resimene* 872 resin
   MPE 706
   geospace dome shelters
   Santicizer* 411 plasticizers
   Nutrium* fertilizer
   Phosgard* organophosphorus compound
   Santofome* resin
   Lustran* resin
   Cadon* nylon
      asphalt roof coatings
      Lustrex* hi-test 88-1A resin
      silicon epitaxial wafers, Czochralski crystals
      gallium arsenide epitaxial wafers
      spandex yarns, fibers
      americium-beryllium (Am-Be) neutron sources
      americium alpha sources
      MPE 36-39
      Syton* C-40 colloidal silica
      Syton* 240 colloidal silica
      Santocel* Z silica aerogel
      Phos-Chek* fire retardant
      Avadex* BW herbicide
      Rogue* herbicide
      PCNB
      Wear-Dated* warranty
      ethylene
      butadiene

1960 (*continued*)

0 1 2 3 4 5 6 7 8 9

Nylon molding powders
single crystal indium arsenide
single crystal indium antimonide
Vyram* 2763 resin
Vyram* 2764 resin
rigid vinyl siding
Lambast* pesticide
vanadium catalyst type 11
Monsanto* oscillating-disk rheometer
Pan-O-Lite* leavening agents
Leven-Lite* sodium aluminum phosphate
Stabil-9* leavening agent
Santicizer* 462 plasticizer
Santoset* 1 plasticizer
Santolube* 314 oil additive
prilled pentachlorophenol
Santicizer* 480, 481, 483 plasticizer
synthetic lactic acid
Acrilan* anti-static acrylic fiber
Monsanto* automatic size emulsifier
   Chemback* carpet backing materials
   hydrogenated bisphenol A
   MPE 73
   Scriptite* 435 resin
   calcium saccharin
   Opalon* 4700 resin
   tributoxy ethyl phosphate (TBEP)
   Niran* 10-G insecticide
   blow-molded rigid vinyl plastic containers
   Dequest* deflocculating and sequestering agents
   "soft" alkylbenzenes
   Polyflex* 0404 film and sheet
   Mould Coat* synthetic bone ash
   Santicizer* 160 butyl benzyl phthalate
   rigid vinyl rain-carrying system
   Silent-Cor* sound deadening board
   translucent cold-drink vending cup
   Vyset* 69 coating resin
   Coolanol* 15 dielectric coolant
   Santolene* M oil additive
   nylon 6/6 resin
     Ramrod* herbicide
     CWS* fumaric acid
     Thermo-lath* insulating panels
     MCS 310

1960 (continued)

0 1 2 3 4 5 6 7 8 9

ammonium phosphate fertilizer
Pydraul* 312 hydraulic fluid
transparent plastic meat trays
Therminol* FR-O heat transfer fluid
   12MHZ multi-function counter/timer—Model 100A
   Therminol* 77 heat transfer fluid
   Gelva* multipolymer solutions 263, 264, 269, 270
   Wallop* herbicide-insecticide
   Opalon* 740 resin
   Santoflex* 13 antiozonant
   Phos-Chek* P/30 fire retardant
   Santicizer* 266, 268 plasticizer
   AstroTurf* surface
   Santolene* T fuel additive
   Butvar* B-79 resin
   Pydraul* 135 hydraulic fluid
   hydrazine fuel cells
   Santovac* vacuum diffusion pump fluid
   Modaflow* resin modifier
   Santicizer* 148, 192, 194 plasticizers
   Stymer* RT-270 copolymer resin
   Scripset* 520 paper coating resins
   nylon 6/10 resin
Interpass sulfuric acid plant designed, sold
   RA-315 resin
   Gelva* multipolymer solution 260
   Therminol* 66 heat transfer fluid
   Therminol* FR low-temp heat transfer fluid
   Syton FM* silica sols
   AstroTurf* track surface
   Model 1500 plug-in universal counter/timer
      Resinox* exel 530, 533 laminating phenolic varnishes
      Vykan* engineered composites
      Mooney rheometer
      Gelva* multipolymer solution RA-387
      soybean beverage
      Montase* industrial enzymes
      Cadon* 2nd generation nylon
      Model 3100A frequency synthesizer
      Model 110A programmable universal counter/timer
      Tetrathal* tetrachlorophthalic anhydride
         Lasso* herbicide
         colored vinyl siding
         Tytron* flooring system
         dislocation-free gallium arsenide

1960 (*continued*)

0 1 2 3 4 5 6 7 8 9

TiRamic* tile panels
cure simulator
Curetron* data acquisition unit
Tel-Tak* tack meter
Flair* synthetic grass display material
Therminol* 55 heat transfer fluids
VX2020 series of X-band cw oscillators
Mersize* ExCL rosin size
MD1, MD2 silicon pin photodiodes
WD-2 polyester
MV50 solid-state light
learning aids
ME2, ME5 series high-power LED series
Cerex* spun-bonded nylon
A07 nylon tire yarn
100B 50MHZ universal counter/timer
Model 107A automatic computer counter
Cavitrol* 1 valve
ac^2* analog instrumentation
AstroTurf* brand doormat

1970

0 1 2 3 4 5 6 7 8 9

Tytron* and TyBlox* rigid plastic surfacing material
Skybond* RI-7272 polyimide resin
Santocure* NS-50 vulcanization accelerator
MAN-3 monolithic alphanumeric readout
Model 120A 150-Megahertz universal counter/timer
ME6—Ga As LITE* infrared-emitting diode
di-undecyl phthalate (DUP)
Santosafe* W/G hydraulic fluid
Skylube* 450 hydraulic fluid
Fibralloy* 300 molded products
VX272ET Gun-effect oscillator
304A pulse generator
Elura* hairgoods of modacrylic fibers
MCS2 rectifier, MCD2 photo-diode coupled pairs
511A digital printer
Lytron* 897, 898, 899 latices
MV5020, 5040
acetic acid
Model 105A 500 MHZ frequency counter
Whisper Trim* 1 valves
dc²* digital controller
    MV9000 series solid-state cartridge lamps
    MDA111 solid-state alphanumeric display module
    150A automatic counter
    wood protective coating
    oxo-alcohol
    MPE720
    MCA2 photo-darlington optoisolator
    M340FR resins
    Resimene* X-915, X-918, X-963 melamine resins
    MAN1002 hexidecimal light-emitting diode array
    Santotrac* lubricant
    Santomelt* 990 CR ice and snow melter
    dual channel optoisolator model MCT2D
    MPE 380 HDPE
    Machete* herbicide
    EVC1 latex binders
    3½- and 4½-digit digital thermometers and multimeters
    LEDs in multiple colors
    MAN 3 M LEDs
    Gelva* resin emulsion TS-61
        SEF* modacrylic fiber
        Pydraul* E hydraulic fluids
        tire flaw detector
        Stymer* RT-1300 copolymer resin

1970 (*continued*)

0 1 2 3 4 5 6 7 8 9

    Resimene* X-970, X-980 melamine resins
    Monvelle* biconstituent fibers and yarns
    Limit* 33 defoamer
    Acrilan* Plus acrylic fibers
    Vydyne* R nylon resins
    1200/1500 series dataloggers
    270 series digital panel meters
    Model 8110 factoring, panel mount counter timers
    Cavitrol* 2 valve
    Whisper Trim* 2 valve
    Wizard* 3 series controllers
    PM 500 series field-mounted temperature transmitters
    ac^2* panel-mounted computing elements
    ac^2* TS113 shop test unit
    miniature LEDs
    high-brightness MAN 10 LED display
    high-frequency optoisolator MCT2F
    0.6-inch LED display
    MCA 7 reflective sensor switch
    Ga As LITE* diodes
    MCA 8 slotted limit switch
    MP5054 high-brightness illuminating LED
    AC bi-color LEDs
        Vydyne* 21X nylon resins
        Roundup* herbicide
        tensometer 500
        Multiflow* resin modifier
        nylon 9/9
        type 9500 butterfly valve
        ac^2* RD202 and RD205 dedicated and trend recorders
        ac^2* TL155 computer auto/manual station
        MV5074 T-1 size LED
        MCT10 miniature optoisolator
        MAN 50-70-80 LED displays
        MCS 6200 miniature solid-state relays
            2100 series multimeters
            Cycle-Safe* containers
            Whisper Trim* 3 valve
            Cavitrol* 3 valve
            dc^2 batch controller
            MAN 31 LED calculator display
            ME 7120 series of high-power infrared LEDs
            MCT 8 slotted switch with transistor output
            MCT 66 dual channel optoisolator
            bright orange, green and yellow LEDs

1970 (continued)

0 1 2 3 4 5 6 7 8 9

     MAN 3600 orange LED display
     JEDEC registered optoisolators
     MAN 4000 series of .4-inch LED displays
     MV 5753/4 extra-bright LED lamps
     6100 series instrumentation printers
     8500/8700 series counter/timers
        Polaris* plant-growth regulator
        Builder M detergent builder
        edisc* 8500 rotary-shaft valve
        Model 8320 time interval meter
        VeeBall* V100 valve
        dc^2* ammonia controller
        dc^2* gas transmission and distribution controller
        ac^2* PL107 non-liner controller
        Scamper* outdoor sweeper
        T-1 size LED lamps, four colors
        very high brightness T-1-¾ size LED lamps

Index